Burns and Oates

**Flora - The Roman Martyr**

Vol. I

Burns and Oates

**Flora - The Roman Martyr**
*Vol. I*

ISBN/EAN: 9783337272647

Printed in Europe, USA, Canada, Australia, Japan

Cover: Foto ©ninafisch / pixelio.de

More available books at **www.hansebooks.com**

# Flora,

## THE ROMAN MARTYR.

VOL. I.

BURNS AND OATES,

LONDON:
GRANVILLE MANSIONS,
ORCHARD STREET, W.

NEW YORK:
CATHOLIC PUBLICATION
SOCIETY CO.,
BARCLAY STREET.

# PREFACE.

FLORA, the Roman Martyr, is a book without any literary pretensions. It was written during a visit to the Eternal City many years ago, with a view of recording, in their first freshness, the impressions of devotion gathered at many a Roman shrine, and several pages were hastily penned, amidst the bustle of sight-seeing, when the connecting thread of the plot often became tangled, sometimes broken. Indulgence must be asked for on account of certain anachronisms, some slight liberties having been taken with one or two dates; also, on account of the length of the descriptions, when the enthusiasm called up by the classical reminiscences of the Italian land caused the writer to dwell too long on some favourite scene.

It is difficult to correct a work after the lapse of years. Rugged and misshapen though a tree may be, it is best to leave it to bear what fruit it can.

Flora, the heroine, is an ideal character, this much alone being true, that a Saint of that name suffered martyrdom under the Emperor Gallienus, and is buried in the Church of St. Martina, but her connection with St. Lawrence is quite imaginary. With the exception of Claudius, Siona, and Florentius, most of the characters are historical.

Perhaps it will be asked why we have departed from the usual statement that St. Lawrence was burned alive on a gridiron. On a close examination of the iron bars preserved in the Church of San Lorenzo in Lucina, they seemed to us to have formed part of one of those low iron beds found in Etruscan tombs; and as the expression, *lectus ferreus*, occurs in the "Acts of the Martyrs," denoting an instrument of torture used on some occasions, we deem such a bed to have been identical with the *craticula*.

If we bring these long-forgotten pages before the public, it is in the hope that they may benefit the victims of a persecution, going on in our own days, more lingering than that which the early Christians endured, but scarcely less cruel, considering that we live in a more civilised age.

We allude to the nuns of Italy, ruthlessly torn from their convent homes, sometimes in the dead of the night, and left without any shelter except what pious friends offer them. The aged and infirm have been taken from their beds, and carried through the streets by their sorrowing sisters.

It is to relieve such misery that the proceeds of this little work are destined.

*9th January*, 1886.

# INDEX.

## VOLUME I.

### Chapter I.
Villa of Florentius at Aricia. His slave Claudius, a Christian. Siona, the lady of the house.

### Chapter II.
Arrival of Origen at Rome. He meets St. Cecilia with her husband Valerian. Goes to see Pope Urban in the Catacombs.

### Chapter III.
Household of St. Cecilia. Her young Christian friends, Martina, Agatha.

### Chapter IV.
Entertainment given by Lucullus. Sudden illness of Flora, infant child of Florentius. Siona, the mother, fearing it will die, consents to its being baptised.

### Chapter V.
Martyrdom of Valerian, Tiburtius, and Maximus, followed by that of Cecilia.

### Chapter VI.
Flora's early childhood. Arrival of a young cousin, Laurentius, from Iberia.

### Chapter VII.
Roman market place. Baths. Conversation between Florentius and Hippolytus, a suitor of Martina's.

## Chapter VIII.

Hippolytus renews his suit to Martina. She confides to him the secret of her religion. He withdraws.

## Chapter IX.

Accession of the Emperor Gordianus, the younger. Choosing of new Vestals. Volumnia, daughter of Nemesion, selected.

## Chapter X.

Manumission of Claudius. Projected journey to Liguria.

## Chapter XI.

Martina's martyrdom. Conversion of Hippolytus.

## Chapter XII.

Nicæa in Liguria. Flora makes acquaintance with a young Christian girl, Reparata, who becomes a friend, together with Pontius, her uncle.

## Chapter XIII.

Florentius is made acquainted with the religion of his wife and children.

## Chapter XIV.

Friendship between Florentius and Pontius.

## Chapter XV.

Nemesion's home. His second daughter, the blind Lucilla. Icilius, formerly suitor for Volumnia's hand, attempts the life of Gordianus—takes refuge in the temple of Vesta. Young Vestal suspected.

## Chapter XVI.

Icilius condemned. Flora works a change in him for the better.

## Chapter XVII.

A walk on the Via Appia. Hippolytus the hermit.

## Chapter XVIII.

Gordianus and his minister Misitheus. They visit Aricia.

## Chapter XIX.

Games in honour of Latial Jove. Death of Misitheus.

# AUTHOR'S FINAL CORRECTIONS.

P. 18, l. 11 from the top, *for* 'precious the signs,' *read* 'precocious'.
P. 21, last line, *for* 'Teller's,' *read* 'Feller's'.
P. 22, l. 12 from the bottom, *for* 'Slemon,' *read* 'Alcmon'.
P. 187, l. 6 from the top, * after the word *foundation*, instead of in l. 2 from top.
P. 194, footnote, *for* 'statres,' *read* 'res stat'.
P. 226, l. 7 from the top, *for* 'had loved,' *read* 'have'.
P. 254, l. 10 from the top, *for* 'dulces,' *read* 'dulcis'.

## CHAPTER I.

IT was on a summer evening of the year 235 of the Christian era. The shades of twilight were already gathering on the horizon, while the last rays of the setting sun still bathed, as in a sea of glory, the scarce visible outlines of distant Rome.

On the Via Appia, at about two miles from Aricia, a slave, whose dress denoted him as occupying the place of *Villicus*, or superintendent of his master's farms, issued from the gate of a large, handsomely-built country-house, and, proceeding on his way, stopped on the brow of the hill which commanded a view of the Vallis Aurea. The sun, which had been hidden from his view, as he ascended by a shady path, now burst full upon him, bright in its dying glory; he veiled his brow with his hand. . . . As he stood there alone, the evening breeze fanned his bronzed cheek, recalling to him, by its soothing influence, early memories, the love that yet breathed and seemed wafted to him from far-off lands. His countenance evinced strong emotion, and in accents such as he had not used for years, his heart's yearnings found utterance in his native tongue.

"My country! my country! methinks I see thee, looming in the distance, standing out among the golden clouds which surround this land of slavery. Far more beautiful art thou in thy rugged scenery and native loveliness. Happy those who pass their lives among thy white cliffs, against which the ocean waves beat daily, but in vain. Never more shall it be given me to gird the sword which my forefathers so nobly wielded. Other slaves would be content with my lot, for I have much to make me happy. But, alas! golden fetters press as painfully as red-hot iron on one who feels flowing in his veins the noble blood of Car-a-doc."

The speaker was about forty years of age. His noble bearing and proud look sat strangely on a slave; but Claudius was a Briton by birth, descended from one of the ancient chiefs of his own country; his noble pedigree was stamped on his handsome features; his martial gait and elastic step bespoke the freeman, treading unwillingly on foreign soil. He had been taken prisoner of war, and condemned, as such, to serve as a slave. Fortune, however, had smiled on his chains; the family he was bound to treated their servants with a kindness unusual among Romans; indeed the old name of *familiars*, which indicated the position of slaves as members of the family, had its full meaning in this household, especially in the case of Claudius, whose superior merits had so much attracted the notice of his masters that he had risen to the highest post of confidence, and was named *Villicus* to their estates.

No small stir had been going on in the country house for some days. Rich furniture and abundant provisions sent out from Rome had passed on the road. Painters and vendors of marble had come to and fro, employed in repairing the somewhat neglected *triclinium* of the villa; new mosaics had been laid in the *aula;* in the private oratory of the Penates, a small altar had been raised to Lucina. All this had entailed much labour on Claudius. Besides the gathering in of the harvest, he had superintended many improvements in the garden; new avenues had been drawn out under his directions, and the trees bordering them cut into curious shapes, the fish pond had been replenished, a new wall raised round the little island exclusively devoted to the fattening of snails, and the bees which till now had thrived near the uninhabited villa had been removed to a distant and secluded part of the grounds. The functions of Claudius were not confined to out-door work, for he had no wife to take the domestic department into her hands; this was unusual in a *Villicus*, as the Roman laws had regulated that every slave holding an office of trust ought to be a married man. Once only his master Florentius had reminded Claudius of this obligation, but the latter had thrown himself at his feet, imploring a respite. Florentius was rather surprised, but as he prided himself on being a good-humoured philosopher, he dismissed the slave with a joke and thought no more of the matter, till one day his wife presented him with a petition on the part of Claudius which she urged with gentle seriousness,— it was that his masters should not oblige him to marry.

"The man is a barbarian, so he knows no better; but

what makes you plead for him, Siona?" asked her husband.

"I am the daughter of a conquered people, Florentius, and the prayer of the oppressed can never reach my ear in vain."

"You are a Roman matron, Siona, since my love has made you one, and the gods be praised that knitted our destinies together! Let it be with Claudius as he wills if it so please you."

From that day Claudius was looked upon as a privileged slave, and he showed his gratitude by renewed activity at his work, seeking on all occasions to give pleasure to his masters. A new feeling sprang up between them, singularly different from what was usually manifested in Roman households; a deep, grateful affection on the part of the slave, a regard, amounting almost to respect, on that of his owners. In the eyes of his mistress, the constancy with which he clung to the memory of his British home seemed something sacred, and she warmly espoused his cause.

The evening on which our tale opens, the villa of Florentius near Aricia had been prepared for the reception of the lady of the house. Siona was about to become a mother for the first time, and all that Roman luxury could afford had been collected to surround her with every comfort during her stay in the country. This very evening was appointed for her arrival, and Claudius awaited her on the road. It was a solemn hour, when a golden halo overspread the face of nature, and the evening clouds gathered from the heavens a hue of such strange and mysterious beauty as is seen on no earthly horizon but that which encircles the favoured land! Rome lay far away in the distance, reigning in silent majesty from the summit of her seven hills over almost all the then known world. Ever great, though degenerate! more powerful, but less triumphant, than when the virtues and valour of her citizens formed the pride of her republican days. How they had loved her then, those sons of her might! even to the laying down of their lives, and washing in their blood the least stain cast by the stranger on the fame of their beloved Rome! Even now, though the spirit of Cincinnatus and Regulus lived no more in the Roman breast, the love of the Alma Mater yet survived; pure flame, which, like the sacred fire preserved for ages, and burning silently on a hidden altar, guards the old palladium to which is attached the fate of Rome. Is it to be wondered at that when they gazed on that city, so extensive in its power, so eternal in its foundations, her sons proudly asserted that the orb of day would sooner be extinguished, than Rome close her career of glory?

To all those who have known toil or sorrow, evening is the hour of rest; in the uncertain, misty twilight, distant visions come with their brightest illusions to the heart that cannot forget. Like the golden clouds, coloured with an ethereal light, they bear to the soul a dream of life beyond, to be coldly dispelled with the coming darkness, yet treasured up, even though a thing of dreams!

There was a wood sacred to Diana bordering the road. Claudius, after half-an-hour's fruitless expectation, withdrew to its leafy cover; there he knelt down, and taking from his belt a small pouch formed of the skin of an animal slain in the chase, he drew from it a handful of earth: a strange grim smile passed over his features, revealing a fierce spirit which lay dormant within him. "Soil of my fatherland," he exclaimed, "thou art pleasant to the touch! thou hast lain in my breast since the day they tore me from Britain. I gathered this dust with clenched hands, vowing I should tread it one day again, but as a freeman. Small handful of earth! thou art all of Britain I can yet call my own, yet dearer to me than all the splendour and magnificence of this land of slavery. Ah, why have this people brought me here, envying me the humble cottage of my British home!"

He put the little pouch to his nostrils and his mouth, breathing hard over it, as if to inhale the atmosphere of liberty with which it was impregnated; he held it some seconds to his eyes too, and when he withdrew it, their expression was strangely softened; he laid it on the ground. From the breast of his tunic, he drew out a folded linen cloth, which he would require at the Christian assembly he was to attend that evening, where the Holy Eucharist was distributed to each of the faithful, to be carried away by them to their own houses. The memory of the sacred rites returned to the slave, and he examined the dispositions of his heart. He struck his breast with remorse: "Pardon me, oh God, that I know

Thee as yet so little, and have not yet learned to forgive!" He flung himself on the ground, his hand still clasping the linen of the Holy Eucharist, his forehead bowed over the handful of natal soil; the old love and the new faith were now mingled. . . . . The struggle was over in that poor heart, there was a prayer placed on his lips by the Crucified, the slave at that moment was a hero, and the descendant of Caractacus triumphed, even in chains!

When he arose, the twilight had disappeared, darkness had closed around, and the moon had risen; there was a sound of singing and music borne onward by the breeze. He went out upon the road: there were many lights, as of torches seen at a distance; he hastened to his master's villa, summoned his fellow slaves to meet and welcome their mistress, and ranging them in order, gave the signal to set out, heading the ranks himself. As they came near to the new comers, these stopped, and a voice from the litter called for Claudius. He approached, and the curtains being open for the admission of the cool evening air, he knelt by his mistress, Siona, and kissed the border of her *palla*.

"I am very glad to come to Aricia, Claudius, and I hope the gods will send us good health and fine weather; we must propitiate them: These slaves bring offerings to the *lararium;* go on before me with them to the house."

The slave made no answer, but, falling back a few paces, appeared not to have understood her orders. They soon arrived at the villa, where the female slaves were assembled in the *atrium* to welcome their mistress; she led the way to the *lararium* set apart for the worship of the household gods, and, before crossing the threshold, turned back to call Claudius. The slave was holding a torch to light her steps, but did not follow; he looked at her with an expression sorrowful yet firm; he waited till all had passed, then put out his torch and disappeared in the darkness.

\* \* \* \* \* \* \*

The next morning early, Siona visited the grounds where she knew many improvements had been made to please her on her arrival; she loved solitude at all times, and on this day had signified her wish to be alone. Bending her steps towards the beehives, she passed through the flower-plots where a huge basket lying on the ground attracted her attention; it offered a tasteful assortment of variegated flowers disposed as a pyramid. There was a slave weeding the beds; at the sound of her footsteps, he looked up, hastened to take in his arms the basket he had been arranging, and, kneeling before his mistress, presented it to her without speaking.

"Is this an offering for Lucina?" she asked.

There was an unpleasant smile on her face, and a slight tone of irony in her voice, which the slave understood; he looked up at her, hesitated, then said, holding back his gift:

"For you alone, lady."

"Nay, I must offer my own flowers to the goddess, if I choose."

Claudius looked round to see whether any one was within hearing, then whispered very low:

"Do you believe in her power, my mistress?"

A slight tremor of surprise mingled with fear passed over the countenance of Siona, but she recovered rapidly her presence of mind, and, drawing herself up to her full height, she rebuked her slave for the first time in angry terms.

Claudius had presented his offering kneeling to his mistress; he retained that posture, but his gaze was upturned, and his mind rapt in an Invisible Presence; he knelt no longer to her. He knew that she was born of Jewish parents, and the traditional features of her nation had never struck him so forcibly as at this moment, when they were strongly marked by excitement. There was a peculiarity of expression in her eyes which none could read, even those who knew her best; it was not sorrow but rather a restless unhappy look as of one seeking for ever after a good that is lost. Oftentimes her gaze was averted, as if overpowered by a Brightness visible only to herself, and that gaze, when one could meet it, contained an unutterable sweetness and an unearthly radiance. It seemed as though the strange expression of those eyes came from a Bright Vision whose impression had remained, long after it had faded away. As Claudius looked at her long and attentively, these thoughts came to him not for the first time; his mind was conferring with itself, and he seemed to have formed a resolution. He rose suddenly, folded his arms, and said in a calm firm voice:

"You rebuke me, lady, and yet you know what your fathers taught you long ago : 'Thou shalt adore but one God'."

All her passion left her in a moment; pale and trembling she sank back on a garden seat, and covered her face with her hands: "Hush, hush, Claudius; how do you know those awful words which have never visited my ears since childhood? My father and all his household left Jehovah to adore Roman gods long ago."

"And do you believe in their power, you virtuous and pure-minded beyond many of your sex? can you worship divinities whose history is but a tissue of crimes? If you have remained uncontaminated, it is that a ray of light has clung to you, even through the darkness of Paganism; is it not so?"

"And you, Claudius, who speak so boldly, of what creed are *you*?"

"My mistress must have guessed that from my disobedience of last night. My life and death are in her hands."

"Truly, it never struck me until you refused to sacrifice that you could belong to the abhorred sect of the Christians."

"It is so, I am a Christian."

A shudder passed over the young woman, and, glancing at the flowers at her feet, she selected a sprig of sage and with it touched her forehead, to avert the evil omen according to Roman superstition.

"Claudius," she said, "it terrifies me to think thou hast lived with us so long and drawn down upon our household perhaps the vengeance of the gods. Fly! I will help thee, and thy secret shall remain ever sacred with me. Fly! my husband shall not know thy place of refuge, and I will deceive him rather than bring upon his threshold the misfortunes which thy polluted presence may draw down upon it. Go, Claudius, I implore thee, if not for me, yet for my child, on whose birth thou hast cast an evil glance, by not sacrificing to Lucina. Thou dost not answer me: wilt thou not take the proffered opportunity? If thou art a father thyself, ah, have compassion on a mother's fears. In the name of thy own dear ones, leave me for the salvation of me and mine."

The slave's breast heaved violently; he breathed convulsively; his hands were clenched each on the other arm so firmly that the flesh grew livid under their pressure; still he did not speak, but the swollen veins on his forehead told of an internal struggle like that he had gone through in the forest. Life and liberty to be purchased by swerving from duty; on the other hand, slavery, years of toil, ending perhaps in a martyr's fate. But to strengthen him through this, there was peace of conscience, the approval of the All-seeing One; there was above all, and before him at this very moment, a soul to save: the brave heart had soon made its choice!

"Lady, you have spoken to me as to a slave; now hear me answer as a Christian. You would induce me to be unfaithful to my earthly master; I serve a Heavenly One Who has told me He will allow no wrong. You would, from a superstitious dread, forget the duty you owe to your lord and household, for I am my master's property, and you cannot dispose of me without his leave. Forgive me, Siona, for the rebuke. It comes not from me but from Him Whom your fathers worshipped; from Him Who spoke on Horeb, Whose words never change, because He is eternal; from Him Who abhorreth a lie, Who has commanded unto each to be faithful to his calling. He inspires me to be faithful to my masters, because it is better to suffer evil than to do it."

Siona looked at Claudius as one awe-struck. The solemn tones, the inspired look with which her slave pronounced the name of God, all seemed to her as if a dream of her early days had arisen to her view.

Encouraged by her silence, he continued: "I speak to you of a Law-Giver Whose name you cannot have forgotten. Have His divine commandments been torn from your memory? Do you remember His promises? Do you remember the Messiah spoken of to our first fathers, Who is still the expected One of the children of your land? So vivid is the anticipation of that promise among you, that at one of the feasts of your people the youngest maiden of the household withdraws to await in solitude and silence the springing forth of the root of Jesse. That promise has been fulfilled! He came, and His people knew Him not; day by day He sat teaching in the temple, and they did not heed Him. His hour came! the hour appointed by the Father, revealed ages before by the prophets, and He gave up His life to redeem His own; He died by the hands of His people! Siona, shall I tell you more? or do you prefer reading a history traced in the language of your own people and handed down to us who believe? It is a sacred trust confided in me; may I lay it in your hands, and will you guard it even as you have promised to preserve secret the religion of your slave?"

His mistress stretched out her hand mechanically, as if she were lost in thought: "This is like a dream of my childhood," she said; and with an impulse which seemed to follow out the vague feeling of reminiscence, she pressed the sacred volume to her heart, her forehead and her lips. "This was the custom of my father when he called us all to his knee, and told us of Jehovah's written Word."

She opened the little volume, and the characters of a language she had ever looked upon as sacred moved her strangely. She bowed her head, and during some minutes was absorbed in its perusal. Presently she looked up, her eyes suffused with tears; her voice trembled and was hushed like that of a child.

"Claudius," she said, "my mother used to tell me the story of one of my ancestors who had lived in the time of that strange One Who was called Jesus, who had spoken with Him, and lo! his story is here."

The slave looked at the page her finger rested on; it recorded the interview of the Saviour with that young man who, having observed all the Commandments from his youth, was called upon by the Master to forsake all things and follow Him, but *he went away sorrowful, for he had great possessions.*

Claudius glanced at the page, then at her, then at the Holy Writ again.

"Great God!" he exclaimed, "you have then heard this passage before?"

"I can count how many generations separate me from this man; my father spoke of him often to us."

"Oh then, lady, wonder not if a Guardian Spirit moved me to speak to you this day. The Word that went forth to your forefather, that lay hidden for *his* children, has spoken to you now. I no longer marvel that you have remained pure in the midst of Roman paganism, for the Most High has overshadowed you. Nay more! there is a seal set on those who have conversed with the God Who spoke on Horeb. I have often seen on your features the light of another world, the reflection of a superior Brightness which had passed over you, like the glory of God on the face of Moses. You are marked out for a great destiny, Siona; the Word of the Lord is never spoken in vain, and the *call* of your ancestor must be fulfilled! it may be through you, it may be in your unconscious child."

Siona continued listening with clasped hands, and it was some time before she spoke.

"Enough, Claudius," she said, "our conversation has been long, and must remain a secret; thou hast moved me much, and if thou hast not spoken truth, thou hast done me a grievous wrong, for I can no longer be calm and tranquil as before. Do not speak to me again, for I fear thy influence; agitate me no more with these memories of my people and my faith, for my duty calls me to be faithful to my husband's gods. Urge me no more, lest their vengeance fall on my innocent child."

"Yet one word, my mistress. I speak not from myself. He who reigns above," and he raised his hand on high, and his voice was solemn as before, "your Master and mine has spoken to you this day. If you will not be His now, He will call you again, through sorrow and through fear. Beware, for the doom of expiation hangs over your people, and our God is a jealous God, Who punishes the sins of fathers on their children. I now return to my daily toil, and you to the joys of your domestic hearth, but I feel we have not met in vain. Farewell! I ask you only to remember me in the hour of trial, when you will require more comfort than philosophy or Roman idols can give. I may be able to help you then, and I ask of you to call upon me. I ask it in the name of your forefathers, in the name of that precious existence confided to your care, for which you will have an account to render to your God and mine."

He made a profound inclination to his mistress and disappeared. She remained as if transfixed to the spot, and was only roused from her reflections some time after by hearing the voice of Claudius giving orders to his *topiarii*, the slaves appointed to prune trees. He was climbing up a ladder, stretching out cords, and as attentive to his work as if it were his prominent object in life. The young wife retired with slow steps into the interior of the house.

## CHAPTER II.

IT was early in the morning, so early that the shades of night still struggled with the approaching day; the moon dispersed her silver rays over the Latian Campagna, eclipsing the faint brightness scarce visible in the East, shining on each lordly Roman *ediculum* like a sepulchral lamp, while the sculptured stone faces looked up, unearthly and strange. On, on sped the moon, tipping as if in mockery the minium-coloured eulogium engraved over the lamented dead, too often, then as now, a falsehood on a grave; on to the huge paving-stones where the letters V.A. (Via Appia) were discernible in the clear rays, where the neglected blade of grass grew unheeded in crevices of the Regina Viarum; then the pale moonbeams passed to the fields beyond, to the lonely shepherd's cot, and, at last, to the hills, where the queen of night faded away in the light that burst on the horizon.

There was a traveller on the Via Appia at that early hour, and, as the golden clouds arose, he knelt and bowed his head; but, though he turned to the East, it was not the sun he worshipped. His was the mysterious faith known in Rome but to be reviled, scorned, and persecuted; his allegiance was sworn to the mighty

Chieftain Who had conquered from the Cross, Whose army, wide spreading yet invisible, victorious yet oppressed, trod even now the vast realms of the Roman empire in the east and the west; Whose war cry, uttered from on high, called up myriads from the bowels of the earth, Whose adorable Name at which spirits above and below bow in threefold awe must be guarded as a sacred mystery, to be whispered but under cover of the night's darkness, revealed but to the faithful initiated, and sheltered beneath the surface of the soil beyond the profaning reach of man. Therefore, the traveller turned towards the Campagna, and with head bowed low to the earth knelt awaiting the arrival of the brethren who, he knew, must at that early hour be withdrawing from the Catacombs, and to whom he proposed making himself known; meanwhile he murmured the prayer in which all the Church joined at early dawn, while angels bore aloft the hymn of praise from the prison, the palace, and the hiding-place, and round the entire world thrilled the echo of the Catholic Amen!

Who has not heard of Origen? the Church's luminary, who wrote more books than some men can read in a life-time! whose infancy gave such promise! whose ardent thirst for death worthy of a martyr's son could only be restrained by the innocent fraud of his mother, who, secreting the boy's garments, prevented him from running to the prison where his father awaited his sentence! Who has not quailed at hearing that the giant efforts made by that master spirit proved unavailing to keep him in the upward path, and that the Church mourns over Origen as one fallen away? Who has not wondered at his science united to that purity of heart so spotless in early childhood that his father Leonidas had knelt before the cradle of his little son and kissed the breast that was even then the temple of the Holy Ghost?

And this traveller's worn countenance when he rose from his prostrate position and raised his head, what a tale it told! how the energies of his soul had stamped it as with a seal, how precious the signs of age on that forehead wrinkled more by labour and austerity than years! how often that emaciated frame quivered under the excitement of strong feeling, revealing an impetuous nature brought under control by self-discipline and an iron will! how guileless the mind which, born to command the world in the highest realms of genius, could thus forget its powers in the lowliness of self-abasement and seek in the dust of the roadside the traces of its God!

For there was a tradition attached to the spot where he had knelt, and, although he trod that road almost for the first time, he knew it at once. Here St. Peter escaping from persecution had been prevented by a vision of the Divine Master bearing His cross:

"And where goest thou, Master?" asked the affrighted disciple.

"To be crucified anew," was the reproving answer of Jesus to the faint-hearted apostle, who forthwith returned to the death that awaited him in Rome. With lips pressed to the pavement, covering with kisses the footprints of more than human size and of perfect symmetry marked in the stone, the fervent African sighed for the martyr's crown which had once awakened his boyish enthusiasm. "Oh Lord," he exclaimed, "shall there be denied me the glory of being faithful unto death, the triumph of washing in my life-blood the stains contracted in life's dreary path?" And over that powerful frame there passed the quivering of a mortal agony. A prophetic spirit seemed to have been imparted at this moment to Origen: visions arose of a thorny crown woven with the laurels of fame; the robe of calumny clinging to him and consuming his life away; and, lastly, the doubt, dreadful, overpowering, scorching in its fiery breath. . . . . Would the grace of faith be granted to him till the end? Alas! how often is there less danger in the encounter with wild beasts than in wrestling with an invisible enemy! how much easier at times is it to pass through the ordeal of earthly fires than to issue unscathed from the spiritual contest with God's foe and ours!\*

---

\* Origen was born at Alexandria in 185 A.D., and surnamed Adamantius from his assiduity at his studies. He taught the faithful publicly in Alexandria at the request of his bishop, Demetrius; but a sedition arising in that city, he left it and retired to Palestine, at which his bishop was displeased; and Origen having, at the request of the prelates of that province, explained the Holy Scriptures in public, Demetrius manifested his disapprobation at this charge being entrusted to one who was only a deacon. He recalled Origen, who continued for some years to edify the faithful by his holy life and labours. Being sent to Achaia, he was, on his way thither, ordained priest at

During the first half-hour which followed the break of day, the sun rose higher and higher; then came the sounds of animated life: the carolling of little birds, the shepherd's voice and the lowing of herds, the distant hum of population wafted over the fields from living Rome. Presently was heard a noise of wild mirth, approaching nearer and nearer, a jarring of discordant music and strange shrieking. A procession issued from the Porta Capena, headed by maidens in

Cæsarea by the bishop Theoctistus without the consent or advice of Demetrius, who, resenting this, deposed Origen and accused him of having taught several errors, among others that Satan will be saved. Origen cleared himself entirely of this imputation, established himself at Cæsarea, where Theoctistus, Gregory Thaumaturgus, and Athenodorus took him for their master. The bishops of Arabia invited him to go there to convert Beryllus, bishop of Bostra, who denied that Jesus Christ had had any existence before the Incarnation. He accomplished that task and Beryllus expressed his gratitude to him. A council being held in that province against certain heretics who declared that the soul died with the body, Origen was called in and confounded the false doctrine by his sound and powerful reasoning. During the persecution of Decius in 249, he was cast into prison and tortured several times, but not put to death, in the hope that if he apostatized others would follow his example. He was set free and died at Tyre in 254 in his 69th year. It has been alleged that to obtain his deliverance he pretended to offer incense to the idol Serapis, at Alexandria, but this has not been proved. Few men have written as much as he has. His works are "An Exhortation to Martyrdom," and "Commentaries on Holy Scripture". He is the first who went through the entire sacred text; the greater part of this work still exists, and it breathes faith and piety. He laboured at an edition of the Bible in six columns, confronting the different versions already made; he considered that of the Septuagint as the most authentic. Sermons of his had been collected to the number of one thousand. He

yellow robes, playing the tambourine, and dancing to
their music ; behind them a long train of Flamens or
priests bearing poles surmounted by pines, while others
held bucklers on which they rapped with spears to imi-
tate the clashing of arms ; behind these again walked
youths, casting on the ground handfuls of gold-dust
which glittered in the sun's rays as it fell ; these last
surrounded a chariot drawn by six milk-white horses,
and carrying an idol more senseless still than the many

had generally seven secretaries whose sole occupation was to
write from his dictation. In his book of *Principia*, which is not
original, but translated by Rufinus, we certainly find some pernicious doctrines and a system founded on that of Plato. He has
been accused of making God material, but this he utterly denied.
It was immediately after his death that doubts arose as to his
orthodoxy. In the 4th century, the Arians proved their errors by
his doctrine. St. Athanasius, St. Basil, and St. Gregory of
Nazianzen defended him as having spoken in orthodox language of
the divinity of Christ ; St. Hilary, St. Ambrose, and St. Gregory
of Nyssa praise his works ; but St. Basil says expressly that he
did not think rightly about the Holy Ghost. He was condemned by
the fifth general council. St. Epiphanus and St. John Climacus
spoke very strongly against his doctrines, and Pope Pelagius II.
said that no heretic had taught anything so pernicious as Origen.
Pope Martin I. pronounced anathema against him in the first
council of Lateran in 649. St. Augustine and John of Damascus
wrote against him ; St. John Chrysostom and John of Jerusalem
in his defence. In the 3rd century, the Emperor Justinian issued
an edict against him, and he was condemned in the Council of
Constantinople, the acts of which have been added to the fifth
general council. (See on this subject the *Life of Tertullian and
Origen*, printed in Paris in 1675 ; *Memoirs of Tillemont for Ecclesiastical History*, Vol. 3 ; Ceillier, *History of Sacred and Ecclesiastical Writers*, Vols. 2 and 3 ; *Origeniana*, by Huet, who has
published all that remains of Origen's *Commentaries on the New
Testament*.)—[Teller's Dictionary.]

heathen divinities set up in pagan Rome. The object of all this worship was a black stone, taken from the Temple of the Sun at Emesa by Heliogabalus, when he left the altars of his favourite god to assume the Roman purple, continuing, however, to revere him as his tutelary divinity. To this block, adorned with precious gems, and placed in a temple on the Palatine, he had ordered universal homage to be paid; in its honour he had changed his name from Antoninus to that of Heliogabalus, alluding to the god of the Sun. The Imperial fanatic had transported to the shrine of his favourite the Ancilia, the Palladium, and all the sacred pledges of the faith of Numa, and, although these were, after the death of the emperor, restored to their respective places of worship, yet the College of Flamens continued to exercise their functions, during the reign of his brother, Alexander Severus, and kept up the ceremony of accompanying the god in procession each year as far as the river Slemon outside the Porta Capena.

Origen, wishing to avoid coming in contact with the motley worshippers, concealed himself in the shadow of a tomb, and waited for them to pass. Just at this moment, a cloud of dust arose on the Via Appia in the distance, and the tramping of horses' hoofs resounded on the pavement; they were coming towards Rome, and the procession stopped, seized with fear. On, on, sped the horsemen! They were not simply a military escort, bearing messages, as was their wont, from one part to another of that extensive empire, but they were a strong force, ranged in serried ranks, and they went at a regular pace, as if hurrying to the battle-field. The people recognised a goodly detachment of the Prætorian guard. These, under indolent Emperors and overbearing generals, had grown to be more masters of Rome than the senate or the Cæsar; and the efforts of Alexander Severus to restore discipline among them had rendered him an object of their hatred. The Emperor was at that time on the banks of the Rhine at the head of a large army; what then could bring these guards to Rome at so great a distance from the camp? From his hiding-place, Origen watched them, and thought their appearance was ominous of bad tidings. He himself had come to Rome at the secret instigation of Mammea, mother to the emperor; she, having seen and heard the Christian philosopher at Antioch, had grown enamoured of his doctrine. Origen, on drawing near to the great city, had been informed that Alexander, scarcely returned from the Persian war, had left his capital again, to encounter another foe in Germany, but nevertheless he had determined to pursue his journey, and await the Emperor's return. As the band of Prætorian guards approached, Origen was lost in conjecture.

His suspense was not of long duration. The soldiers drove up at a rapid pace, and, as they came near to the religious assembly, they reined in their steeds. Had the priests moved aside, and not intercepted their path, perhaps they would have passed on, but the Sacrificator veiled his head, and, with an angry gesture, ordered them to stop. A hoarse laugh burst from the rude soldiers, who were barbarians for the most part, and a voice called out from the ranks:—" The effeminate Syrian Emperor is no more! Let the same day see his downfall, and that of the foreign gods."

A shout of applause echoed this speech, and, surrounding the chariot and brandishing their weapons, the guards made as if they would have taken possession of the stone god, whose magnificent equipage excited their covetousness, but the multitude shrieked, the Flamens put themselves in an attitude of resistance, or at least of opposition; some of the horses, maddened by the tumult, broke away, the people endeavoured to turn the remaining white steeds towards the city, but were charged by the guards, and all the fields were covered by priests, children, frightened maidens and soldiers in pursuit.

Origen found it impossible to leave his place of concealment, and any help he could have offered would have proved ineffectual. He deemed it wiser to withdraw further into the Campagna; walking backwards in order to keep his eye fixed on what was going on before him in the road, he continued retreating till he came to a low wall; satisfied now that he was at too great a distance to be seen or pursued, he stepped over it, and let himself down on the other side. The ground was less high within than without the enclosure, so that Origen met with a fall which slightly stunned him; he rested on a heap of newly dug earth, and felt grateful for his escape. He reflected over what he had heard. Could it be that Alexander Severus was no more? that kind friend to the Christians, suspected of being a Christian himself? And Mammea, in whose generous heart and superior mind he had hoped to find a protectress for the persecuted faith, where was she? would she survive the son whose infancy she had guided, whose throne she had graced before his hands were strong enough to assume the reins of power? had she perished with him, or did she weep over his loss?

Amid these conflicting thoughts, a wonderful sensation of peace stole over the traveller. Was there something hallowed in the air he breathed, that when the morning breeze fanned his heated brow, he felt as if an Angel of God had passed over him with outspread wings? It was so, indeed! for he stood in the Presence of Him Who is hidden yet revealed, at Whose approach the unbeliever trembles with mysterious awe, and the child of the true Faith rejoices that he has found Him in Whom he liveth, moveth, and hath his being, and to Whom the voice of the spirit of adoption calls out: Abba! Father!

At Origen's feet there was a heap of brambles, collected as if for those fires with which labourers sometimes cover a barren piece of ground to fertilize it with ashes; he stooped to examine and saw a few bricks loosely put together; he moved them aside with his hands and found concealed a fissure in the ground. His heart leaped for joy; this must be a *luminare*, so practised as to give light and air to the Catacombs. He knelt down and looked, but could not see into the darkness; sounds however reached his ear; he must be near the *Presby-*

*terium* or chapel where the Holy Mysteries were being offered, in presence of the assembled Christians. What wonder then, if, like Moses, he had felt that the ground he trod on was thrice holy! There was a long and solemn pause. He knew they were at the Breaking of Bread; he joined with them in prayer and mystic communion. Again he heard a sound, but this time it was no longer solemn and low; the faithful were singing a hymn of thanksgiving, and above them all rose a voice clear, ringing, silvery like an instrument, yet human in its pathos, and drawn from the deep well-springs of a woman's heart. It was such a voice as the Father of poets would have coveted to be the messenger of his inspired accents among men; that music would have kindled enthusiasm, led on warriors to the battle-field, or brave hearts to heroic deeds. Had it thrilled in the halls of pleasure, it might have intoxicated an Alexander, set fire to another Persepolis; but the young songstress had chosen to herself another destiny and another fame! To her, the world was the enemy of her God, human passions the object of her scorn. And love, that fountain once pure in its origin, only corrupted when it passes through earthly channels, that sometimes giver of happiness and frequent destroyer of peace, had only visited Cecilia to leave her unscathed. Between earthly joys and her virgin heart she had raised a barrier, never to be withdrawn, like the holy veil of the temple which divides the external world from the Sanctuary of God.

The sounds died away, and Origen hastened to cover the orifice again as he had found it, and looked round to see whether he could find any one to lead him to the entrance of these Catacombs, where he would be in the midst of brethren. He returned to the wall he had passed over, and saw a poor beggar wending his way wearily on crutches. With that prompt charity which Christians practised in those days as their first duty, he called to him gently, offering him his assistance or an alms. The mendicant drew near, looked at him with surprise, and both remained a few seconds gazing at each other hesitatingly ; at the same moment, there was a rustling sound among the vines, and the tall figure of a man clothed in the garb of a slave, holding branches in one hand as if he were a gardener, and wearing a bunch of keys at his girdle, came before the traveller, looked at him sternly, then over the wall at the beggar, with a glance of enquiry.

"He called to me, offering me charity," explained the latter, "but I do not know him."

An expression of satisfaction was visible on the countenance of the new-comer, yet he still doubted.

"I seek brethren," resumed Origen, "in the name of" ——he put his hand to his forehead and made with his finger a sign so imperceptible as to be only recognized by the initiated. Such were the two in whose presence he stood ; the cripple shouldering his crutch, waved his hand, and the slave dropping the branches he held, kissed his fingers,* and both said, " Stranger and brother, hail ".

* The customary salutation in Rome, from which was derived the word *adorare* (putting the hand to the mouth).

The mighty talisman had done its work, the Sign of Him that was crucified had rallied to the Master's call those three brave hearts, each doing His Will in his separate calling; the luminary of the Church, the outcast of society, and the captive warrior become a Christian slave. After the recognition, there was a moment's silence, which Origen was the first to break: "I am a stranger," he said, "come from Palestine on a pilgrimage to the city of the Apostles; a tumult occurred on the road which obliged me to take refuge in this lonely vineyard, of which thou seemest to be the guardian," he continued, addressing the slave; "is it not so?"

"For this hour, I keep guard in order to warn the faithful of any danger; to passers-by, I seem but a gardener."

"And that is of good augury," replied the new-comer smiling; "when our Master had arisen, and sought to veil His glory to men, He assumed that disguise. But He is near, nay, under this very soil; I would wish to kneel to Him like the Magdalen of old, calling Him Rabboni. Wilt thou lead me, brother?"

"It is late, and the Mysteries have drawn to a close; but here come noble Romans, Valerian and Tiburtius, they can inform you on all subjects."

The slave went to meet the young men whose names he had mentioned, exchanged a few words with them, then fell back a few steps behind them, joining a group of Christians who also were coming away from the Catacombs. The patricians addressed Origen in terms of extreme courtesy, saluting him as the slave had done before with the name of brother.

"Can we serve you in any way?" asked he who seemed to be the elder; "you are a traveller and must require a resting-place. Will you share our house in Rome?"

"Thanks, I am weary indeed, but I wish to see our common father before taking any rest, and I know he has taken refuge somewhere near this spot."

"You are well informed."

"Perhaps the guardian I met on entering this vineyard may conduct me to the feet of Urban."

"Certainly. That is Claudius, slave of Florentius; let him guide you and accompany you to Rome; I can easily explain to his master the cause of the delay."

"Florentius!" exclaimed the traveller, drawing a little tablet from his breast; "I know that name, I bring letters to that worthy Roman."

"How singular! how plainly we see that our Heavenly Father watches over us! I will not detain you, but when you have paid homage to the Pontiff, come to us near the bridge in the Via Salutaris; my wife and my brother, Tiburtius, will rejoice to see you, as indeed all my household." So saying, he went to the group of Christians where the women and men had come out in separate bands from the place of worship, a practice rigorously enforced by the Church in those days, and, taking by the hand a lady of very low stature and uncommon beauty, who was leading a little girl, "Cecilia," he said, "come to welcome a stranger!"

She greeted the traveller as her husband and brother-in-law had done; then as Origen looked enquiringly at the little girl by Cecilia's side:

"This is Agatha," she explained, "the child of a friend of mine who is a Christian. She sent her to me from Syracuse under pretext of her health requiring the climate of Rome, but in reality to remove her from the influence of her Pagan father. Kiss the hand of the stranger, little one."

"Does he love Him?" asked the child, looking up to heaven.

"Yes; do not fear, my child. You must excuse her," continued Cecilia, addressing Origen, "Agatha is a fierce little Christian; her childish soul has drunk in the Saving Word with such eagerness that she longs for God, and asks me continually when His hour will come."

The traveller looked down at the little girl with a pleased smile. "And so you want to go to God?" he asked.

"Oh, yes," she replied; "I have prayed to Him that I may wash my garments in the blood of the Lamb, and He will hear me." She clung to the stole of her protectress and kissed it. Origen placed his hand on the child's head. "Amen!" he exclaimed. "Yea, verily from the mouths of infants Thou has perfected praise, Oh Lord. And now, my noble friends, I thank you for this kind welcome, and shall visit you later; let me now follow this trustworthy slave."

They parted, to proceed in opposite directions, Origen

carefully treading along the barren field—a pathway which he could not discern, but which was perfectly visible to the practised eye of the slave.

"And of what nation are you, Claudius?" he asked, wishing to show kindness in return for that he had met with.

"Britain," was the answer, in a tone of voice that was solemn, as if a deep chord had been touched.

"The love of country seems strong within you. I feel for you."

"Yes, I suppose we all love our native land; but my feeling for Britain is something more."

"You speak the language of Rome as if you had dwelt here a long time. How comes that? Will you tell me your past history? I am a stranger, but I have known suffering."

"You have unlocked my heart, noble stranger, and I shall tell you what I have kept secret for years. I was a child when I followed my captive father to Rome in the triumph of the Emperor Severus. I was his companion in slavery, but not for long; the love of liberty burned within me, and the flame was kept alive by his words. My father was a chieftain, a relation of him whom the Emperor Claudius restored to his country unfettered and redeemed. But woe to the race of Cara-doc! His descendants would not submit to be dependent on Rome. They renewed the old strife, were taken prisoners, and had to endure the galling yoke and the hated chain. My sire expired under the blows ordered by a cruel master, and I, burning with the desire for revenge, concealed my feelings so well that I asked and obtained a place in Rome's mercenary legion. My extreme youth had saved me from the ignominy of being branded a slave. I was strong. They took me to serve in their ranks, as they thought, and I followed them in the reinforcements which were sent to guard the Roman possessions in Britain. But, ah! no sooner had my foot pressed the parent soil than I executed my long-formed resolution. I stole from my sentry's post in the night, leaving my *sagum, lacerna,* and armour on the ground; the latter I besmeared with blood, the garments I tore, to make those who found them suppose I had fought a deadly strife. I hurried away, and, after long seeking, found again the mountain home I had left as a child. I gladly assumed the arms of the Britons, the dirk and the heavy sword, whose clang, while dangling at my side, incited to pursuit, and the lance, and my target for only defence. The children of my tribe welcomed the wanderer, whose heart had never forgotten freedom in a foreign land; they linked me to a beautiful maiden, in order that the race of Caractacus might live again. She was a Christian; and, had I remained by her side, I should have learned earlier the high lesson which forbids revenge; peace and the island home might still be mine! I was called to the battle-field only two years after my marriage, which was solemnised according to the rites of her religion by a solitary missionary, who had watched over her childhood, and been long sheltered by her father. The old man baptized our first-born, and would have pressed me too to bow my head to the saving waters, but my heart was yet too full of glory and revenge. The last time I went out to battle, my wife girt on my sword, and wept that I should go. I reproached her with her weakness, but her forebodings were fulfilled, that was the hour of our parting; I was taken prisoner, and the doom of my slavery was sealed."

"And then you returned to Rome?"

"I did! by the will of Him who punished thus my pride and spirit of revenge. Yet I bless the chain which He has blessed, it has fettered me for ever to my Master's cross."

"How did you become a Christian?"

"When the British chieftain, from whom I descend, came in chains to Rome, and obtained from the Emperor the gift of freedom, his daughter, Rufina, was detained here as a hostage, assumed the name of Claudia, and married the Roman Senator Pudens, who became the disciple of St. Peter. Their children were Pudentiana and Praxedes."

"What, Claudius! do you indeed belong to that family? then you have a claim to glory far higher than lies in your affinity to the British chief."

"The great-grandchildren of Claudia were still living in Rome. I remembered the tie of relationship, and sought them in those hours of despair, which are only known to the heart that has lost its all. I found them youths and maidens of a pure life and of loving goodness, employed in ministering to the wants of their suffering brethren, visiting them in prison, encouraging them to die, consoling their orphan children. I went to them often, for I had a kind master who allowed me to enjoy comparative liberty. I found them, nightly, watching and praying, after a day of good deeds; I saw them guardians of the sanctuary hallowed by Peter's dwelling and Pudentiana's prayers. When my hand sought theirs in friendship, I could see, and they proudly showed it, stains of a roseate hue impressed on their delicate fingers, a glorious and hereditary mark which had passed to the nephews and nieces of Praxedes and Pudentiana, in reward for the zeal with which those holy virgins had collected the blood of Christ's martyrs, and devoted their lives to that special work. I learnt the Christian faith, implored the grace of baptism, and, on that very font where the granddaughters of Caractacus preserved the gore of those that were slain, I inclined my head, formerly too proud to bow to an earthly master's yoke. And, oh! that water washed out all that was sinful within me, and I arose with an ardent thirst to do and to suffer for my heavenly Master's name. I sighed for the baptism of blood, and as if a foreshadowing dream of that last victory had arisen before me, when I issued from the holy font, my head was bathed in a purple stream, for a long-preserved relic had been used in the holy ceremony. To me, as a relation of Praxedes and Pudentiana, Baptism had been administered with a shell with which they were wont to scoop up the earth, saturated with blood, after their brethren's martyrdom."

Both Origen and the slave had reached the entrance

to the Catacombs and lingered without, while the narrator, speaking from the fulness of his heart, made his hearer thrill with sympathy. Tears stood in Claudius' eyes as he concluded, and, wiping them away, " Forgive me," he said, "for thus detaining you, the memories you have evoked are strong."

"Nay! I am to blame for questioning you, but, believe me, you have spoken to the heart of a friend. May I ask one question more? You speak as one who has frequented schools. Where have you acquired knowledge?"

"In extreme youth, an insatiable desire to learn drew me to hear the lessons of the Druids; the bards of our climes also found in me a willing pupil, and I might have sung the glories of our people and of our name, but, now that I have studied here," and he placed his hand on his breast, where lay concealed a small volume, " I seek to know but Our Lord, and Him Crucified."

"Amen!" responded his companion. "May the same grace be granted to me. But how comes this? where are you leading me? I have been in Rome before, when I was much younger—only twenty-six years of age, and though I made but a short stay, I remember full well coming often to the cemeteries, but the entrance was very different, not on this side of the road at all."

"Your memory has not failed you, but we are obliged to be much more on our guard now; we have blocked up the old entrance, cut a private staircase, communicating by a movable ladder with this *arenaria* which has been quite abandoned since the workmen extracted all the material they could find, and we are very safe."

The slave drew two small lamps from a hiding-place they were secreted in, and gave one to his companion, telling him they would light them at the foot of the steps. They descended with great precaution until they reached a staircase cut out in the tufa litoide, and found themselves in the Catacombs, where they began to thread the narrow passages, on each side of which lay brethren asleep awaiting the resurrection. There they lay ! the first fruits of the glorified saints, and on their graves the palm of triumph, the dove of innocence, were rudely engraved ; the phials of clotted blood inserted in the cement, while it had been yet fresh, told of many a hard-won victory and gory triumph on the battle-field of God. Origen pressed his forehead reverently to many of the marble slabs, on which a few letters, a few words, at most, barely indicated the great deeds which Angels had already registered at the Judgment Seat of God. Claudius, still leading the way, now told him they had reached the chapel of Pontiffs, and, raising his voice, uttered the usual formula, at which two acolytes came forward. The slave told them his errand, and confided the stranger to their care. Origen then entered alone the vaulted chamber which the venerable Urban had chosen as his place of refuge. It was sufficiently spacious, and received light and air from a large *luminare*. At the further end was a step of marble on which stood an altar supported by four pillars, and in the wall behind this was an older and more simple kind of altar—a sepulchre hewn out of the rock, the flat covering of which was once the *mensa* whereon the holy mysteries were celebrated; the front was of brickwork. St. Zephyrinus, the immediate predecessor of Urban, held this place of honour in the cemetery he had himself designed, and occupied the principal tomb. This cemetery he had entrusted to St. Calixtus, from whom it took its name, and it was ever after under the exclusive care of the Popes. This is why we find Urban abiding here\* as guardian of the sacred deposit which has been transmitted from the Catacomb to the Vatican, imperishable then as now in the hands of a decrepit old man. Surrounded by the mutilated remains of his august predecessors, leaning perhaps against the very grave which was to close over his fast-sinking frame, Urban reigned, a Sovereign and a Father, more truly *Imperator et Pontifex Maximus* than the Cæsar on his throne. Here, he daily offered the Holy Sacrifice, here he found consolation in his solitude, by praying for his flock and receiving their visits. Even now, some of the faithful had lingered after the celebration of the Mysteries to expose their spiritual wants to their common Father, and seek his advice. At the entrance of the stranger they withdrew, and Origen fell prostrate before the earthly representative

---

\* This passage is taken *verbatim* from *Roma Sotteranea* by Dr. Northcote. Pages 87, 131.

of his God. As he had that morning pressed his lips on the foot-prints of the high road, so now he covered with tears and kisses the feet of him to whom Christ had confided His authority. The Pontiff raised and welcomed him, for the science and piety of that son were well known. He heard gladly from him of the welfare of those distant Churches all referring to Rome in the bonds of unity. Origen respectfully alluded to the sorrows that were clouding the Pope's life, but the holy man gloried in the trials appointed by God to strengthen His Church. They spoke of the Empire too, and its vicissitudes. On hearing of the tumult on the road, which the traveller had witnessed, Urban observed, "Yet I do not think with you, my son, that this denotes our Emperor is no more. Certainly the return of the Prætorian Guard portends a revolution, but it may be that they only came to give the senate an account of the dispositions of the army. Some conspiracy is probably on foot, headed perhaps by the barbarian general Maximinus, who has long been suspected of aspiring to the purple. He keeps his royal master in Thracia, with the view of promoting his own ends; yet, methinks, if he had succeeded, we should have known it before this. The proclamation of his accession to the Empire would have been made with more pomp. It could not have been published on the high road by a few Prætorian Guards. No, my son, Alexander still lives, but, alas! the mildness of his rule has passed away, or rather in his absence the Prefect of Rome, Almachius, outsteps his orders, and endeavours to become popular by persecuting the Christians. Many of our brethren have been seized, and taken before the judges. Instead of the high mission to which the Emperor's mother called thee, thou hast come in troubled times, my son."

"Oh, Father, that I were worthy to meet here with torture and the palm!"

"No, thou art not thus called to serve the Spouse of Christ. Thou must uphold her to friend and to foe, make her light so to shine before men that they will grow enamoured with her beauty; thou must carry others to the fold, but thou canst not lay down thy life for them as He did," and he raised his finger towards an image of the Good Shepherd painted on the ceiling. "Ay, my son," he continued, "it is a noble task to disentangle the poor erring one from the thorns of the world, and bring it to His feet, to employ the energies of thy mighty soul in promoting His glory; but wonder not, nor tremble, if thou find that a path long and rough has been allotted thee, for the sufferings of the mind are very poignant; thou hast drunk deep of science, thou must ascend a special Calvary more toilsome than the way of the Cross assigned to all."

He paused, gave a long sigh as if he saw into the future, then changed the subject. "Thou art a traveller, and thy weary limbs require rest. Share with us the food brought by Christians for our daily sustenance," and he reached an *ampolla* with some bread and dried fruit from a niche in the wall. "And where wilt thou seek shelter in Rome?"

"A noble Roman, by name Valerian, accosted me on my way here, gave me a trusty slave as a guide, and invited me to reside under his roof in Rome."

"He is our dearly beloved son, newly called to the faith; thou surely didst not meet him alone?"

"No, his brother was by his side, and a lady of great beauty, his consort, but small and slight as a young girl."

"That is Cecilia, and with her modest, unassuming manner, she is an apostle. Oh, the noble things done by that great mind and weak frame! How many has she brought here to be baptized! A Christian from her childhood, she has been the joy of my heart when I had cause to mourn. She has been as a lamp lit by Christ's love in the midst of her Pagan home, and has not shone in vain, for many that saw her have been brought to the faith by her sweet influence. Called, as many of our Christian maidens are, to that holy state in which a Heavenly Spouse closes their heart to all earthly love, Cecilia was faithful, and made me witness to her solemn vow. A few months ago she came to confide to me the anguish of her mind. Her father had affianced her to Valerian, a noble Roman, and the day fixed for her nuptials was at hand. A despair, such as the fear of death could never awaken, had taken possession of her soul, and she asked me what she could do to avert the dreaded fate. The old Roman spirit spoke within her, for among her ancestors she numbers Caia Cecilia Tanaquil, the wife of Tarquin the Ancient. She asked me whether she might not choose death rather than break the faith she had pledged to Christ. 'Father,' she said, 'there lives in the annals of my country a woman who has been praised, though the dignity of the Roman matron had expired in her before the poniard had done its work; might not a higher motive justify in me a similar act? would God accept the sacrifice of Cecilia even as Rome has exalted Lucretia?' I rebuked her sternly, although by the eyes of Paganism the very idea would have been looked upon as suggested by an exalted virtue. I told her her life and death were in God's hands, and bid her trust in Him who preserved Daniel in the lions' den, and the three Hebrew children in the furnace. She prepared to comply with her parents' behest, and I offered up unceasing prayers that Heaven would protect her: a vision had forewarned me of the triumph of the maiden, and I marvelled how God's word would come to pass. The nuptial day arrived, and I, unseen, mingled in the throng that awaited the bride coming to her husband's home, veiled from head to foot in the yellow veil of the *Flamen Dialis*, an emblem of conjugal fidelity, because the wife of the Flamen alone can never be divorced. Cecilia wore the Vestal dress and her hair, like that of those priestesses, in six braids; Roman maidens always pay thus, on their marriage day, a last public homage to virginity. Little did the bystanders know of the feelings that agitated her. I alone prayed for her from the depths of my heart. The bridal procession passed before the Taberna Meritoria which Pope

Calixtus had, by the permission of the Emperor in less troublous times, received for the use of our brethren and consecrated as a church. I dwelt on the precincts, and, from the threshold, could see the pomp of that procession. This church is near the house of Valerian, and dear to Christians, as a prodigy took place on its site at the birth of Our Lord. A fountain of oil had sprung up in that spot; thereby revealing to Pagans the Reign of the Just One Who had come, and brought plenty and peace. Cecilia bowed her head as she passed the holy place, and I was so near that I could hear her repeat the ejaculation I myself had placed on her lips: '*Fiat cor meum et corpus meum immaculatum ut non confundar*'. She disappeared from my view; I came here and ceased not to pray till the morning; sleep then oppressed my eyelids, nor was I aroused till a man's voice called loudly on my name, and a noble youth, kneeling before me, poured forth in burning accents his profession of faith, and told me he was Valerian, the spouse of Cecilia. Thus much I have told thee, that when thou goest to reside with these Christians, thou mayest treat them as privileged ones of God; the remainder of their history thou wilt learn from intercourse with them. And now, son, thou must be weary. Leave us for thy noble hosts; we shall await thee at our next assembly. Farewell."

Again Origen knelt, and kissed the old man's feet as he had done on entering, then sought in the passage the slave who was waiting for him. "I have kept you long, good Claudius," he said.

"I fear me, I have indeed prolonged my absence beyond my usual time, and my master will perceive it."

"Then do not conduct me any longer. But stay, here is what will explain the long delay. Present this to Florentius." He took a tablet from his girdle, and traced some lines on it with a stylet. "Tell him the stranger who sends this will come with Valerian to see him. Go now, I shall find my way alone."

They had returned to the light of day and the open air; the traveller and the slave parted, bending their steps in opposite directions.

# CHAPTER III.

"WHAT strange clients you have, Valerian," remarked a young soldier who had stepped aside from the street, during a shower of rain, and was taking shelter in the outer portico of the noble Roman's house, at the same time that Valerian came from within. "By Mars! there is not one of these but is blind, or lame, or deformed; and yet, their dress is decent, so they cannot be mendicants."

"And is every citizen who is welcome to my *atrium* during the rain obliged to be as fine a fellow as yourself?"

All Roman houses were divided into two: the public part which every one could enter, contiguous to the street; and the private, separated from the former by an intermediate court, where clients and parasites used to assemble every day to salute their host as he passed out, and were rewarded for their assiduity by receiving each a small loaf of bread, called *sportule*. There was a tie, akin to relationship, established between patron and client; he patronised them, and took their interests to heart, and they often accompanied him to the Forum, forming a goodly train about him, and endeavoured to prove their gratitude by voting for him, applauding when he spoke in public, and doing his bidding at all times. But these who crowded round Valerian were Christian poor, not parasites. He feared lest the soldier might discover his secret and theirs; he made a private sign to them to disperse, at the same time saying aloud, "You are welcome to stay here during the rain, citizens". At which they dropped off quietly one by one.

"Now you must not remain in the *atrium*, Maximus, but come in and honour us with a visit. You must salute my wife Cecilia."

"I shall be highly flattered. I heard that you had become a married man while I was away at the wars, and I wonder I have not met you or your lady at the Campus Martius."

"I have become very domestic, as you shall see." Valerian knocked at the door of his house, which he had closed on leaving it a few minutes before, and a porter answered the summons with alacrity, calling a slave who took off the visitor's military cloak and shook off the drops of rain which had fallen on it.

"I see you have neither a dog nor a chained slave to guard the entrance," observed the new-comer, "and the cheerful face of this man seems to greet your return, whereas my porter looks up at my face as if he feared a beating."

"Perhaps you may have sometimes given occasion to him for that."

"Well! I own I am rather a rough master; but you were not gentle either when we were youths together. What has altered you?"

Valerian did not answer, but led the way to the *exedra*, the room generally set apart for conversation; it was unoccupied, and a slave being asked as to where was his mistress, replied she was occupied in distributing work.

"Ask her to favour us with her company."

They sat down, and in a few minutes Cecilia came, bearing a large basket of fruit in her hands, and followed by two slaves, carrying wine and small loaves. At the sight of a stranger, she stopped, a little confused.

"You expected another visitor, Cecilia," said her husband, "but he has not yet arrived. This is an old friend of mine, by name Maximus, just returned from the wars."

"He is welcome," said the young woman, with a sweet smile. "And how fares our august Emperor?"

"Why, well! as long as we can keep base conspirators from plotting against his precious life; here is to their confusion, and to His Eternity," he exclaimed, as accepting the glass the slave handed to him, he held it up in the air; "but, first to the gods and the guardian divinities of this hearth!"

"Stop!" cried Cecilia, as, with a quick yet easy motion, she held back the libation the officer was about pouring on the floor. Her husband understood her impulse, but trembled lest she should betray herself; a woman's ready wit, however, came to her aid. "The mosaic of this *exedra* has been laid only a few days, it is yet fresh, and the strong Falernian wine will stain it irrecoverably; the pattern is of my own design, so I am rather partial to it."

"The gods forbid I should spoil it, and, verily, the wine is too good to spill. Thus do I honour the genius of the Emperor and yours," and he quaffed it off at a draught. Next, moving his chair the better to examine the pavement, "Then you deal not only in the works of your sex, lady, the artist's talent is also yours. A strange device this is; water, water, on all sides, hills half submerged, a ship, and a flying dove with a branch in her beak; it is perhaps the deluge of Deucalion, but there are no figures."

"No! I wished to have a water-scene for the sake of trying a new colour the artificer has invented. I like the style our Emperor has introduced of uniting mosaic to *lastri;* if Valerian consents, all our *cellæ* shall be paved in *opus alexandrinum.*"

"I shall not wonder now, lady, if you are not seen in the public walks, when your time is so usefully employed."

"Cecilia does not forget the cares of the household either," continued her husband. "Not a day passes but she must needs make the rounds of the *Cella Panaria,* the *Vinaria* and *Fructuaria;* even now, we called on her in the midst of her occupations."

"These fruits come from our hortus at Tusculum," she said, holding up a large pear. "The gardener is quite proud of his production."

"So he may be," replied Maximus, "as well as my friend Valerian to see himself master of such a well-directed household. I thank him for having allowed me to take a glimpse of his happiness, and I thank you, lady, for permitting a reckless soldier to contemplate virtues he had supposed to belong to former days. Worthy daughter of Caia Tanaquil, may your days be long, and the thread of your life spun of gold."

About half-an-hour elapsed, during which the friends entertained each other with pleasant conversation. The rain ceased, Maximus rose to take his leave, and, saluting Cecilia respectfully, he bade his hosts farewell.

Scarce had he gone when a slave came to announce another visitor, who would not tell his name. They knew this to be the traveller they had met that morning and hastened to receive him.

"Will you go to the bath or the *triclinium*?" asked Valerian.

"I am afraid I am too much exhausted for the bath, after my long walk, yet I am ashamed to appear before this noble lady in my traveller's garb."

"Say not so; has it not been enjoined to the pilgrim to travel but with one cloak, and without money in his purse? My slave will conduct you to a *cubiculum* where a tunic and toga are prepared for you; we will await you in the *triclinium*."

A few minutes after, the African was ushered into the banqueting hall of the Christian household; Tiburtius, the younger brother of Valerian, was there too; the men stretched on the beds ranged in order for their reclining on during meals. Cecilia sat at the table, and the slaves passed round with ewers and perfumed water to pour on the hands of the guests.

"How pleasant," observed the lady, "to be able to speak without fear. When Valerian has Pagan guests to dinner, I am at my wits' ends how to perform the duties of hospitality without the idols interfering."

"Oh! clever Cecilia," exclaimed her husband, laughing, "how you cut short our friend Maximus, when he would have poured forth his libation."

"Poor centurion! he looks so good, may he be enlightened. Our guest does not know perhaps it is the Roman custom to begin dinner by the eggs. *Ab ovo usque ad mala.*"

"Noble hostess! there are many hermits in the desert who would consider an egg too great a luxury."

"Alas, alas!" said Cecilia, "my lot has been cast in towns, and I must partake somewhat, I fear, of the corruption of Rome."

"Speak to us of our dear Pontiff," resumed Valerian; "did you converse with him long? Do you think his health is good? We who see him constantly cannot judge as well."

"I noticed nothing," replied Origen; "I knew only that I was at the feet of God's representative, and felt that a great grace and a great power were given to that venerable man. With an overflowing love and an inspired wisdom, he spoke to me of the churches of my land, and of their several wants, and of his children of Rome whom he seems to bear all in his heart; calling them, even as the Good Shepherd, each by his name.

Is it long since he has been obliged to seek the Catacombs as a place of refuge? for he spoke to me of a church given by our good Emperor to Pope Calixtus, which the Christians made use of until lately."

"Yes, that was the *Taberna meritoria*,* which was given to us. We were able to congregate there, and when the *popinarii* (wine vendors) grumbled and asked to take it back from us, the Emperor said: 'I prefer God being honoured in this place, no matter how, rather than give it back to wine vendors'. It was a noble answer, but alas! times are strangely altered since our good Emperor is gone to the wars."

"You all speak," observed Origen, "as if a persecution were at hand; even that sweet child I met with you this morning, lady, talked of martyrdom. May I not see her again? I thought she lived with you."

"Cecilia has a private little assembly of young maidens within our walls," explained her husband, "but she guards them with jealous care."

"We so often have pagan visitors, that I must needs watch over my sweet lambs, lest the ravishing wolf come among them, and take what the Good Shepherd has marked for His own; but I shall send for them."

She beckoned to a slave, and in a few seconds, a troop of young girls came in, varying in age from five years old to eighteen; all were dressed simply; there was beauty on many of those young faces, and, on all, a modesty and sweetness of expression which bespoke

---

* Now the church of Sta. Maria in Trastevere.

an inward purity of heart, and the blessedness attendant thereon.

"Where is my little friend of this morning," inquired Origen, "where is Agatha?"

"Here!" cried the child, with ingenuous simplicity, as leaving her companions, she ran to the stranger and kissed his hand: "Do you know," she said, looking at him with an earnest, inquiring expression, "you remind me of St. Peter? I saw him last night," she continued musing, with a pretty little air of seriousness.

"You, *puella*, where?"

"In my sleep. I had fallen down yesterday and hurt myself very much; I prayed to St. Peter before going to bed, and he came to me and cured me; he put a sweet unguent on my arms, the perfume is on them still."

"God bless thee," said the stranger, and put his hand on her head. "May the vision come to pass, and in all thy troubles and sorrows, may the Apostle watch over thee and keep thee from evil; may his guardian hand heal all thy wounds."

Those words proved a prophecy to be fulfilled in after years.

The young girls gathered round Cecilia, but Agatha, with the satisfaction so natural to a child that is noticed, continued prattling to the visitor.

"It was so nice," she observed, "the perfume the Apostle left on me, it was like the sweet smell that comes from Cecilia's hair; have you perceived that?" she asked in a whisper.

"No," he replied, amused, and in the same confidential tone, "she surely is not vain enough to take great care of her hair."

"Oh no! but do not tell, and you shall know what I see; every morning, when she calls us round her to teach us our prayers, there comes an Angel near her and puts on her head a crown of lilies and roses; she always wears one, but no one can see it, only we little ones, Lucia, Rufina, Secunda, and I; the elder ones only smell the perfume, but they don't know what it comes from."

"Hush, *puella*, I think thou hadst better not speak of this."

"Only to you, and you'll not tell."

"No! I shall not, but go to your companions now."

She obeyed, and slipped into a seat by Cecilia's side.

"What say you to our juvenile circle?" asked Valerian of his guest.

"Oh, it is a blessed sight! I am only surprised how you have influence enough over their parents to get them to trust you with their children."

"I attract them under different pretexts," explained Cecilia, "sometimes to teach them a pretty embroidery, sometimes that they may sing with me; they come to me a few hours each day, and thus we learn and pray together, and help each other upwards."

All the young faces turned towards her as she spoke, and their glistening eyes and beaming smiles told how they loved her.

The conversation glided on to other things. Origen, for the amusement of the young people, told them tales of other lands, but nothing pleased them so much as the life of the Fathers in the desert. They all petitioned their kind teacher to allow them to make mats as the hermits did. He then told them there were holy virgins who served God without retiring to the desert. He spoke of one Dorothy of Cæsarea in Cappadocia, who had vowed to Christ her love and her life; he went on to say how, brought before the Prefect Apricius, she had been ordered to sacrifice to false gods, and then given in charge to two Pagan sisters, Christa and Callista, whose influence it was thought would move her from her high intent. But just the reverse took place; her firmness and virtue opened their eyes, they embraced the true faith, and after confessing Christ in the midst of torments, died all together for the glory of His name.

A burst of applause broke from Origen's hearers; they begged of him to tell more.

The heavy viands had by this time been removed from the table, and fruit disposed in fanciful baskets took their place, together with pastry and confectionery, shaped so as to mimic architectural designs. There were pyramids and obelisks and temples without end, and fountains of spun sugar with silver spray. Wine was handed to the men, but refused at the table, according to Cecilia's custom.

"Is there no chorus to-day," asked her husband, "to finish the repast as is our wont?"

"Yes," she replied, taking her lyre from the hand of a slave. "Martina has a pretty song, neither too profane for the company, nor yet so sacred that it may not grace a feast."

She struck a few chords, and chiming in with the eldest of her pupils who stood by her side, they sang together on the pleasures of friendship and the sorrows of separation, but Cecilia's voice rose high above that of her young friend. Now joyfully cadenced like the fluttering of a little bird, now deeply toned like a recitative, now still and hushed, then bursting forth in a long, deep wail, warbling melancholy notes like the mourning nightingale, slower and slower it sounded, then was only heard at long intervals, and at last expired, while the hearers still listened anxiously for the melodious accents that yet floated on the air.

Origen was the first to break the silence. "I heard that voice already," he exclaimed, "in that very field where you met me this morning; I found out a *luminare*, and from it I heard quite plainly the hymn that was being sung in the Catacombs."

"That is a fearful risk," observed Valerian; "we must tell the *fossores* to repair that opening. And now, let us go and take a walk in the garden. Tiburtius, will you show the way to our guest."

The girls gathered round Cecilia, offered up a prayer with her, then followed into the small *hortus* attached to the house.

"We were speaking of your singing," said Valerian, as she joined him, "and I was telling our friend how its accents first awoke in my heart those feelings which——"

"Brother!" she interrupted, checking what she feared was praise, and calling him by the name she always used towards him when they were alone.

"Nay!" said Valerian reverently, "it is good sometimes to tell the secret of God, you know, and Origen has just asked me how it was Tiburtius and I became Christians. I had long courted the daughter of the Cecilii, and, the more reserved was her demeanour, the more grew towards her my then earthly love. I won her at last, and the nuptial procession brought her to this threshold; out of respect for her religion, for I knew her parents had brought her up a Christian, she was not raised over the threshold of her new home, but entered freely, and sat on the woolsack, and accepted the keys and the distaff, emblem of her domestic dominion. When I drew near to claim her, she firmly uttered the words which custom has rendered so full of meaning, *Ubi tu Caius ego Caia*. I welcomed her, as the descendant of Caia Tanaquil, who was to bring glory to this house, but, ah! far beyond what I deemed. When all those who belonged to her had withdrawn, I sought her, and found her kneeling in her *cubiculum*, her hands stretched out in prayer, and her head still covered with the *flammeum* (nuptial veil). I stood by her side, and she rose and spoke; the words of that hour my heart has repeated each day, and I cannot forget them now. 'Valerian,' she said, 'I am in the care of an Angel who watches over my virginity, therefore, I cannot be thine, lest thou draw on thy head the vengeance and anger of God.' Overpowered by the majesty and power of her words, I asked her if I might be made worthy to see her Angel. She explained to me the doctrines whose beauty had formed her study since childhood. I was seized with a mighty thirst for the living waters, and having learned from her that Urban dwelt among the sepulchres of the martyrs, I sought him and was baptized. I returned to my spouse and found her praying still, as I had left her, but no longer alone. An Angel was at her side, he covered her with his wings, and a fiery sword was in his hand, to punish with the vengeance of God all such as should lay claim to her. I knelt before the Heavenly Messenger, and was dazzled with his brightness. He extended his hand to me, and placed on my brow a crown of roses and lilies, and I could see that Cecilia wore the same, and I asked her wherefore, and she answered, 'The lilies are the emblem of the virginity I have chosen; the roses foretell the blood we are called upon to shed for the faith; art thou ready?' I answered I was, and she placed on my lips a prayer which shall be my last ere I am called to the dread combat: '*Fiat cor meum et corpus meum immaculatum ut non confundar*'."

He ceased speaking, and Tiburtius resumed :—

"I entered the room where my brother and sister-in-law had spent so long a time as to alarm the household; they were both kneeling in prayer, and a perfume of unutterable fragrance filled the *cubiculum*. I looked for the flowers which emitted the odour, but they were hidden from my view; they told me an Angel was present, but he too was invisible to me. Cecilia spoke to me as she had done to my brother, and my conversion was prompter even than his. I too sought the Pontiff, became a Christian, and, at my return, the Angel placed on my head the martyr's crown, and now, in their dear company, I await the fulfilment of the promises of Christ."

"Happy young men!" exclaimed the philosopher, taking a hand of each and pressing them affectionately. "Happy that your path is already marked out for you, that your course will be rapidly run, and that the reward is almost within your hands,—happier far than I!"

Cecilia saw the cloud of anxiety overspread her guest's features, and, with a view to divert his mind, "Let us to merrier subjects," she said to her husband; "our guest is unacquainted with the details of a Roman house, and will perhaps see with pleasure our *Pinacoteca*" (kind of repository for works of art), and she led the way, telling the children to play in the garden, while Martina, the eldest, followed her. This girl was about eighteen, and of a noble birth that stamped her features with dignity, softened down by Christian meekness. Her fringed eye-lashes veiled eyes whose expression was of sweet languor, revealing a character unfit for the world's strife, had not its latent energies been called up by a potent stimulus; her face had all the roundness and colour of blooming youth and health, her hair, too long to be confined by the fillet, encircled her head, and was brought back over her forehead, braided in a knot. She was an orphan, and, having lost her parents at an early age, employed the wealth she had inherited from them in relieving the poor. Prayer and good works filled up the life of the young virgin, who often came to seek by Cecilia's side the strengthening influence of a superior mind, and the sweet solace of friendship.

"I fear," she said, stepping quickly after them into the *Pinacoteca*, "that the new vase, which the slaves laid on the ground while waiting for the pedestal, may be upset; it is covered up."

"Thank you, Martina, you are always careful."

They unveiled together a vase in terra cotta fresh from the Etruscan fabric, which stood in the middle of the floor; Valerian admired the execution of the design, while Origen went round examining the pictures and objects of art which filled the rich museum.

"You look surprised," observed his host, "and you perhaps wonder that we do not better carry out the precepts of evangelical poverty, but we are obliged to conceal our religion under a show of splendour, and these manufactures, besides, employ Christian labourers, and are a harvest for the needy; in days of want we give them to the poor to sell for their profit."

"I am quite sure, my friends, that all you do is from an exalted motive. This dish!" he exclaimed, touching a silver vessel,[*] slightly hollow, and having a rim

---

[*] The effigy of St. Martina, in the church dedicated to her near the Mamertine prison, where her body was found, represents her with her head lying on a dish answering to this description.

studded with precious stones, "how singular! it is so like —— "

"Like what?" asked Cecilia, who heard the incoherent observations. "It belongs to Martina, and she has entrusted it to me."

"It is like," he resumed, "one we preserve in Jerusalem, which tradition venerates as having been that in which the head of John the Baptist was placed after its decollation."

They passed on, but Martina remained transfixed to the spot; a gleam of ineffable joy lit up her usually calm countenance; her eyes were fixed on the dish, and what she saw there she never revealed to mortal ear. Presently, however, she returned to Cecilia's side, and held her back, as they were passing to another room.

"Return that dish to me," she said.

"Willingly! but what is the matter?"

"Do not speak of it; but that man's words have moved me strangely. I have often prayed that a prompt death might be mine, that the agonies of torture might be spared me, for my weakness is so great, and I fear temptation. If my prayer be heard, if I am allowed the prompt death of decollation, let my head lie there. I shall take the vessel, and pray before it daily, that my last hour may be constantly uppermost in my mind. Thus will I strengthen myself against that martyrdom which I feel will be my lot, unworthy though I be to bear off the glorious palm."

Cecilia took her young friend's hands within her own, and spoke to her soothingly, she kissed her flushed cheeks, and urged her to be tranquil. She succeeded in calming her, and they went on to the *biblioteca* where Valerian and Tiburtius were engaged in displaying to the learned Origen the fruits of many researches, and the collection of many years. He was deeply interested, for there were manuscripts he had longed for, and copies of works he had believed to be extinct. Pleased at his attention, Tiburtius had undertaken to pull down the rolls of parchment, while Valerian explained them by degrees; while so doing, the younger brother happened to put his hand on the wall, and suddenly exclaimed, "What an extraordinary heat! there is a fire here! . . . brother, . . Cecilia, call the slaves, quick! help!" And the young man rushed out of the room; but Cecilia went at once to the baths which were separated from the *biblioteca* only by a wall. She perceived that a great fire had been lit in the *hypocaustum*, a double vault below that of the *sudationes*, or vapour bath; hence arose an intolerable heat, and steam issued from the pipes in thick, wreathed columns of smoke. Slaves came now hurrying in, and large water-vessels being poured on the fire below, it was soon put out. What, it was inquired, had caused the accident? One of the slaves came forward, and sorrowfully yet fearlessly, as one who speaks the truth and knows he will be heard, explained that he had been desired to prepare the bath, and, supposing the wood to be wet, had heaped more of it than was requisite on the fire, and then neglected to watch it. A mild, firm rebuke was his only punishment, and his mistress bade him return to the *hypocaustum*, for the embers were still smouldering. As he did so, and all followed him to see there was no more to fear, Cecilia remained alone, wishing to examine whether the mosaic or tiles were injured; while stooping over them, she felt a sudden giddiness seize her, the blood had rushed to her temples, and she fell fainting on the floor. A few minutes after, her friend Martina missing her, went back, and found her stretched on the pavement. Alarmed and anxious, she sprinkled some of the cold water which had remained there on the sufferer. Cecilia opened her eyes, and, recognising her: "Help me to get up," she said, "and do not call any one".

"You fainted from the excess of heat."

"I do not think it was that," she said, rising with an effort.

"What then, Cecilia?"

"Do you see those three children?" she said, pointing to a fresco which represented the Hebrew youths in the furnace. When I was a timid girl, Urban told me to remember them and not to fear; thankful for the courage with which their example inspired me, I had them painted there. Just now, as I stood alone, I thought they fixed their eyes on me strangely, steam was issuing from the pipes, and a vision arose before me, and a voice seemed to whisper in my ear that I too should be cast into a furnace, and a dire fear overcame me. Oh, Martina, I am willing, the Lord knows it, but the poor frame sinks under the thought of combat. Take me away, and pray that I may be worthy to meet the fate that awaits me."

The young girl wiped her friend's forehead, which was clammy and cold in the midst of that heat, and the two brave hearts bore up together, and each forbade the other to despond.

They went out to the garden, that Cecilia might breathe the fresh air; the children were still there, and their innocent caresses made her smile again. Soon she heard the voice of her husband enquiring after her, and went to meet him.

"You look pale," he said; "perhaps you are too tired to see another visitor, Lucullus, one of my earliest friends."

"I pray you, brother, to excuse me, I am not well!"

"He invites us to a feast he gives on his natal day in his gardens at Tusculum; a refusal would pain him, may I accept for you?"

"Whatever Valerian chooses for me will give me pleasure."

"Thanks, dearest Cecilia. Take care of her, Martina," and he withdrew.

## CHAPTER IV.

THE gardens of Lucullus were situated at Tusculum, near the Villa of Cicero. Thus the epicure and the philosopher had chosen the same retreat, but the sage had placed his classical home on a hill, whence he could look down on the haunts of men, gaze from afar at the scene of his triumphs, and dream of distant Rome, whose murmuring applause seemed to lie hushed at his feet. It is strange how solitude becomes a craving want in those who have lived for fame; for falsehood and fleeting glory are not the meed of man; much as the heart pines for fame, it will tire of the sickening draught and turn for refreshment to the well-springs of truth, which are seldom in a noble nature deviated from their course, and are ever ready to gush forth anew at the secret touch of sorrow or disappointment.

The *horti* of Lucullus occupied the slope of the same hill lower down; the gateway formed the arch of a portico whose double row of columns supported a vaulted roof, thus affording a pleasant retreat from the noonday sun. Niches in the wall sheltered statues whose beauty was even then renowned, and whose mutilated remains call forth to this day the admiration of visitors to the Vatican gallery. The portico, extending on four sides, formed a complete hollow square, in the centre of which rose a white marble temple, bearing on the frontispiece the title *Amicitiæ*. That edifice enclosed a statue of immense beauty, conveyed from Corinth by Lucullus, when, returning from the Persian wars, the conqueror of Mithridates and Tigranes brought countless treasures to Rome, the fruit of his victorious expeditions. So great indeed was the luxury introduced by him into Roman customs that Pompey used to call him the Xerxes *togatus.*

An open arch, corresponding to the gateway, led into the flower-garden where the *ambulationes* or footpaths were distinguished by green arches cut out of box, while the wider paths called *gestationes* were covered with shady trellis work, and disposed for such as disliked walking and were carried in chairs by their slaves. Everywhere, the sand of variegated hue, yellow, grey, or red, which latter was made of pounded bricks, and blue, of crumbled slate, was so disposed as to form mosaic patterns, which were as often renewed as the foot of the passer-by spoiled them. Here towered the tall plants bearing flowers with which the guests were wont to crown their heads at feasts, and there crept the smaller highly-scented herbs used in perfumery. There was the Chamæ-melon, the rose, the Milesia of twelve leaves, the Græcula, the Spineola, the Mosceuton, with olive-shaped petals, the Prenestina, which survives frosts; there was a glass hot-house for the tender nurslings. The strong perfume of orange-blossoms attracted the visitor towards one sheltered spot where he soon found himself involved in a mimic labyrinth of no inconsiderable extent; many gardeners had the exclusive care of this grove, which was the principal ornament of the grounds, for oranges clustered in abundance on the branches, and only dropped off when the highly-scented blossoms filled the neighbourhood with their fragrance, and announced the return of spring. Whoever had the patience to wind his way through the intricate paths, found in the centre a pleasant fountain, the surface of which rose and fell with the numerous *siphunculi* which poured their tribute at intervals into its basin, now crossing each other, now shooting upwards, now describing graceful curves. A secret spring, too, would dash the water into the face of an incautious looker-on; and if he endeavoured to escape the bath, he trod on other concealed pipes, which also turned against him. Round the entire flower-garden ran a *pergola*, thickly covered with vines, forming a verdant verandah of about the same extent as the marble colonnade already mentioned. A cavity, hollowed out of a rock, led, by a secret passage, to the *Nymphæum*, where art seemed to be combined with the most refined luxury. It was divided into two semi-circular grottoes, leaving between them an open space, where a monument of white marble rested on the shoulders of huge Egyptian figures; each of these held before it a vase of granite, from which grew laurel trees, whose leafy branches served to bring out in relief the figures of the nine Muses, placed above all. These bore their characteristic attributes save that, to harmonize with the nature of the *Nymphæum*, the *tibia* of Euterpe, the globe of Urania, the scroll of Clio, and all the other instruments were so many fountains, spouting water into a porphyry reservoir below. At the secret touch of a hydraulic machine, the water ceased to flow, the streamlets turned in another direction, and set in motion a musical instrument. Of the grottoes, one was paved in mosaics, representing the four seasons, round which ran a border of a coarser kind, recording in black and white stones the adventures of Ulysses; the walls were covered with marble, encrusted with lapis lazuli; all around, niches of alabaster contained the statues of nymphs, the tutelar divinities of the place, and the architecture was as choice as that of a temple. A dome crowned the whole, admitting the light through a small circular aperture; a rich mosaic ceiling on a gold ground looked brilliant, even in that subdued light, and cast refulgent rays on a group of Galatea placed in the centre, reclining on crystal waves, and surrounded with Tritons. The other grotto was of a more rustic kind; shells of various colour and shape lined the sides, among them being inserted branches of coral. The pavement was of coloured pebbles; sea-weed grew in an artificial aquarium; old Ocean occupied a majestic position, his arm resting on a reversed urn, while fish, carved in variegated marbles, and open oysters filled with pearls, bore witness to the careless opulence of the master of this enchanting retreat. There seemed to be no outlet to this part of the *Nymphæum*, and a stranger might seek for one in vain; but to the initiated, a bronze statue of Harpocrates lowered its finger, a piece of mechanism being contrived for that purpose in the pedestal he stood on. A key he held in his hand was then visible, and a serpent, coiled up against the wall behind him, slowly untwined itself, thereby displaying the lock of a door leading up a stair-case, that gave out on a wide-spreading, verdant piece of ground, elevated above the rest of the gardens, and commanding a pleasant view. Here was an amphitheatre, which was generally considered almost indispensable in a luxurious country-house; beyond, another building of smaller proportions served for the recitals of poets and for dramatic performances; beyond this again stretched a wood to a considerable distance, through which several paths led to the temple of Latial Jove, which could be seen on the summit of the hill bearing that name.

Slaves were hurrying to and fro over the grounds on the day appointed for the banquet which the master of the house gave in honour of his birth-day. The dinner was to be laid in the *Nymphæum*, the heat of the weather rendering that resort most enviably cool. By a refinement of taste, the dining table was made to represent a boat; a mast-head rose in the centre, ornamented with a sail of purple and white silk worked in gold; a gilt poop and prow figured at the head and foot, and the slaves who were to wait at table were all dressed as sailors; even the musicians who, as was customary in great entertainments, filled up the intervals between each course, bore silver oars on which they gracefully rested. Those who were charged with the preparations of the feast had passed many a sleepless night for weeks, and the fantastic devices, the choice fish fattened for the occasion, the new inventions both in the culinary and decorative arts, had occupied the household more deeply than news of the wars or an Imperial triumph. Lucullus was a kind master, good living being supposed to encourage good humour, and, although his fame was far removed from that of his forefather in the days of Augustus, yet he held to the pleasures of the table, as much from natural inclination as out of what he termed respect to his family name. On this eventful morning, he was not above taking a turn through his vast kitchen, where a goodly array of slaves were employed in cooking, dressing, pounding, chopping, making such a noise that he could not hear his own voice, whereupon he passed to the bath-room to prepare for his visitors. These came very early; hardly indeed had the voluptuous Roman freed himself from his anointing slaves, than he found himself surrounded by his most intimate friends, who wished to be the first in offering their congratulations for his natal day.

"The gods return you your good wishes a hundredfold, my dear friends," he said. "And you too, Valerian, have come thus early? ah, this is kind. I hope the noble Cecilia will deign to grace our feast?"

"My bride is of retired habits, and seldom quits our home, but I spoke of you as a friend of my youth whose courteous invitation I wished her to accept; I ventured, besides, to assure her"—this he whispered with an inquiring smile—"that since you have become a married man you do not allow any excess at your table that might be offensive to a Roman matron."

"Truly, friend Valerian," replied the other laughing, "I too have a model wife who may well consort with yours. But this stranger, is he your guest? you mentioned his name to me the other day."

"Yes, I present to you Origen, an African philosopher who loves Rome for herself, and still more for her sons whom he honours."

"As I doubt not the friends of my noble guests are their equals in worth," said Origen courteously, "I have come too, Lucullus, to mingle in the ranks of your well-wishers."

"Friend of my friend, I salute you," replied the host, taking his proffered hand. He then invited them to proceed to the gardens, where he thought they should find more visitors awaiting his welcome.

"Yes," observed Valerian, "on our way hither I saw some ladies assembled in the flower-garden, and I left my wife among them."

They went towards the labyrinth, and on their way thither were joined by several acquaintances, who were profuse in greetings to Lucullus and compliments on the extreme beauty of his villa.

"It is embellished by the sunshine of your presence, my friends. Noble Florentius, we greet you."

"Are you seeking the lady Pudicitia, Lucullus? She is there, and my wife too."

The mistress of the house was doing the honours of

the garden to her lady friends, but, as her lord drew near, she was the first to meet his glance and they advanced to meet him. She was richly dressed, as became her rank, but she wore her ornaments more in obedience to custom and her husband's wishes than with a view to vanity. A snow-white garment fell round her in long folds, and the cameos which fastened it bore no idolatrous image. Her hair, drawn back, left uncovered a low, child-like forehead, whose very repose betokened a happy, confiding spirit; the features were regular, but not striking, a pleasant smile lighting them up when she spoke, and the simplicity of her manners formed her principal charm. The contrast was great between her and her stout, good-humoured Epicurean-like husband, yet it was easy to see how he prized her, and how her sweetness subdued him.

"You will not be displeased, Lucullus," she said; "I sent a message to my friend Siona to bring her little child with her, for she never will lose sight of it, and she would have staid at home, had I not urged her."

"Quite right; I hope I shall see the little stranger later. Is it a boy?"

"No!" said Siona, "my little girl is called Flora, after her father; she is only two months old."

"Rather too young to grace our banquet, at which we shall expect you soon, ladies."

Shortly after, a burst of joyful music gave the announcement that the feast had opened in the *Nymphæum*, and the guests took their places, the men reclining, the women sitting round the table. The device of the ship excited such universal admiration, that hardly any one could partake of the *antepastum* or fore meal, consisting of eggs, fish, pickled fruits and small delicate fish, preserved in salt to excite the thirst and the appetite. During this time slaves went round, bearing baskets of wreathed flowers with which the guests crowned their heads: of these, some were supposed to prevent the effects of wine, others to avert malefices, others again were used as a homage to the gods. The mistress of the house was a Christian, in secret, and had provided wreaths of lilies, a flower not generally used on such occasions, but she had done so to preserve her brethren in faith from the very semblance of idolatry; the flowers, emblematical of innocence, formed a fit ornament for those brows, many of which were destined to fall, guiltless, under the lictor's axe. Again the slaves passed round, bearing silver ewers whence they poured perfumed water on the hands of the guests, and then the dinner began in earnest. There were pheasants, which, although cooked, bore their feathers so ingeniously stuck into an exterior coating of paste, as to appear alive; ranged on a huge silver dish with their brood around them, they seemed to have been settled by the hand of an artist, rather than that of a cook. There were peacocks, with their beautiful tails preserved by the same method; there were birds of every country, and other animals, more remarkable for their exotic rarity than for their flavour. The richness of the dinner service too was proportioned to the reputation of the giver of the feast. Glasses of rock crystal were served to the guests, many of them in such curious shapes as to tantalize the thirsty; some were double, so that the wished-for liquor could not moisten the lips that approached it; others were in the shape of a syphon, others open at both ends, so that it required much dexterity to use them at all, and the trial caused great laughter among the lookers on. Again, the good Falernian wine was contained in dragons' heads, and had to be sucked through the animal's ears and snout, another occasion of merriment. The plates and dishes were for the most part of chiselled silver, and Etruscan workmanship. The first course being over, an entertainment of a different nature interrupted the pleasures of the table; musical echoes resounded through the *Nymphæum*, and a troop of dancers disguised as sea divinities, and water nymphs, flitted lightly over the mosaic pavement, and executed divers dances; they then disappeared in the recesses of the grotto.

"Valerian, I hope the feast meets with your approbation," observed the master of the house to his principal guest.

"It were vain indeed to praise the feasts of Lucullus, but I do admire the dignity with which the entertainment is conducted; that dance was artistic and refined."

Meanwhile, Origen had got into conversation with Florentius, who, piquing himself on being a philosopher, was charmed to find a kindred spirit in the African who had called on him the day after his arrival in Rome with letters he brought from the East. The Roman patrician was endeavouring to explain to his learned opponent that he held a system differing from that of the senate with regard to the gods.

"The first things that existed," he said, "were Foundation and Depth, to these were added Silent Thought, for all must exist in pairs. They engendered Νοῦς and Ἀληθεια, which are Spirit and Truth. These first couples formed a *tetrad* or square, which is the root of all the system. These superior gods are Æones, for they represent lives and centuries. From Nous and Aletheia came Logos and Zoe, which are the Word and Life."

"And these," continued Origen, "gave birth in their turn to about ten others—He who grows not old and Union, Depth and Mingling."

"What!" exclaimed Florentius with delight, "have you too studied in this school?"

"The Gnostics who teach this doctrine are at Antioch, where I dwell. In my search after truth, I have gone to many a source."

"But you have not found it?"

"I have."

"Pardon me if I disbelieve you. Everything on earth is doubtful, hazardous, probable rather than true. Men, weary with seeking truth, rest in one opinion rather than another, that is all. Certain ignorant men, perfectly devoid of the knowledge of human letters, have dared to decide on the divine nature, which so many philosophers have been disputing about for centuries, and with reason, for we know neither what is above nor what is below us, and happy should we be could we know ourselves. If it be true that, in the beginning, the germs of all things were concentrated in nature, what has that to do with God? If the different parts were joined together by a congregation of atoms, fire lit the stars, the earth grew firm under our feet of itself. It being impossible to believe anything true, we must let each nation keep to her traditions; therefore, Eleusis has a Ceres, Phrygia owns Cybele, Epidaurus honours Æsculapius, and Rome, which adores the mall at once, has received the empire of the world in reward for her piety."

This concluding remark was uttered with an ironical smile, but a burst of applause from the guests drew the speakers' attention to what was passing at the table. An extraordinary masterpiece of the culinary art was brought in in triumph, escorted by slaves gaily dressed. A wild boar, roasted on one side, and boiled on the other, afforded a puzzle which no one could solve. The animal was perfectly whole, and yet, when a slit was made with the knife, a number of little live birds flew out, to the delight of the guests, and fluttered over their heads. Besides the feathered tribe, the boar was stuffed with sausages, puddings, roast fowls, and other cured and minced meats. This was verily a triumph, and the question went round the table: "Had the two halves, one roast, the other boiled, been cooked separately, then united, and how had it been done?" Lucullus appealed to the guests to know whether the cook did not deserve to be sent for. All assented, and the happy man being ushered in, was loudly applauded. He explained that the boar roast and boiled was an invention of his own.

He had covered one side with a thick paste which effectually saved it from the action of the fire, and gave it, when removed, a colourless look as if it had been boiled, while the other part, on the contrary, was exposed to a brisk fire; the happy inventor was amply rewarded by the satisfaction universally expressed. Considerable time having been given to the discussion of this dish, and all due honour paid to it, the dinner service was entirely removed, the table remained quite bare, and from the vault of the *Nymphæum* there descended a wide-surfaced apparatus; it was lowered gently, and to the sound of music. It was so well calculated as to fit the table exactly, being already prepared and laid out with sweet dishes and confectionery. The centre piece was the figure of a syren, sitting on a bed of coral, apparently singing to enchant the seamen of a mimic ship which floated in white wine in a silver trough disposed around her in a spiral form; little sugar figures sat up, holding tiny oars, and a similar image was fastened to the little mast. The guests immediately recognised Ulysses resisting the allurements of Scylla. The other dishes were also arranged with great taste and skill, and small fountains threw up little jets of scented water. Fruits of prodigious size, and flowers of great beauty, varied the appearance of the dessert, and wine began to circulate freely.

Lucullus, seeing that convivial gaiety was at its height, turned once more to Valerian: "Will you present a petition to the Lady Cecilia?" he said; "we know her to be gifted with a voice as rare as it is beautiful;

may we request of her to grace this poor banquet, if not for my sake, whose birthday feast she has deigned to honour, at least for that of my wife with whom she is linked in friendship?"

Cecilia bowed assent to the prayer so courteously presented, and made a sign to one of the musicians present to bring her a lyre, but her manner was visibly agitated, as if her mind were occupied with restless, uneasy thoughts. A few words whispered to her by Pudicitia made her grow more calm, and, as the latter left the table, following her friend Siona who had risen abruptly a few minutes before, she determined to sing, as was her wont, when requested. She raised her eyes, seeking for inspiration: "What a Sappho!" exclaimed Florentius to Origen, but the latter knew far better what was the source of her genius, and the soul of her poetry. She thought, and, borrowing the words of the swan of Mantua, she sang like him the reign of peace and plenty, the golden age of Augustus; a graceful cadence interrupted the rich, deep tones, and she told the praises of their host, even as Virgil had praised the Lucullus of his days. Again she spoke of Justice and of its glory, then, in the accents of the Sibyl, prophesied of the Just One who was to come. Her voice grew so solemn that all present were hushed in expectation, then there was silence for a few seconds, then again came a few notes which seemed to drop one by one into the listening ear of the Future. . . . *Et pariet Virgo.* . . .

It was no longer Cecilia that sang or impressed her

audience, it was an Invisible Spirit speaking through her voice! and, as she rose to retire, no one thought of retaining her, or even applauding her, so solemn and Sibyl-like had been her strains. The men continued to remain at table; the ladies withdrew. Cecilia passed on alone to Pudicitia's chamber, where she knew Siona was awaiting her in great anxiety.

The young mother had not joined the banquet till it was far advanced, being uneasy about her child, and, when at table, a message from the nurse had summoned her away. Cecilia now found her, bent, with clasped hands and tearful eyes, over the frail little form that lay on the bed before her, writhing in childish convulsions. Female slaves were around, practised in household cares from their youth, skilled in the arts that cure. There was one aged woman who had attended on the sick for years, and healed many: by her orders, the child was bathed and chafed by turns, a decoction of simples was being prepared to relieve its internal sufferings, but the little face was distorted by pain, the eyes were closing, the violets of death had tinged the baby features. Cecilia saw it all, and, with a firm though mournful voice: "Siona," she said, "it is your duty to summon Florentius".

The poor young woman understood she must give up all hope, and uttered a wild shriek: "No!" she cried, "it must not be; his little one, his idolised Flora, cannot be torn from him thus. Oh gods, rather take me!" and she sank on the floor, beating her forehead on the marble pavement.

"Hush, Siona," exclaimed Cecilia, "do not blaspheme; the pagan gods neither hear nor help us."

"What do you say?" cried the hapless young woman, as if aroused by a sudden recollection; "that is what Claudius said! he told me to call on him when I should be in sorrow, and he promised to help me. Claudius, Claudius! Summon him quickly," she cried to the slaves around her; "call him, he came with us this morning, where is he?"

The good slave had indeed followed his masters, apparently in compliance with their kindness, for they had wished him to take a holiday, but in reality, owing to the Providence of God, he was at hand to fulfil his promise to his mistress, and comfort her in her hour of need. He knew of the child's illness, and was even now watching and praying in an adjoining chamber, imploring help and light from above. On hearing himself called, he came, and standing before his mistress as he had done once before in a commanding attitude, he raised his hand: "Lady Siona," he said, "your child is dying, but, in the name of your forgotten God, my Eternal Saviour, I bring you His Promise: let her be a Christian, and she shall live".

Siona covered her face with her hands; she was calm now, and without looking at the slave whom in this moment she reverenced: "Save my child," she exclaimed, "for I believe!"

Claudius disappeared, and the anguish of expectation fell over them all, for the breathings of the little one seemed stifled. Cecilia took a cup, filled it with clear water, and stood uncertain what to do. At that moment the slave returned with one of the guests by his side. It was Origen.

"Noble Cecilia," said Claudius in a low voice, "send away all the attendants, for this stranger, who holds the office of deacon in the Church, will administer the sacred rite. And will you stand sponsor, promising for the little one she will be faithful to the end?"

Origen took the water, and turning to the young mother who knelt by the bed in anguish: "Have courage, daughter, for, behold, it is even now done to thee according to thy faith".

He breathed on the infant, and behold! its little frame ceased to writhe; he held the water over it, and its eyes opened, and its childish gaze was peaceful; he saw the danger was no longer imminent, and turning to Cecilia: "There is no necessity for abridging the usual ceremonies," he said; "will you allow the Christian slave to stand sponsor with you, noble lady?"

"He who has obtained this child's recovery by prayer is far nobler before God than I am," answered the descendant of the Metelli. She took the little child from off the bed, and placed it in Siona's arms, but she kept her hand gently on it.

"Dost thou renounce the devil, the world, and its pomps?" asked the deacon.

"*Abrenuntio*," was pronounced at the same time by the patrician woman and the slave.

"Dost thou promise to believe in Jesus Christ?"

"*Credo*," repeated the sponsors.

"Dost thou wish to be baptized?"

"*Volo!*" and the two voices blended again in the solemn protestation.

"*Puella, Flora, ego te baptizo, in nomine Patris, et Filii, et Spiritûs Sancti.*"

The mystic rite was accomplished, a new Christian added to the Church, the Guardian Angel of that little child clothed it in a robe, which it was to bear spotless, till it went to wash it in the blood of the Immaculate Lamb. The little one uttered a childish cry when the water touched it, then, exhausted by previous pain, it fell asleep immediately. Cecilia kissed it with unutterable gratitude: "Siona," she said, "let us magnify the Lord, for He has done great things for thee this day".

The young mother had passed so rapidly from grief to joy, that she was overpowered for some time, and could not speak, till a torrent of tears came to her relief; the first words she could utter were: "Let the water which has saved my child be poured upon me too".

"Dost thou speak from impulse or from conviction?" asked Origen.

"From my heart! from my heart!" she replied. And, placing the child again on the bed, she knelt down by the side of it. "I believe from my heart in the God of my Fathers, and in the Messiah Who has long ago visited His people. I truly repent of my idolatry, and I promise, calling to witness the God of Moses and the Christ of Claudius, that I will be faithful unto death, professing Christianity with my child."

"God hears thee, daughter, and will grant thy

request; but thou hast been a voluntary Pagan, and for thee the path cannot be so easy. Thou must do penance first, and then after due instruction thou mayest be admitted into the One Fold."

"From this day forward," she replied, "I shall live in that hope."

Origen and the slave then withdrew, leaving the ladies together, who did not join the company again. That same evening, Siona and her husband returned to Aricia, but she did not trust herself to speak of the child's illness, and he supposed the excursion had fatigued his young wife, who was unusually silent. A few days after, Origen came to spend a little time with them, according to Florentius' invitation, and this afforded a good opportunity for instructing Siona in the Christian religion. She drank in with avidity the stream of truth for which her heart thirsted, and on her return to Rome in the autumn, she improved her acquaintance with Cecilia, and was prepared by her for the grace of Baptism. She could no longer endure the sight of the household gods, but could not ask for their removal without suspicion. Origen turned them into ridicule however, and Florentius was so charmed with his friend the philosopher, as he considered him, that he took down the Penates of his own accord from both his town and country house. Thus the false divinities of that household disappeared, and there arose One who established His Empire gradually, in the hearts of the slaves first, of the masters last, a Hidden God.

At the recommendation of Cecilia, Siona was admitted

to the assembly of the faithful, and allowed to join the ranks of those who were under instruction preparing to receive Baptism the following Easter. And that blessed Holy Saturday night came at last, and Cecilia and Claudius were the happy witnesses of that conversion towards which they had so much contributed; but, impressive as was the beautiful ceremony in the eyes of all, it had a still deeper meaning for them who knew the previous history of the neophyte, and they were not surprised to see her remain bowed down in prayer even after the signal for dispersing had been given. Cecilia, raising her up gently, asked her what she felt: "Speak not," answered the radiant Siona, "for I have heard and seen Him. His Presence is even here, and you all shine in it! He has repeated to me the words He spoke to my ancestor: *Si vis perfectus esse, veni sequere me.* And I will follow thee, oh Master, to prison and to death!"

She raised her clasped hands and streaming eyes to Heaven, and, verily, in that moment, she saw what mortal eye may not gaze upon. They waited a little to give her time to compose herself, then hurried her off; with that peace in her heart which surpasseth all understanding, she re-entered her pagan home.

A few months passed; the silent work went on; a gleam of sunshine seemed to play on the Christians of those days, but it was only the presage of a coming storm. Valerian and Tiburtius having been discovered burying the dead, and it being reported that they distributed great sums among the poor, they were called before the tribunal.

## CHAPTER V.

ALTHOUGH the sun shone brightly, and though it was the busiest time of the whole day, yet there reigned in the Roman Forum a hushed silence, like the eagerness of expectation. A crowd of people surrounded the temple of Antoninus and Faustina where the Præfect Turcius Almachius sat in judgment on two young patricians, accused of honouring the bodies of martyred Christians. There was no edict in force at that time against the followers of Christ, but Almachius had seized upon a frivolous pretext to incriminate the noble Romans whose wealth had excited his cupidity.*

"Which of you two is the elder?" was the first question put by the judge.

"There is no difference between us," replied Tiburtius. "God, the True, the Only One, the Eternal, has made us equal by His grace."

"Can you tell me that which is hidden, yet true?"

"The eternal life which you refuse to see."

"You speak not according to your own spirit."

"No! but according to the spirit I have received from our Saviour Jesus Christ ——"

---

* The whole of this interrogatory is taken from the Acts of the Martyrs.

"Withdraw! You know not what you say. And you, Valerian, is your mind more sound than your brother's?"

"There is a heavenly Doctor who has deigned to take charge of my brother's mind and mine, Christ, the Son of the Living God."

"Do not speak so foolishly."

"Your ear being false, you cannot discern the truth of my words. I have seen in the depth of winter men devoted to pleasure pass along the country, and laugh at labourers who tilled the earth, planted the vine, and grafted the rose, and they said to them: 'Men of toil, leave this superfluous work, come and partake of our amusements; why waste life in such occupations?' and they clapt their hands in derision. The pleasant spring succeeded to the days of cold; the country was covered with verdure, and rose trees with leaves and flowers, the vine descended in graceful festoons from the trees, and these too bore fruit. The labourers were filled with joy, but the men of the city who had laughed at them, now felt the effects of want, and they said: 'Verily! the toil of those working men hath seemed to us a shame, and their company a disgrace, and behold! they were wise, and we foolish; we derided them, and they are now surrounded with flowers and honour'."

"You have spoken eloquently, but not in answer to my question."

"You have considered us foolish and senseless," resumed Valerian, "because we give hospitality to strangers, and succour widows and orphans, and give an honourable burial to the bodies of martyrs. According to you, our folly consists in refusing the pleasures of voluptuousness, and disdaining the privileges of high birth. A time will come when we shall gather the fruits of our privations; for now is the time to sow, and those who sow in tears in this life shall reap in joy in the next."

"Then you mean that we, and our invincible sovereigns, are doomed to sorrow, while you will possess true felicity."

"And who are you and your princes? You are only men, born on a given day, and destined to die when your hour shall come. You have to render a strict account to God of the power entrusted to your hands."

The altercation was touching on dangerous subjects; the Præfect endeavoured to cut it short.

"No more of these lengthy words; offer a simple libation to the gods and you may retire without any punishment."

Both brothers answered at once: "Every day we offer sacrifice to God, but not to the gods."

"And who is your God?"

"I wonder at your question. Do you think there are more gods than one?"

"Tell me, at least, the name of this God you speak of."

"The name of God," returned Valerian, "is a Name you cannot discover, even if you had wings, and could fly in the air."

"Then you imply that Jupiter is not a god."

"It would be a great mistake to suppose it. Jupiter is a homicide, a monster of vice, and the name of God is only befitting to Him Who is Virtue itself."

"And is the whole universe in error, and are your brother and you the only persons who know the true God?"

"Christians are spread all over the empire; it is you who form the minority, poor planks cast on the ocean after shipwreck and only fit for fuel."

The judge, irritated beyond all bounds, ordered the noble Roman to be scourged by the lictors. A suppressed cry was heard in the crowd, and a patrician lady, closely veiled, was borne away by her attendants. Valerian recognised the voice, and as he was led to the pillar where criminals used to undergo this punishment, preliminary to death, he cried out in joyful accents, so as to be heard: "This is the hour which I have ardently sighed for, this day is brighter for me than all the feasts of this world".

Like unto the Master, Whose name was engraved on his heart, he stretched out his hands to the executioners, and unclasping his patrician toga, he bowed under the ignominious strokes; but his voice was not hushed, each blow seemed to strengthen it, and the people listened as he cried to them: "Roman citizens, let not the sight of my torments hinder you from confessing the truth. Remain constant in the true faith, destroy the gods of wood and stone, to whom Almachius offers incense; reduce them to dust, and may those who adore them be eternally punished."

The number of blows prescribed by the law being filled up, Valerian was unbound from the pillar. As the lictors threw their bloody scourges on the ground a slave came and petitioned to have them, offering gold in exchange. They laughed at him, but took the proffered bribe. The man stooped to pick up the rods, and in so doing, kissed, unperceived, the feet of Valerian, who whispered to him: " Tell her I am strong of heart, let her pray for me to the end ".

The slave rolled up his prize in a linen cloth, and disappeared.

The noble Roman, undaunted, was again led before the tribunal, where his brother awaited him, and a like sentence was passed on both. They were to be conducted to the fourth mile-stone of the Appian Way, to the Pagus Triopius where they were to sacrifice to Jupiter, or be condemned to death. Guards now surrounded the prisoners, and they set out in order on their march. As Valerian cast his eyes on the officer who was at their head, he could see the brave man pass his hand over his eyes, and lower his helmet to conceal his emotion. He recognised him, and exclaimed: "Maximus, how come you to have been named to this duty?"

" Because noble patricians like you require a noble escort, and they would not confide you to a subaltern. Oh, the mockery of this feigned respect, when we know what they have in store for you. Noble and brilliant flower of the Roman youth, brothers united by so tender a love, why will you persist in offending the gods, and how can you run to death as to a feast?"

"And think you," replied Tiburtius, "that we could show such joy at this hour were we not persuaded that the next life is better than this?"

They went on, and as they came near to the Tiburtine gate, the people, who at first had crowded round them, began to disperse, several returning to the city. Maximus drew nearer to his friends, and asked in a low voice: "What is the next life?"

"Even," replied Tiburtius, "as our body is covered with clothing, so it is with our soul clothed in a mortal envelope. Our body, which draws its origin from the earth, shall be restored to it, and turn to dust to rise again like the phœnix, when the dawn of day shall come; but as to the soul, if it be pure, it will be taken to Paradise to enjoy there eternal felicity, and await its re-union to the body."

Again the young officer drew back a few paces, and a strange conflict arose within him, such as he had never experienced before; it was the first fruit of the martyrs' sacrifice; their blood was baptizing his soul, even before it was shed. After a short silence, he resumed: "If I could acquire the certitude of this future life you speak of, I too would feel disposed to contemn the present life".

"Then," said Valerian, "in the name of Him for Whom I am about to die, accept the promise I make to you. In the hour in which my body shall be immolated, your eyes will be opened to see the glory into which we enter, on one condition alone, that you repent of your past errors."

"I accept," replied the young man, "and I devote

myself to Heaven's anger if in that hour I confess not the True and Only God." *

Thus was his act of faith pronounced; it had burst forth from the almost unconscious heart of the soldier, touched by a mighty grace. The brothers wished that the work might be fulfilled before they left him.

"Can you not," they said, "order these men, over whom you have authority, to take us to your house? There they can guard us; our execution can be delayed one day; meanwhile we shall send for him who is to purify you, and this very night you shall see Him we have promised to show you."

Maximus complied; he directed the soldiers to skirt the town walls, and this brought them to a country-house which belonged to him. There ranging them in a circle, he placed Valerian and Tiburtius in the midst, and listened to the truths which they expounded. They continued their instructions till nightfall, when a messenger who had been dispatched in secret to Cecilia, returned with her and two priests, bringing with them the substance which was to be changed into Sacraments, the bread and wine of the Sacrifice, and the mystical oil which was to anoint those athletes of God! Cecilia, at once a wife and an apostle, reassumed at this dread hour the charge she had already fulfilled towards Valerian. Like the Angel of Gethsemane, she had come to them, holding to their lips a chalice which was soon to pass away, and strengthening them to pro-

* This conversation is taken from the Acts of the Martyrs.

nounce that sublime Fiat which tore her womanly heart with even more suffering than they would have to go through in their approaching martyrdom. The waters of baptism were poured on all those willing men, and the house of Maximus was turned into a house of prayer. Morning came, and it was Cecilia who broke the silence first in that pious assembly: "Soldiers of Christ,"* she exclaimed, pointing to the dawn which broke upon the east, "cast away the works of darkness and clothe yourselves with the armour of light. You have fought manfully, you have run your race, you have preserved your faith. Go then to receive the crown of life which the just Judge will give you and all those who welcome His coming." Then she left them, walking out hand in hand with Valerian, and on the threshold thanked him for the brotherly love he had borne her, and for the happiness of their short holy union, and there she remained, watching them until they were out of sight. On they went, an invincible phalanx; they passed the spot where the Master had appeared to Peter, and all knelt and touched with their foreheads the consecrated spot. On again, the monument of Cecilia Metella casting its shadow over them, and Valerian could see the name so dear to him engraved upon the marble; it was the last thing of earth he gazed upon. They reached the village of Pagus Triopius; there was the temple of Jupiter, and his priests, standing at the foot of his altar, presented the martyrs with incense. They

* *Acta Sanctæ Ceciliæ.*

only answered by kneeling, and offering their necks to the executioner; all the soldiers, now Christians, ranged themselves around them; they could not comply with the Præfect's orders, they refused to lay a hand on their brethren in the faith, and others had to be summoned to do the cruel office. At that moment Maximus fell prostrate, for he saw the heavens opened, and the martyred brothers enter into glory. The bodies remained until night on the very spot where they had fallen. Then came a woman, clothed in mourning patrician robes; she was accompanied by slaves, who gathered the dead together, wept over them, and bore them away.

Meanwhile the soldiers had returned to Rome; their commanding officer seemed to be seized with a strange hallucination, and for some days he never ceased repeating, even while walking and sleeping: "I have seen, I have seen".

He was summoned to the tribunal of Almachius; threats and the judge's anger could only draw from him the confession of his faith. His punishment was most severe, for, having betrayed his trust, he was condemned to be beaten to death with whips armed with leaden balls; in this atrocious torment his skull was fractured, and he soon expired.

The same pious hands which had buried the mortal remains of Valerian and Tiburtius, laid Maximus by their side, and in memory of that last conversation which had brought faith to his heart, a phœnix was engraven on his grave. From that day, the house of

Valerian in the Via Salutaris became a place of refuge to sufferers of all kinds; every day, abundant alms were distributed there by Cecilia, who used to go round to the poor, speaking words of comfort to each of them; sometimes she told them she was soon going away, and must send her treasures before, to wait for her, there where the moth could not devour them, nor the rust of the world consume. She often had a little child in her arms, she loved it as the solace of her widowhood; it was brought to her daily, and seemed to know her well, for a baby smile would play on the little lips, in answer to the oft repeated injunction: "Flora, thou must love Jesus".

Siona did not dare to visit her friend, for the Roman widow was well known to the judge, and the sentence of death was already hanging over her, but she sent her little one in her stead, for she believed a mysterious sympathy existed between those two pure souls, of whom one was about to leave the world the other had scarcely entered; perhaps she fondly hoped that the inheritance of Cecilia's virtues would be infused into her child, for, each time she returned to her, she received her with a kind of respect, and gazed upon that little face, which seemed to her to bear the foreshadowing of a great destiny.

Six months passed away. One day, Cecilia reclined in her *cubiculum* after her solitary repast; the young virgins she had been rearing for Christ were dispersed; she had sent them to the shelter of their respective homes, as a gardener cares for his nurslings at the approach of a storm. Flora alone was playing quietly with flowers, on the floor. Suddenly, there was a noise outside, and a slave entered with consternation in her manner, announcing that the emissaries from the magistrates had come to seize her beloved mistress: "Do not let them see you," she added. "Fly through the garden. I have bid them tarry awhile, so as to give you time to escape."

"Silence, woman," replied the noble lady; "look only to the safety of this child."

She went out to where the men stood. Their attitude was so respectful, so full of compassion and admiration, that when they entreated her to sacrifice to the gods, she felt she could address them: "Citizens and brothers, hear me," she said, "you are brave soldiers, and in your hearts, you detest the impious conduct of Almachius. As to me, I glorify in confessing Jesus Christ, and suffering for Him, for I have never cared for life. I pity you for being compelled to obey so unjust a judge. To die for Christ is not to sacrifice one's youth as in your pity for me you seem to think, it is only giving dust in exchange for gold, a perishable gift for an eternal reward. Would not you too joyfully barter a vile coin against a precious metal, if it were offered to you, and would you not invite all your friends to share your good fortune? Jesus Christ does more: He will return to you a hundredfold what you offer Him, and add thereunto life everlasting."

Several of the men were already won by the inspired accents of the noble virgin, and she saw by their manner the advantage she had gained. Stepping on a pedestal to raise herself: "Do you believe," she asked, "in what I have just told you?"

A thrill of enthusiasm ran through the ranks, and they answered with one voice: "Yes! we believe that Christ, the Son of God, is the true God".

"Go then," she resumed, "and tell Almachius I require a delay; he can defer my condemnation for a little while. In that interval you will return here and find one who will teach you."

They went and, as God had so decreed, the will of the brave virgin prevailed over the bad man's heart; he granted her a respite. To her it was the time of an abundant harvest, to be gathered for her Heavenly Father. All those who lived in that part of Rome drew round her, hearing they were to lose her soon; almost all hearkened to her words, and Urban the Pontiff, in order to console the last days of his beloved daughter, and crown her last work, came to dwell in her house, and pour the regenerating waters on those she had converted.

Four hundred neophytes knelt before the Common Father, a Christian army girding their loins for the day of combat. Cecilia consigned her house to one named Gordian that it might serve henceforward for the Christian assemblies. Urban remained in the midst of his new flock, comforting and exhorting them. In that gathering of Christians, Flora was known as the child of the house, she would play innocently by the Pontiff, or listen to him when he spoke, for she reverenced him with childish awe.

One day he was reading the Gospel to his hearers, and as he came upon the words, "If you become not like unto this little child, ye shall not be worthy of the Kingdom of God," that little girl was crouched before him, gazing at him with those singular eyes she inherited from her mother. He held her up as illustrating the Master's words.

"Oh Father!" exclaimed Cecilia, shuddering, "do not apply those words to my god-child; the little one whom Our Saviour pointed out to the Apostles was in after years devoured by wild beasts."

"What then! art thou not preparing for martyrdom, and dost thou dread a similar glory for Flora?"

"Ay, Father! but that child is connected with the old tale of Our Master's unrequited love," and she repeated to him the history of Siona's forefather.

The venerable Urban listened, looked again into the face of the child, and seemed to read therein with a prophetic eye; for he made the sign of the cross on her, and said in a low voice: "Flora, thou must fulfil thy destiny, the grace which thy ancestor threw away has descended upon thee, it must bear thee through the Virgin's path to the Martyr's crown."

A few days passed, and the messenger of Almachius returned; Cecilia was summoned before the tribunal; slight in stature and simply dressed, she looked but a young girl, and, as such, the magistrate addressed her, "Puella, what is your name?"

"Men call me Cecilia, but I have another name far more noble, and that is, 'I am a Christian'."

"What is your condition?"

"I am Roman-born, of a noble and illustrious race."

"I am enquiring about your religion, the nobility of your family is well known to us."

"Your interrogation was not exact then, since it required two answers."

"Whence do you derive so much assurance?"

"From a pure conscience and a sincere faith."

"Do you not know my power?"

"And do you not know Who is my betrothed?"

"What is his name?"

"The Lord Jesus Christ."

"Are you not aware that our Masters, the Invincible Emperors, have given orders that all who refuse to deny themselves Christians are to be punished, and all who deny themselves as such, acquitted?"

"Your Emperors err as well as yourself. The law you bring forward only proves one fact, that you are cruel, and we innocent, for, if the name of Christian were a crime, it ought to be your duty rather to make us confess it."

"But the clemency of the Emperors thus offers you a means of saving your life," interposed the Judge.

"And we," replied Cecilia, "consider the title of Christian as great and sacred, we cannot deny it. You wish to hear a lie from our mouths, but, in proclaiming the truth, we inflict on you a torture greater than that to which you subject us."

"Either sacrifice to the gods or simply deny that you are a Christian, and you shall depart in peace."

A disdainful smile curled the lip of the virgin; "Truly," she said, "what you propose is most humbling to yourself as magistrate; you wish me to lie. I triumph in the accusation, and death shall be my victory."

"Unhappy woman! Know you not that the power of life and death are in my hands?"

"That is false."

"How say you so?"

"You have only the power of death; you can take life from those who enjoy it, but you cannot restore it to such as are dead. Say then that your Emperors have constituted you a minister of death, but nothing more."

"Lay aside this audacious language, and sacrifice to the gods."

"You must have lost the use of your eyes, for I and all here present can see nothing but statues of stone, bronze, and lead."

"I am a philosopher, and have disdained your taunts when only addressed to myself, but I may not suffer the gods to be insulted."

"Not a word have you let fall, but I have proved it to be unjust, and now you have even lost your sight. You call these stones gods; feel them, they wear away, and cannot defend themselves from the injuries of the weather. Every one knows that God is in Heaven. Christ alone saves from death, and condemns the guilty to be punished by fire."

The intrepid virgin ceased; for only thus far had it been given to her to speak. She was mindful of Him

Who had told her not to reflect beforehand, for in that hour He would inspire her with what she should say before men. The judge feared to spill the blood of one of such illustrious birth, for he had already infringed on his orders. He now commanded Cecilia to be conducted to her own house, there to be put to death privately. She was to be shut up in the *caldarium* of her own baths, a great fire being lit in the *hypocaustum* beneath ; the steam would thus suffocate her, and she would die untouched by the lictor's hand.

Joyfully the virgin entered the place of her martyrdom ; devoutly she fell on her knees and kissed the pavement which was to receive her dying form ; triumphantly she stretched out her arms as if to seize the palm so soon to be hers. How strange, she then thought, was that prophetic foresight which had caused her to paint on the walls of the *caldarium* the three Hebrew children in the furnace ! it was now a peaceful vision given to her to comfort her agony. She looked on the happy faces till they seemed to swim before her in the dense clouds of steam that arose ; her breathing became difficult, her brain reeled, her eyes shed tears that did not relieve her ; she called upon her God, and fell fainting and exhausted on the burning pavement. She thought death was at hand, and composed her limbs modestly for the eternal sleep, and drew over her head the veil that was to hide her features from mortal eye, when lo ! an angel stood by her side ; he who had been through life the guardian of her virginity, now revived by a sweet dew from Heaven her sinking strength, fanned her with his wings, and cooled her temples with a moisture distilled from his bright hands; he told her the hour was not yet come, though near at hand, then her voice returned to her, and, rising from the ground, she broke forth into a hymn of praise, and in tones which the vaporous atmosphere rendered more clear and ringing, sang the triumph of that hour.

Those who stood without shook their heads with compassion, and many eyes were moistened with pity, and they said: "'Tis like the swan that sings when about to die".

The morning of the third day dawned; the executioners opened the *caldarium* to withdraw the body of their victim: lo! she lived! a fire more ardent than that lit by mortal hands supported her still, the love which is stronger than death had annihilated the destroying flames.

News of the prodigy were conveyed to Almachius; the enraged tyrant despatched a lictor with orders to cut off her head. The man of blood came, but he quailed in the presence of her who had conquered death. Twice he brandished his axe in vain; at the third stroke, Cecilia fell, an unslain victim on the floor. The Roman laws did not permit the executioner to strike more than three times; he was obliged to withdraw, leaving Cecilia to her fate. The door of the noble lady's house was opened to such Christians as wished to honour her remains, as they thought! but oh! wonderful interposition of God! from that head, bleeding and disfigured, yet still attached to the trunk, a voice came forth, faint and weak, yet sweet as the martyr's tones had been through life, and exhorted the brethren to be faithful unto death. Maidens surrounded her, and steeped linen cloths in her blood, men knelt at a respectful distance, and listened to her dying words; pagans came too, and, as many as saw and heard her, went away believing. She taught them the mystery of the Holy Trinity; with the three fingers of her right hand extended, she continued to hold up one of the left, and repeated in accents which lived in the hearers' minds long after the voice that uttered them was hushed for ever: "Believe in One God in Three Persons". Death has respected the burning eloquence of those motionless hands, the tomb has revealed the modest beauty of that attitude, sculpture has immortalized it; from her stony vault and marble figure, Cecilia repeats: "One God in Three Persons". She recognised the poor she had loved and commended them to the charity of the faithful; she spoke to the young girls whose mistress she had been so long; to Martina who knelt by her side, and wept unceasingly, she whispered words of solemn import which made the girl's cheek grow pale at first, then radiant with ardent desire.

"Watch over my little Flora," she said in conclusion, "I entrust her to your care."

Then Martina left her for a few minutes, and returned with a little child in her arms; she knelt down and held the little face close to that of the martyr. The child looked frightened at the sight of so much blood, but did not cry; presently with that Christian instinct which she had imbibed from the example of others, she dipped her tiny finger in the streaming cloths and signed her forehead with the cross. Cecilia saw the impressive act. "Even so," she said, "my blood has marked her for Jesus! · I shall recognise her before God's Judgment Seat! . . . Let her prayer be through life '*Fiat cor meum et corpus meum immaculatum, ut non confundar*'. Now, take her away, and let a messenger be sent for Urban, our Pontiff and Father, for I cannot die till I receive his blessing."

Her desire had been forestalled, and the Pope now stood by her side; he had seen her grow in virtue under his eyes, he had received the revelations of her sinless heart, and the aspirings of her brave spirit; he came now to receive her last sigh. Her voice which had been growing fainter and fainter, became almost vigorous at his approach:

"It is well," she said, "I had implored of God a three days' delay that I might see you once more and confide to your Beatitude * the poor whom I have loved, and also this house that you may turn it into a place of assembly for the faithful. Now, bless me, Father, for I go to the Bridegroom who saith: Come!"

And as the pontifical hand which had often blessed her, was raised over her once more, she turned away as if unwilling that men should gaze on her in that last moment. The prayer she had so much loved hovered on her lips, but was not concluded: "*Fiat cor meum et*

* *Acta Stæ. Ceciliæ.* A striking instance of the antiquity of this title.

*corpus meum immaculatum,"* . . . they heard no more! she had ceased to live!

Urban had placed her in her grave, even thus, as death had left her, with her head bowed down, and turned away, and knees modestly joined, and the outstretched arms stiffened and motionless, yet teaching still, in their death-like attitude, for the fingers repeated Three in One!

Even thus! in her noble, patrician, gold-embroidered robes which veiled to the world the depths of her penitential spirit, but not entirely so, for when Martina's arms gently raised the beautiful corpse to her bier, she felt through that rich tunic the iron chain with which the virgin girt her delicate frame; mysterious armour, known to those who fight the battles of the King of kings.

Even thus she was found hundreds of years later, unchanged; thus she now lies under the altar with the instrument of penance concealed under her golden robe.

She was placed in that catacomb which Calixtus had devoted more especially to Pontiffs, but at its furthest extremity, near to that of St. Pretextatus, where lay her husband, in order to unite, as much as possible, those who had been linked on earth in the holiest of bonds.

And there she began her long sleep, awaiting the resurrection in the shadow of that great mausoleum which has carried the name of her ancestress, Cecilia Metella, far and wide, and men little knew, when they passed by, that a greater glory and an undying fame lay hid beneath the soil.

## CHAPTER VI.

THREE years passed away. Maximinus, the Thracian peasant who had at first won the Emperor's favour by his agility in a horse-race, had risen from thence to command the 4th legion, later, the Prætorian guard, and finally, the whole army, now wore the Imperial purple. But alas! the first dignity of the empire sat ill on the barbarian, he never visited the land he was unworthy to call his own; Rome never saw him, that humiliation was spared her, but from his camp on the Danube, the despot reigned by the terror of his name. Italy was covered with spies and informers, more apt to discover those whose riches rendered them an object of envy, than to distinguish merit or accuse the guilty. The senators were the first victims of the absent tyrant's cruelty, for those days were no more when the Fathers of the Roman people would sit peacably in the attitude of command when danger was nigh, prepared to repulse the invader by the awful majesty of their presence alone. Alas! how much was gone of the old greatness, and the respect for the past, and the consular dignity, and the republican pride! Degenerate Rome! had he who wore the purple been less a slave, the humiliation might have been less crushing; but now! the gods themselves were not respected, the army wanted money, and the temples were stripped of their silver offerings and golden shrines, the idols themselves were to be seen remorselessly carried away on carts, to be melted down for base purposes.

The ashes of the good Alexander had been brought home by pious hands, and Roman gratitude erected a monument to him* together with his mother, Mammea, the guardian-parent who had formed his youthful mind, and trained him to virtue and science; one among the many women who have in all ages been praised for the vigilant care with which they guarded the offspring confided to their widowhood. How often has a youthful hero been developed, and a man risen to renown, because the fostering hand, the woman's wit, and keen discernment, guided as wisely as the father's rule. How many great men have owed their education to their mothers, from Cæsar to Napoleon!

And therefore they slept together, the mother and the son, and as men passed outside the Porta Celimontana, they saw near the mountain of grain, a huge mausoleum which many looked upon with tearful eyes, for it brought back the memory of happy days. Many entered it to pay an act of homage to the illustrious dead. In its sepulchral chamber, there was a marble sarcophagus of more than usual size; bassi rilievi ran round it, and they told the history of Achilles, his love for Chryseis, his quarrel with Agamemnon, the death of Patroclus and Hector's direful fate; the scene between the kneeling Priam and the haughty Achilles occupied

* To be seen in the Capitoline Museum at the present day.

the fourth side, as if the image of death must not be brought forward with that of glory, and above, on the cover of the urn, lay, half-sitting, half-reclining, the mother and the son. Time has respected those marble figures, which show to this day the absence of those signs of animal life, too often to be met with in the busts of Roman emperors. There is intellect in the woman's well-developed forehead, more perhaps than in Alexander's, where openness of character and goodness are more conspicuous. Mammea's hair, drawn back, and confined under a fillet, shows a head where men's qualities predominate over feminine features, the pose in both is natural, devoid of indolence, and indicates an energetic character, ever ready to arise for the work to be done.

Time went on; the Christian faith flourished in darkness and persecution; yet sometimes, for the heart of man is weak, the brethren grew weary of their trials, and raised their hands to God, asking Him to be their Judge, and praying that His reign of peace might come. It was spring! there was joy on the face of nature, and a corresponding exhilarating feeling raised the heart even of such as had cause to mourn. Siona stood on a terrace in the garden of her house situated on Mount Aventine, where she and her husband used to resort during the summer months, their town house, near the Tiber, being better suited for the cold season. She was looking down sadly on the edifices of that city, where the pride of life and public corruption were drawing down on its inhabitants the vengeance of God.

Before her, there stood out on the horizon the hill of the Janiculum on which St. Peter breathed his last, consecrated, even in those days, as a spot sacred to pious pilgrimage and fervent prayer. From that, the first stage in the long passion of Christ's martyrs, she could trace out the long Dolorous Way which they had trod like their Master, from the Gethsemani of trial to the Calvary of expiation. How many, dear to her, had fallen in that Road of the Cross! how the wounds of her heart bled afresh as the houses they had dwelt in, the places they had frequented, rose to her view in that busy city! Cecilia, who the first had initiated her in the divine truths, how soon had she winged her flight to Heaven! and, of those friends who yet remained to her, how many were destined to fall victims in the daily strife! As for herself, she did not know what was in store; in her Pagan home, the light of truth had shone for her alone; her religion was a profound secret which she kept concealed from her husband, and if anything happened to her, what would become of her child, her precious lamb, marked with the sign of Christ's flock? Thoughts of mourning regret, of hopeless fear, of nameless despondency, came to her in that hour, and weighed down her spirit; she bowed her head on her hands. Presently, a tiny foot-fall disturbed the pebbles in the gravel walk behind her, and as she turned to look round, a child's face, the miniature of her own, gazed at her with infantine wonder and tenderness, and her little daughter whispered: "Mama, why are you sad? please do not cry!"

Flora was in her fifth year: many thought her a precocious child, but it was the consequence of early Christian training; for religion is a natural element to the human heart, and those who are from childhood steeped in its doctrines show a vigorous health of mind which seldom or never gives way under later struggles. Oh the marvellous secrets and the prodigious learning of those little souls to whom Jesus has come early and taught His divine lessons; theirs is a wisdom the world does not know, and theirs a conscience full of depth, of beauty, and poetry, to which the children of this world, learned though they be, can never attain!

Flora, though a mere infant, was already a little companion to her mother: Florentius was absent at this time, having gone to Iberia to receive, in his wife's name, property which she inherited from her sister who had lately died in that country. Siona was in the habit of taking her child by the hand, when she used every morning go round the house to superintend domestic arrangements: the little girl missed her mother this morning, and having looked for her in the garden, came up to her gently, pulling her by the dress.

"Mama, why are you crying? is it because you have not received any letter from my father?"

"On the contrary, dear child, he sends me word he will be here soon."

"Oh joy! has the *tabellarius* come from Iberia then?"

"Yes," said Siona, "he has brought these;" and she took out from the folds of her *stola* tablets engraved with the point of a stylet.

"From my father!" exclaimed the child kissing them, "I want to hear every word he says; that is, if you will please to tell me, Mama." She climbed up to the top of the low wall against which Siona was leaning, and sat down, putting her arm round her mother's neck.

"Florentius has been detained by bad weather; he had besides much business to attend to, and he has been obliged to look out for a person who will attend to the property when he leaves."

"Does that mean a *Villicus* like Claudius?"

"No, not a slave. I am very sad at having lost my sister; her husband died only a few months ago, and your father and I wished her to come and live with us, together with her little boy. We heard she had fallen ill, and Florentius set out at once, but he only arrived in time to see her die. She left her orphan child, Laurentius, in my charge, and your father is bringing him home to us. You will be very good to your little cousin, will you not, Flora?"

"Well! I wish it were a little girl."

"The poor little fellow is only two years and a half old, much younger than you, you see, so you must help me to take care of him, and teach him, and make him good."

"I understand!" replied the little girl, quite satisfied now, and assuming a little air of importance; "you will be his Mama, and I his big sister. Oh, how nice! may I go and tell Claudius, and ask him what I can do to amuse my little cousin?"

"There is time enough, my good little girl."

"Oh, but Claudius will be so pleased, may I go?"

"Certainly," and her mother handed her down gently, but a new thought struck the child.

"Mama! what a pity you sent away my nurse Concordia, she would have been so useful now that my little cousin is coming."

"No, my child, you were growing too old for a Pagan nurse, and Concordia was a constant hindrance to me, owing to her great dislike to Christians."

"Yet her daughter, my foster sister Barbara, wishes very much to be baptized."

"Oh Flora, what have you been doing?"

"I have been instructing her, Mama; indeed it was not I that began, but Lucia, and she is so good, she must be right."

"You must never speak of religion unless Claudius or I be with you."

"But, Mama, Barbara will never, never tell, she is so afraid of her parents, and besides Claudius was listening to us, while he was at work, very near."

"Oh, then, I am not uneasy. But see! what a large party of children that is, coming up the hill, they must be on their way to see you, let us go and welcome them."

Flora's young friends and playmates were frequently in the habit of coming to spend the day in the pretty gardens of Florentius' house on the Aventine hill, but, on this occasion, they had sad news to announce; Agatha, their favourite companion, was about to leave Rome.

"What a pity," cried Flora, "oh, where is she? she is not with you?"

"No!" said Lucia, "she came this morning to bid me good-bye."

"She came to our house too," said Rufina and Secunda, two sisters; "she told us she would spend this afternoon with you, and we came to meet her."

"Oh! what shall we do without her?" they all repeated.

"She taught me to embroider," said Bibiana.

"And me to read," interposed Lucia.

"And she is so very, very good," continued Flora, "and we all love her so much, that it is of no use to think we can ever be happy again without her."

"No! never again!" repeated the juvenile chorus.

Meanwhile the object of all this childish praise and regret had passed into the house through the street door, led by Martina, who, at Cecilia's death, had taken charge of her, and kept her in her own home. They now reached the garden, just in time to hear the lamentations of the little circle.

Four years ago, Agatha was a lively, clever, impetuous child, too headstrong for easy management, but Cecilia had foreseen all the good that might come of that strong will, if well directed. The child's parents lived in Sicily, they had come to Rome for a short stay, and, finding the climate agreed with their child, much better than that of her native island, they were glad to accept the kind offer of their friend Cecilia, who proposed to them to let Agatha remain with her for a year or two, until the symptoms of childish delicacy had passed away. Family circumstances, however, had prevented her parents returning to Rome as soon as they had intended, and, since Cecilia's death, Agatha had remained as we have seen in the charge of Martina. She was now nine years old, a child of prayer and of grace; her docility corresponded to her early training; there was a seriousness about her, and a slight degree of authority in her manner which commanded respect without repelling affection; her young companions looked up to her, and no one of those older than herself ever made free with her.

As she came forward now, her soft delicate features bearing the traces of tears, they said, "You are also sorry at leaving us, Agatha?"

"Oh yes! but it is wrong to give way to sorrow when I am going home, because it is the will of God," and a strong effort repressed the rising tears, "indeed, I never expected to have remained so long in Rome: but now, my father has come as ambassador from Sicily to the senate, and he is taking me back with him."

"Dear Agatha, what will become of you?"

"What God wills! I am thankful that my childhood has passed here, in the city of St. Peter, where I have learned to know my God. I have ever prayed to the Apostle that he would choose for me the path which would lead me most surely to Jesus, and, therefore, I know I am safe. I was told, years ago, to trust in the Apostle, for he would be near me in my sorrows, and cure all my wounds."

"Lady," she added, turning to Siona, "you remember him who thus spoke to me, the noble stranger who was a guest of Cecilia, and who, I heard, baptized Flora. What became of him?"

"Do not ask, my child, for men say that in his wonderful writings he has fallen into error. For myself, I cannot believe it, for his was a noble nature, and I do not think God could have abandoned him to himself; nevertheless, pray for him, that the Holy Spirit whose temple he has ever been, may enlighten him to the end."

Agatha joined her hands in prayer, and a deeper sorrow passed over her pale face.

"Come, my dear children," broke in Martina, "you must not unnerve Agatha who has made up her mind to obey her parents cheerfully: let her carry away a pleasing remembrance of you all."

They took her by the hand, and went over the garden together, visiting their favourite nooks. Martina and Siona remained alone, and fell into deep conversation. The young Christian orphan told her friend of the constant anxiety she lived in, how she had been asked for in marriage, and she dreaded lest her refusal should arouse suspicions as to her religion; for it must appear strange in the world's eyes that a lonely girl should prefer to a wealthy and suitable alliance, the solitary vigils, the loveless life of a recluse, the company of the poor.

"I fear," she said, "lest Hippolytus, angry at my apparent slight, should denounce me to the judge; and, though God forbid I should blush to confess my faith, yet I know my extreme weakness, and I would fain put off the day when it may please Jesus Christ to call me before the tribunals."

"Although self-diffidence be a virtue, I am afraid you carry it too far, Martina; He who has promised to be a Father to the orphan will stand by you; still, I should advise you to leave your home for a time, for greater security; I am lonely in my husband's absence, will you come and stay with us? Flora's childish prattle will divert your mind, for you are preying on past sorrows, and now that you are losing Agatha, you must love my child doubly."

The arrangement was accepted with equal pleasure on both sides, and, after a few minutes' more conversation, they bent their steps towards an arbour where the children had assembled.

"Look, Mama," exclaimed Flora in high glee. "Look at what clever Claudius has done for us," and she showed her a verdant canopy, constructed with branches of trees interlaced; benches and seats were ranged in a circle, in the centre of which was a table, whereon stood an urn. The little girls had hastily put a band of purple round their dresses in imitation of the Laticlavium.*

"What are you playing at?" asked Siona.

"We are senators, Mama, and we are holding a *plebiscitum*, and Agatha is a general going to the wars, who is bidding farewell to Rome, and promising to remain

* The distinctive mark of the Fathers of the Senate.

victorious in the battle-field assigned her, and that is the urn in which we all drop our keepsakes for her, and each tries to prove that she loves her best."

"Poor children! it is very kind of you, Agatha, to enter into their innocent amusement."

"Nay, dear lady, my little friends are very thoughtful and kind. Before long, perhaps, I may have to speak before men, it is as well I should try in this little circle words I may one day be called on to repeat before an unmerciful judge."

She took the place they had assigned to her in the midst of them, and, with an eloquence which, though childish, thrilled the heart from its simple pathos, she exposed to them what they had been taught in common and endeavoured to practise together. She exhorted them to love Jesus Christ above all, and promised them in return, the rich reward of His imperishable love. With her cheeks glowing, and her voice almost hushed by depth of feeling, she told them of the glory there was in dying for Him, and of her ardent hope that such would be her portion. If ever they heard she had been called to the great strife, she told them not to mourn, but to pray for her until that day had come to pass. And then she spoke of Heaven, such as her innocent mind could imagine it and best understand: of its brightness, it glorious phalanx, its long unceasing songs of unutterable love. She bade them all to meet her there, and the young hearts accepted the solemn invitation.

Then each went to the urn and dropped her offering.

Flora collected them all, and brought them to Agatha. They were not vain baubles, but such devotional memorials as Christian children would treasure up and cherish: rings that had been steeped in the blood of martyrs, fragments of chains picked up from their prisons; there was also a fibula, being one of those long pins the Roman ladies used to fasten their dress; this had an ornament in the shape of a little palm.

"That is my gift," said Flora smiling.

"Then I accept the happy augury," replied Agatha, inserting the pin in the folds of her stole, "it shall not leave me, Flora, until the lictor's hand tears it away."

And the word proved true, for no hand ever despoiled the virgin of her white robes, until the cruel command which, in the hour of her agony, added the insult of public shame to the tortures of martyrdom.

She bid them good-bye and went her way, and they saw her no more, but some years later they heard of her triple victory over the world, over sin, and over death, and not they alone, for, as long as time lasts, and the Sacrifice of the Altar is offered up, the name of Agatha shall be honoured, and the virgin's memory live in the hearts of men.

## CHAPTER VII.

THE short-lived Roman winter had already come to a close; the sun's cheerful glow rested on the golden-roofed temple of Jupiter Capitolinus, and penetrated into the narrow streets of the Eternal City; all classes of citizens seemed to have revived with the spring to the alacrity of business. In those days, and among that people where so much of life was spent in the open air, the streets offered a merry sight, and the markets a rather disorderly display. It required a practised step and firm nerves to walk through those thoroughfares, where the *plebs romana* roamed in careless liberty, and raised their lusty voices, unfettered by the restrictions of modern civilization. There, passed the butcher, with different meats strung on a hoop, which he held above his head; here, a news-vendor gathered crowds around him, detailing the accounts of the revolution in Africa, how the Proconsul having pronounced an unjust sentence upon some youths, these had rebelled, assassinated him, revolted against the Roman Emperor, and compelled Gordianus to assume the Roman purple.

"No longer," exclaimed the speaker, "shall we, fellow-citizens, tremble for our possessions, for our gods, for our Senate; the barbarian who esteemed the lives of Roman citizens as nothing, and coveted our wealth, is our

Emperor no longer! Gordianus is a Roman; the pure blood of the Gracchi flows in his veins; with him we shall be restored to our old liberty. Let us, one and all, go to the Senate House, and, urging the Conscript Fathers to ratify this choice, let us implore them to arise and repel Maximinus, who will doubtless come at last to Rome, hoping to enslave us. On, on to the Senate, citizens, and let us cry: 'Life to Gordianus! the inheritor of the virtues of Trajan!'"

The self-elected orator moved forward, and many followed in his train shouting. Hardly had he left the place than a team of oxen, dragging heavy carts, full of marble, just unladen at the Tiber's port, stepped leisurely into the midst of the crowd; many, trying to get out of the way, were jammed up against the walls of houses, scrambled into door-ways, and through windows. The uproar attendant on this scene of confusion tripled the noise, which seemed to have been at its height before; housewives came out screaming, a cry of "Thieves" was raised which perhaps suggested to some the idea of taking advantage of the moment to invade their neighbours' property; the howling of dogs, trodden under foot, added to the din, and many vegetable stalls being overturned, the ground was soiled, slippery, and more than one Roman citizen tumbled down in the mud.

"Good day, Florentius," called out a young man, who, carefully holding up his white toga, was endeavouring to make his way safely through the scene of confusion. "What would a stranger say were he to enter Rome on one of these market days?"

"I am afraid, Hippolytus, he would think us fit descendants of the robbers who first peopled the Lucus Sacer; look at that young knave," and he pointed out a boy who, following a slave with a well-laden basket of provisions, seized every favourable moment when the latter stopped to make some purchase, and pilfered at his ease. The rogue, however, met with his reward, for just as he was plunging his hand once more into the inviting *cophinus*,\* a sound blow on the back recalled him to better manners, and looking up, he saw a man in a patrician garb standing over him with a stick he had just seized from the hand of an ox-driver.

"Begone!" he cried, "is it thus slaves get punished for not fulfilling their master's orders, while young thieves like thee despoil them before they get home?"

The boy skulked away to avoid a repetition of the chastisement, but when he was safe beyond reach, he turned round and showed a Roman spirit in his rustic pride: "May the evil eye fall on thee, stranger," he cried, imitating the slightly foreign accent his fine ear detected, "thou art no patrician, or thou wouldst not strike a Roman citizen"; and, running behind the rostral column of the Forum, he was soon out of sight.

"Well done! brother," exclaimed one of the lookers-on; "thou hast done thyself justice, but, hardly in time, I fear, to save thy dinner."

"Ah, Hippolytus, I did not know you were so near me. Florentius, I wish you a good day. Where are you going together?"

\* Basket.

"We have only just met by accident," replied the last named person. "I am on my way to the baths; and you, Adrias?"

"I have a dinner party at home to-day, and thought I would take a walk through the Forum Olitorium to see that my cook got the best of everything, and I have just saved the poor man from the clutches of a young thief."

"Come with us to the baths. You are over-excited and require to cool yourself."

"Let us all go," interposed Hippolytus; "come, Adrias, and keep us company."

They went on their way together, passing between the Grecostasis, a building of which three Corinthian columns are still standing: it was used to receive ambassadors before they were admitted to the senate. Between it and the Senate house, known as the Curia, ran the meridian: the friends stopped before it to ascertain the hour, and then turned to the right, down the road, which ran along the foot of the Palatine to the Circus Maximus. A lowing of herds and the energetic exclamations of their drivers told of their drawing near to the Forum Boarium.

"I think I must be doomed to-day," cried Hippolytus, "to meet with cattle; I don't think there were ever so many oxen let loose in Rome as have crossed my path since morning!"

"Ha, is this a feast day with Hercules that he is anointed and dressed in triumphant robes? and offerings are placed before the temple of Pudicitia Patria.* It

* The modern church of Santa Anastasia.

must be in thanksgiving for some victory we have gained. Hail Hercules!"

He put his hand to his lips, kissed it, and waved it to the demigod; his brother followed his example, but Florentius disdained to join in the act of adoration.

"How!" exclaimed both the brothers at once, "what religion do you profess?"

"That of common sense and reason," replied the philosopher, draping his toga closer about him, "it is only custom, not conviction, that can make us adore a statue, and I think it impious to sacrifice to a stupid custom."

"But where is your God, Florentius?"

"Within me, I feel him in the divinity of my mind, in my superiority of intellect, in an innate fortitude which enables me to consider pain as no evil, and all the ills that may attack this body as nothing, for life and greatness and immortality come from within."

"You speak somewhat like a Christian, Florentius!"

"The gods forbid! Their chief died on a cross. I follow the divine Plato, and believe like him in the innate divinity of man. The world will never be governed rightly unless a republic be formed upon his laws. Plotinus has planned to build a town in Campania, to be called Platonopolis in honour of the great Master, where all who wish to live according to his precepts shall assemble; the project is about to be submitted to the emperor."

"To whom?" asked Adrias, in a whisper, "for we do not know at this hour the name of the emperor who rules over us."

They now reached the baths of Caracalla, well known in our day by their magnificent ruins, and the treasures of art that have been found in them. These buildings occupied an immense space: the body of the edifice was quadrilateral, comprising the different halls used for the baths. This formed the centre of a vast area, which was surrounded with walls, and, within these, were gardens for exercise in fine weather, covered porticoes and halls, dividing the rest of the enclosure. To the south-east was the *stadium*, set apart for games, together with the *xystus* and *palestra*; to these were joined the *spoliarium* where the bathers left their clothes and received clean ones from their slaves; the *conisterium* where such as used the bath more for health than luxury, were dried in sand; the *coryceum* or *sphærristerium* where they could play at ball, and the *ephebeum* for the exercises of young men only. Thus, these baths were to a Roman what modern clubs are in the present day, for he was there supplied with amusement, occupation, conversation, news, he met his friends there and discussed with them politics and private business. Even dinner was provided at the Thermæ, where the idle part of the population spent almost the whole day long.

"To which hall shall we go?" asked Florentius, as, passing through the garden where young men were playing at games of strength, they made for the *Laconicum*, being that part more exclusively appropriated to bathing.

"Come here!" called out a voice, which they recognized as that of their friend Lucullus, and they entered the *unctuarium* whence it proceeded; the bather was stretched on a bed; one slave was bending his arms and legs at every joint to restore pliability to the muscles, another rubbed and thumped him to circulate the blood, a third held ointments for the body, which required much care and refreshment owing to the continual use of woollen garments next the skin, linen being unknown in those days as an article of wearing apparel; another held the white toga, another the sandals with richly embossed silver thongs, and the chalk with which to rub his master's legs and make them look whiter, but not till another menial called *epulator* had extracted every little hair.

"How I pity you!" cried Florentius laughing, as standing a little distance from the victim of all these attentions, he raised his hands with a gesture of dismay.

"And what do *you* come for, stoical philosopher?" asked the other in a voice rendered almost inaudible under the vigorous exertions of his slaves.

"To be washed like a man in the *baptisterium*,* or to sit in the *solium*† as fancy leads, but not to be pounded, and have all my bones broken by bondsmen whom you would at any other time punish severely for laying a little finger on you."

"Florentius, were you born a Spartan?" asked Hippolytus.

"I have studied Greek philosophy."

"I am a Greek philosopher," cried Lucullus from his

* Public bath for swimming.     † Bath for one person.

couch, "I follow the Epicurean system; let us live in joy, ere we close our eyes in sorrow."

"Oh man of sense and flesh! what do you do with the noble faculties of your intellect? with the strong power to do and to suffer? Joy and pleasure are bad teachers; they weaken and destroy all that is noble within us. Suffering is food for the soul, its purifying element, the light of the mind, by which it sees clear into life, into nature and her secrets. There is no spectacle more worthy of the Gods than to see a good man struggling with adversity."

"Pooh! I would never struggle at all; life is not worth living if spent in struggling."

"And virtue?"

"Is but a name!"

"Lucullus! you are not sceptical as you would make us suppose; you believe in virtue, and honour it in the person of your wife."

"Well!" replied the Epicurean, "I said just now that virtue is a name, and she bears it. Yes, I believe in her, and in many things besides—in the power of love, the benefit of friendship, in the wearisomeness of wisdom and philosophy, in the comfort of a bath. Farewell, Florentius, lest I should vex you longer."

He was now ready and prepared to leave the Thermæ, followed by his numerous slaves. Adrias proceeded to the *sudationes* or vapour bath, Florentius and Hippolytus to the *frigidarium*.

"You are given to musing, to-day," observed the latter to his friend.

"Do you believe in innate ideas?" was the reply.

"In what?"

"Do you believe that our minds receive impressions through the channel of exterior objects, or by the reflection of an interior world?"

"Wait! let me think—here is a good subject to reflect upon; that group strikes my senses first, and then stirs my heart."

They were just then descending a few steps leading to another hall when they stopped before a gilt niche in the wall; there was a small enclosed area, below the level of the marble pavement, and there stood the group known as the immortal Laocoon.* It was always customary to have a window opening to the south in the bath-rooms, and thus, the golden rays of the god of day fell on the features of his own high-priest, the most sublime representation of mortal agony, in which the sculptor's art has idealized and made beautiful the contortions of the suffering human frame. It is difficult to say which is the most striking of the figures of that group, which is the most life-like in its acute suffering, whether the father as, with upturned and reproachful glance, he seems to call upon the gods he has served, who have abandoned him in this, the hour of his distress—there is something of a stern defiance too in his brow, as, clenching the serpent he has just torn from his eldest-born, he would, in his impotent despair, hurl it back again against the heavens of whose vengeance it

---

* It is supposed, from some parts of the group being unfinished, that it was meant to be viewed from above.

is an instrument; or the children, whose writhing is more of pain than of scorn, as they turn to their father from whom they have been accustomed to seek protection and succour. How the fiery bite changes the cry on their lips from an appeal to their parent to a shriek of pain! how the youthful breast seems to heave under the cold marble! how the looker-on feels his own pulse throb, and his breathing oppressed, as he contemplates and watches the serpents' folds, coiling closer and closer around the manly frame and the childish forms! And, in that dread hour, how the dispositions of those youths reveal themselves; the eldest partakes of his father's nature, the youngest has been moulded by his mother's love. In the first, there is despair; in the second, the compassionate eyes are fixed on his parent's suffering countenance, and seem to find more anguish there than in the monster's poisoning embrace. Death awaits them all: but the eldest boy will die first, of the sheer torture of physical pain; the father will hardly wait till the serpents have done their work, but his own vigorous arms will close the final struggle, and the young son when he has seen them both fall dead at his side, will drop down over them, supported by love to the end.

Often and often visitors to the baths had passed before the Laocoon, but few lingered to study its beauty, so accustomed were men in those days to see the works of art strewed around them with the profusion of a genius-gifted land, but Florentius and Hippolytus were both inclined to muse to-day, and they stood long before the marble group; Florentius studying whether physical pain be an evil or not ? Hippolytus thought how powerless is man against the decrees of fate ! for there he was himself, young, handsome, seemingly favoured by the gods and by fortune, and yet ! he alone knew of the secret sting that disturbed his repose. How he had placed all his hopes in an absorbing affection, which, rejected, had recoiled upon himself, and stifling, poisoning, gnawing, like the serpent before him, clung to him, and could not be shaken off. At last Florentius touched him on the shoulder, " We are both dreaming," he said, " let us go to bathe ".

They bent their steps to the *tepidarium*, which was connected with the *sudationes* or vapour bath; it was very high, being vaulted ; in the centre was suspended a chain holding a concave bell which rose and fell, increasing or diminishing the heat. The pavement and walls were double; the upper floor being supported by little columns of square bricks cemented with argile and chopped-up horse-hair, because clay would not have sufficed to resist the fire. Over this, was a layer of *astracum*, half-a-foot deep, and above that, mosaic. All the pavements were very beautiful, and finely executed, some of them represented subjects, with the same precision as a painting.

In the *sudationes*, stood a porphyry vase of such large dimensions that, at the present day, it fills a room adapted to it in the Vatican Museum ; beneath it, the floor was of a beautiful design, and exquisitely coloured mosaic, round which ran another pattern of less fine workmanship, black and white ; representing Nereids, Tritons, and sea-horses.

"The *labrum* is private at this hour," observed Hippolytus to his friend, "and I wish to speak to you alone."

"I am glad to hear it, for your strange manner puzzles me."

They went forthwith to the public bath, where porphyry seats, placed in the water, awaited those who preferred sedentary bathing to swimming.

A pause ensued, and then the younger man, making an effort, said:

"You are a philosopher, Florentius, and must not wonder if I disclose to you a state of mind far below the heights in which you soar. In your science, in the resources of magic which I believe you study, teach me a remedy against the torments of love."

"Cold water and oblivion!" replied the other, playfully sprinkling his companion; "use these and you will soon be cured."

"I am beyond that, Florentius, my passion is of long standing."

"Have you interested the parents of the maiden in your suit?"

"She is an orphan."

"But has she no guardians?"

"She lived alone till a few months ago; when, after rejecting my suit, she disappeared mysteriously; I never see her in any place of public resort, nor can I make out where she resides."

"And what is her name? I shall keep your secret."

"I do not like to mention it, but I know you will not trifle with my sorrow; you must know Martina!"

"Martina! yes, she is my wife's friend and guest. She has been dwelling under my roof this last year: during my absence, she cheered Siona who was lonely, and, on my return, I asked her to continue to stay with us."

"Is it possible! have I indeed found her! Can you tell me who is my rival? for she told me with a noble frankness I admired while it pained me, that her heart was taken up with another love."

"How can that be! she never sees any one; when she goes out it is always in company with my wife, and she always looks calm and happy as if she thought of nothing but the duty of the present hour, just like Siona."

Hippolytus relapsed into silence, and, when his friend had finished his bath and began to dress, he mechanically followed his example, walked out with him, and, having accompanied him to the exterior portico, awaited there the arrival of his brother.

Adrias was just the opposite of the sentimental Hippolytus: a plain, matter of fact citizen, interested in the politics of his country, but still more in the good management of his own private affairs: being a wealthy merchant, he had realized a good fortune by trading in corn with Sicily, and in oil with that part of Liguria which, being sheltered by the Maritime Alps, produces olives of a growth and quality unequalled in the Italian Peninsula. Adrias had his tablets in hand as he joined his friends, and was making up the arrears of a calculation.

"Hippolytus," he said, "I have business to transact in Liguria, but it is inconvenient for me to leave Rome at present. Will you go on this journey in my stead? You are falling into ill-health, and a trip will do you good."

"I cannot leave Rome."

"You! who care for no amusement, no business, no politics!"

"I have an object in view, far more important than business or amusement."

"I hope, brother, you are not a conspirator."

"Against whom or what? I do not even know who reigns over us at present."

"The wisest man in Rome is just as ignorant on that point; Maximinus is expected to invade the empire: we have known nothing of him but his tyranny, and the senate has issued an edict for the citizens to arise and repel him. Gordianus is recognised as sovereign, and his son is associated to him, for the elected Emperor pleaded his own great age, and wished for a younger head and a more vigorous arm to sustain, with him, the fatigues of the throne; but what is the use of my speaking to you, brother, who are not listening to one word I say?"

They were returning from the baths by another road than that which they had taken on going there; they were now in the vicinity of the temple of Vesta, and the priestesses were conveying to the Tiber the materials for their sacrifices and their own robes to be cleansed. They were veiled, as was customary for the virgin votaries, but Hippolytus had been struck by the bearing and walk of one who preceded her companions by a few paces: " How strange," he muttered, "were it not for the information I derived from Florentius this very day, I might have imagined" . . . .

'Have you lost your head!" cried his brother, dragging him away. "Why do you stare that way at the Vestal Virgins? come to my house, it is not safe for you to go about alone. You must have been in the vines and seen a wolf; you require a few grains of ellebore." *

So saying, he took him gently and persuasively by the arm, and, avoiding to pass through the Forum, took a long walk round the city walls.

* The sight of a wolf was supposed to bring on madness, against which the herb *ellebore* was used as a remedy.

## CHAPTER VIII.

"BROTHER! brother! where is he? where has he gone to?"

And Flora, darting out of the house, ran all about the garden, into every hiding-place she could think of; at first, she was half in play, but soon became anxious. She came near a great pond which was railed in all round—she had often fed the fish through the bars; the murrains were so good, they knew her as their little mistress, but, since she had undertaken the care of her little cousin, Laurentius, she never went near this place, lest it should prove dangerous for him. But the sight of the cold, transparent water eddying in circles round the fish as they played, chilled her with horror. Where could her little brother be? She leaned against the railing, looked in . . . . nothing! She fell on her knees, and, putting her hands before her eyes, she prayed as she had been taught to do, earnestly, confidently, to the God of little children and of pure hearts.

Presently, she heard her own name called upon; she listened to hear the voice again, but did not wait long, for a child's merry laugh sounded in her ears, and a little boy ran up to her, tossing a many-coloured ball before him, and exulting in innocent glee.

"Oh Laurentius," she cried, "where have you been?

why did you run away? you have frightened me so much."

The little fellow was a fine, healthy-looking child, contrasting with her delicate figure, but so strikingly like her in feature, that they looked much more like brother and sister than cousins. The same oval face, the same handsome features, cast in the Jewish mould; the same eyes, soft, half-closed, slanting, and reflecting, like those of Flora and her mother, something of that unearthly Vision, that Immortal Beauty which had been gazed on by their ancestor. If there was a destiny written on Flora's brow, then Laurentius was like her, a child of doom, and, as had been predicted, the Word, spoken to the young man in the gospel, and the rejected Call, must be fulfilled in them.

The little boy had now been a year in the house, and endeared himself to all around him. Florentius revelled in his infant intelligence, and declared "that child must never go to school, but be formed by himself on Plato's principles". Siona loved the orphan babe for her sister's sake as well as her own, but Flora, who felt her importance since she was the elder, delighted in taking care of her little brother. Laurentius must learn everything from her; when he was first brought to the house he could hardly walk, and it was beautiful to see the little girl holding him by one hand while he clung to her with the other; she, meanwhile, encouraging his baby efforts, singing to him, and soothing him when he cried. She thought no longer of play, but inasmuch as it might amuse Laurentius; her little pets were neglected, and she only resumed the care of her birds, when she found it necessary to teach Laurentius to be kind to animals. She seemed to have no will but his, and if her little brother, as she called him, were pleased, she was sufficiently rewarded. Had he proved a selfish, instead of a wilful child, she could never have clung to him, but the impetuous little boy, so passionate in his fancies, so sorry and good when his trifling bursts of temper were over, was the very nature suited to Flora's gentleness, and she exercised a good influence over him. Child as she was, the little girl had within her the germ of her future womanly nature; she could bear all but indifference; capable of great affections and heroic self-devotion, she had that sensitiveness of feeling which would make her hereafter turn away from such as did not understand her, and take refuge in that One, Eternal Love, alone capable of satisfying the cravings of her heart. Go on your path, little children! there is within you the spark of a yet unkindled light, which will one day shine before men; go on, fearlessly, for a high destiny awaits you, and a great seal is put upon you! you are marked out for the Most High.

Laurentius saw that his sister looked very serious, and understood she was going to remonstrate with him for running away, so, trying to look penitent, he flung his arms round her. "Don't!" he cried, "I've been so good!"

"No, Laurentius; you are not good when you disobey, and, you know, Mama desired you were never to run away so far as to be out of sight."

"Oh, but I have been comforting a poor beggar."

"That was right, certainly. Was he asking for alms? where did you meet him?"

"Down there, where the beehives used to be; there is a hole in the wall since they were pulled down, and it is just high enough for me to reach, and big enough to put my head through."

"Then it cannot be high or big either, you are such a little fellow, but go on."

"Indeed! but I *am* big! The beggar said so."

"He was surely not in our garden?"

"No! but on the other side of the wall. He was looking in, at the hole from the road, wasn't it odd! I said good-day to him, and asked him if he was hungry, but he said he was ill, and unhappy, and tired."

"I hope you did not talk too much; if he was poor he wants alms."

"I had a honey cake which Claudius had given me, and I offered it to the beggar, but he only broke a piece off, and returned it to me. He seems to be a very good man, for he gave me this," and the child held up the variegated ball he had just been rolling along.

"This is a mistake, Laurentius, the man you spoke to must have been a weary traveller resting on the road; beggars never give presents."

"Well! he said he was very poor, and asked if Martina lived with us; he wanted me to let him in, so that he might see her walking in the garden; he said he would wait in a hiding-place till she passed, but I told him the door was well secured and I couldn't reach the bolt; I offered to call for Claudius."

"And did you?"

"No! for the man begged I would not; he said all he wanted was to see Martina, and asked me so much about her; what she did, and how she looked, and said he had a message for her."

"Then we must go and tell all this to Martina, before you forget what the beggar said."

Off they went, hand in hand, to the aula, or inner court of the house, where Siona sat, weaving tapestry with her friend. Flora explained all she had gathered from her little brother's broken story; the little boy being by this time quite taken up with his ball, which rebounded beautifully.

"It must be," observed Siona, "a messenger sent to you from the Pontiff, who, knowing this to be a Pagan's house, did not venture in. To-morrow we will send Claudius with the child, he shall introduce the beggar, who can then deliver his message safely; perhaps he comes to warn you of some danger, or brings you orders from Pope Lucius."

"That is very likely," observed Martina, who had of late distributed the greater part of her fortune to the poor, and held an important charge in the Christian community.

They resumed their work; but the children did not leave them again, for this was the hour at which Flora was accustomed to receive daily instruction from Martina, who, endeavouring to carry on the work begun by her lost friend Cecilia, loved to explain to little children the lessons of Christ. Flora's little friends used to join her on these occasions, and came regularly to share this class of religious teaching, which was generally followed by some quiet recreation. While they were expecting their usual young visitors, and Flora was preparing seats for them, they were surprised by the sudden entrance of Lucia, one of the eldest; she came alone, her face was flushed and her eyes swollen with crying: she ran up to Martina, hid her face in her bosom, and sobbed out,

"Agatha has suffered martyrdom!"*

All present uttered an exclamation of anguish.

"How have you heard this sorrowful, yet glad tidings," asked Siona, "painful to our human affection, glad inasmuch as we are Christians?"

"Mama received this from Sicily," said the young girl, drawing out a scroll of parchment she had kept carefully concealed. "The Bishop of Catania, my uncle, wrote out all the account of her trial and death."

"Mama sends it to you, that you may present it to His Holiness to be preserved in the archives of the Church. Oh dear, dear Agatha!"

"How soon! how very young she has been chosen by God to give her life for Him," sighed Martina. "Let

* St. Agatha died in 254 A.D.: it is therefore an anachronism to have placed her death at this part of our story. The writer tried to change it, but finding that would entail the erasure of many passages in preceding chapters, or the substitution of another character, it was thought preferable to trust to the indulgence of the reader.

us wait till the other children arrive, we could not have a more solemn lesson than this, let us read it all together."

Lucia sat on a low stool, while Flora put her arms round her, and both wept bitterly, each trying to soothe the other.

One by one the other children came in, and all looked wondering and sorrowful at the sight of their companions' grief. When all were assembled, Martina with a faltering voice told them what had befallen Agatha since she left them; how she had lived, modest and retired, in her home, devoted to good works, under the eye of a Christian mother and an unsuspecting father. She then read the sequel of her life from the bishop's narrative. She had been taken by her father to a public entertainment, where her beauty and high rank drew upon her the attention of the governor. Being disappointed in his suit, and finding that she was a Christian, he had ordered her to be torn from her home, cast into prison, and brought before the tribunals. She had offered herself up to God, and prayed for strength. Then the narrative went on to say how she had been placed for a month in the hands of a wretched woman, and her virtue had conquered vice. Brought before the judge, and questioned as to her birth and name, she had proudly professed herself a Christian, refused to sacrifice, and scoffed at the hideous pagan gods, so much so, that the irritated governor condemned her to a torture lingering, cruel, slow, wounding alike her mortal frame and her maidenly modesty. The most atrocious sentence ever pronounced by one born of woman had been passed on the young virgin, who, lacerated, bleeding, yet living, was conducted back to her prison. One had visited her there, one who in her childish dreams, had promised to be with her always; the great apostle, head of Christ's church had appeared to the girl-confessor of the faith, and her wounds had been healed by St. Peter himself. She was again summoned before the iniquitous judge, when, more impressive in her beauty, since her features bore no trace of suffering, more firm and almost commanding in her attitude, she had again refused all overtures made by the cowardly tyrant, who, crowning at the same time his cruelty and her glory, had condemned her to be rolled on sharp stones, until, finally, her head fell under the lictor's axe.

The account was lengthy; it entered into the minute details peculiar to the Acts of the Martyrs, which serve, even in our own day, as glorious records of our brethren in the faith. By the time Martina had concluded, her youthful auditory were all in tears; they then knelt down and commended themselves to the protection of her who had once been their companion, and was now sitting at the Lord's right hand.

"Children," said their kind teacher at the close of their prayer, "God has permitted us to hear the last act of a pure life; it has pleased Him that this recital should reach us for some good purpose. Perhaps, Agatha has asked of her Heavenly Master that this legacy of her love might be left us, that the fire with which she burned for His glory may survive her and be kindled in our hearts; her example is a challenge to us all; are we likewise ready for the coming of the Heavenly Bridegroom?"

As she put the question, she rose from her seat, and all the children with her; amid the tears and sobs they gave to the memory of their young friend, one answer burst from all those girlish hearts. "Yes, with His grace, we are ready!"

But all eyes were fixed on her: she who was to precede them in the glorious strife stood among them with upturned gaze and folded hands, and a triumphant smile was on her lips; a foreshadowing of future glory on her brow; and then, she bowed her head and murmured: "Even now, O Lord!" as if in answer to One she alone had heard. Was it the voice of the Spirit and the Bridegroom that say: Come?

Some time elapsed until the conversation reassumed a more calm tone, and at the usual hour the young people took their leave: the day wore on. The next morning, Martina, remembering what Flora had told her about the inquiries of the man on the road, consulted Siona as to what she had best do.

"I still think it is a messenger from the Supreme Pontiff," replied the lady, "let us send Claudius to meet him with the child who will recognise him. Claudius will at once see whether the stranger be one of us, and will lead him into the garden where you can speak with him on the subject of his mission."

Accordingly Claudius went to the wall where little Laurentius pointed out the hole which had attracted his attention : and the ladies sat down by the artificial lake, awaiting the arrival of the mysterious visitor. He was not long in making his appearance: clothed in tattered garments, and leaning on a stick, he seemed to be a decrepit old man, although he trod very lightly; his head was covered with a bandage, which partially concealed his features, and he looked down on the ground.

"I am sorry to see," said Siona kindly, "that you seem to have been wounded or hurt."

"Yes, Lady, I am suffering from a wound which nothing can heal."

The sound of that voice made Martina start; she had heard it before, but thought she must be mistaken, this stranger looked such an object of compassion.

"I have been told your business is with me," she said, "perhaps you seek for alms?"

"I do! I have been told you are kind to the needy."

"What can I do for you?"

"One word from you can make me rich and the happiest man in Rome."

"And what is that?"

"Lady, I must speak to you alone."

"Whatever message you have to deliver, do so in the presence of this lady, my valued friend."

"I cannot. I must then leave you, my mission unfulfilled."

Siona arose, and whispered to her, "I shall be near at hand, call me if you feel uneasy;" she then went away.

The moment the beggar found himself alone with Martina, he dropped his stick, let fall his tattered *penula**  which concealed a rich tunic beneath, tore off the bandage from his head, and displayed the features of her lover, Hippolytus.

"There is a treasure you can give," he cried, "and I will prize the gift well. Have you, who are known for your compassion, no affection to give me in return for that I offer you once more? Have I not been faithful to you?"

Surprise, fear, a passing movement of indignation, compassion too, all were visible in Martina's countenance. She did not call for any one, however; a certain delicacy forbade her disclosing the secret of a love which had been so constant, and which she was bound to reject. There was, besides, such sincerity in the young man's tone, his handsome features were so worn and altered, that she saw he had suffered much.

"Hippolytus," she said, with gentle reproachfulness, "is this right? to force your way by stealth into the household whose hospitality I have accepted; to lure the little child of my guest, as if you were a thief seeking for admission? And you a patrician!!"

"A *pius dolus* is always lawful in love and in war. See you, I must; I therefore invented the stratagem."

"Why importune me, when you have had my answer already?"

"You told me then that your heart was taken up with another love, and that is not true."

"Martina has never uttered a falsehood," she replied.

"Pardon me! but Florentius, whom I met at the

* Traveller's cloak.

baths, and who accidentally made known to me your abode, assured me you received no suitor."

"He was right."

"Then how can you reconcile that? Martina, I have a right to know the truth from you; I cannot support this moral torture any longer. If you do not care for me, at least clear yourself in my eyes; let me not carry away the painful impression that the woman I love so truly, harbours thoughts and feelings she is ashamed to acknowledge." Martina's lip quivered, and tears sprang to her eyes; she remained a few moments silent, communing with herself, then said: "Your words are harsh, but appearances are against me, I will speak to you as you desire, truthfully, boldly. I will confide to your Roman honour a secret which must never transpire. I ask you as a friend whom I trust, and whose esteem I value, will you faithfully guard what I am going to reveal?"

"I swear!" said the young man, "by the . . . ."

"Hush!" she interrupted, "your word is enough! invoke no false gods who cannot hear you. I am a Christian! and the love I have refused you is given to the One, Only, Invisible God!"

Poor young man! he could not have looked more horrified had she confessed herself a murderess; he grew pale as death, then, averting his gaze from her, hid his face and wept, bitter, passionate, yet manly tears.

"Why tell me this?" he cried. "I had rather have believed you cold, ungrateful, even deceitful, than a criminal!"

"Hippolytus!"

"You, whom I had hoped to call my wife! are you indeed a member of that sect, whose crimes draw on them the vengeance of the gods and of the immortal emperors?"

"Do you think I would have embraced their creed if I knew as little of them as you do?"

"They have worked upon you. You have been won over by magical art."

"I have made use of my reason, withdrawn my adoration from stocks and stones, and given it to One Who is All Wise, All Good, the Author of Nature; your Maker and mine."

"And yet the Christians commit great crimes."

"That is false!"

"Where then is this Invisible God, and how came you to know Him?"

"His Word is here," replied the maiden, reverently taking a small roll of parchment from the folds of her dress, and pressing it to her lips. "If, as I believe, Hippolytus, you have regarded me with that feeling I cannot respond to, then read here what is told by Luke the Evangelist, and when you have learned to know the Master I serve, you will not wonder that I prefer Him to all the world can give."

He took the gift from her carelessly, his eyes still fixed on her. "Is there no hope?" he asked mournfully, "no hope that time, reason, and years will alter you?"

"Does a soldier prove untrue to the colours he has

sworn to defend? Does a Roman heart belie its *fides data?*"

"Noble girl! Then if your choice is irrevocable, may you prove as invincible when called upon to defend your faith, as you have been powerful now. I had thought to win you, and I retire conquered."

"Farewell, Hippolytus; seek me no more! Think of me but as one who sighs for your real happiness, who dreams for you a fate far superior to the world's glory. I will pray for you, Hippolytus, that your eyes may be opened to the light which has shone on me; that, pure of soul and great in heart, you may tread the walks of life with a higher end in view, and meet me one day in another world."

"You mean in Elysium."

"No! I speak of that future life which is eternal. May the day come when you will understand it, till then farewell! If I see clear into the future, you may hear of me as being called to choose between my God and death. In that last hour when my soul, hovering on the brink of another life, may fearlessly ask of the Great Giver all I desire, then I shall bear your name as a hallowed memory to the Eternal Throne, and hope to be heard! Farewell! resume your disguise. I shall send the slave to lead you away."

She waved her hand to him and passed on towards the house. He remained as if riveted to the spot until Claudius came, followed by the children, who were continually under his faithful care. Flora looked timidly at the beggar; Laurentius, proud of his acquaintance of the day before, ran up to him to show him his ball.

Hippolytus took him up in his arms, and kissed him, exclaiming, "Beautiful child, mayest thou be happy, ay, happier than I!"

He set him down, and then, turning to the slave: "I am ready," he said; "let us go!" and resuming his stick and limping gait, he followed Claudius out of the grounds.

## CHAPTER IX.

THE reign of the Gordians proved to be so short that they never visited the capital of their vast empire. Their accession had been greeted as the commencement of an era of peace and justice, for the people were worn out by the tyrannical cruelty of the barbarian Emperor Maximinus. The Roman Senate confirmed the choice of the people, but scarce six weeks had elapsed since the new Cæsars had assumed the Imperial purple, when both father and son fell in battle. Maximinus then turned his victorious arms against Rome itself, and advanced to the frontiers to reconquer his lost empire. The Senate met in great alarm, and held a secret council, wherein, without appealing to the people, without even the intervention of the Prætorian guards, who had of late grown to exercise a despotic sway, Balbinus and Pupienus were called to the supreme command. Both were old men, but born in different classes of life; the former being the son of a cart-driver, the latter a poet of illustrious birth. It seemed as if, in this hour of danger, Rome was choosing her emperors as she had once chosen her consuls, when, to satisfy the people, she had named together a patrician and a plebeian. The good fortune of the old republic had not expired; for scarce was an army in the field and the plan of the campaign organised, than victory had already declared for Rome. The emperors marched to Aquileia, which was invaded by Maximinus and his son; famine, disaffection, and despair alienated the tyrant's soldiers from him: he was slain, together with the younger Maximinus, and their heads, stuck on lances, were brought to Rome.

But the triumph of the two old emperors was short lived; their interests were too separate, their education had set them too far asunder for them to combine their efforts for the welfare of the empire; the people had never loved them, and, in order to conciliate public favour, they found themselves obliged to associate to the purple a third Cæsar, Gordian, grandson to the old Gordianus. When Pupienus and Balbinus fell victims to the jealousy of the Prætorian guards, who could never forgive the emperors they had not elected themselves, the people were quite unconcerned, and applauded the accession of the young Gordian, who remained sole emperor. The young sovereign put himself under the guidance of Misitheus, his minister, who advised him well in all matters tending to the good of the state.

And now persecution ceased for awhile; the Christians breathed and came forth from their hiding places; the good news of the Gospel spread; the daily business of life went on, and the Roman citizens hurried to their pleasures, their affairs, their busy schemes, thus weaving that intricate web of toil, hope and trouble, called life, now and then mingled with pleasure, which the pagan must needs seek from the cradle to the tomb, for there is nothing for him to look forward to beyond. Thus the Roman Empire pursued its course, rolling its mighty waves to the great ocean of eternity, tossing in its troubled waters and heedless course ruins of human greatness and worldly riches, men's sighs and disappointed ambitions and broken hearts. On, on it rolled to the great ocean, where a Fisherman's bark awaited to shelter its ruined grandeur and its living wreck! and the waters dashed over that boat, but it rose with their anger, and for as many as took refuge in it, it expanded still more, until it grew high and deep, and rooted in the soil: the waters struck again and again, but in vain .... the boat had disappeared, in its stead was .... a rock.

On sped the mighty Empire, like a colossus, big with the fate of nations, but carrying within itself the seeds of corruption and decay which caused its ruin. And thus, each day brought its wasted genius, its mistaken glory, its useless misspent lives, a dreary waste of all nature's gifts! and brought them to false gods, gave them with false hearts, swore them away with false lips, devoted all their energies to the maintenance of a falsehood! How then could that structure stand!

It was a morning in the autumn season; the Tiber had been swollen in the recent rains, and lazily rolled its yellow waters, thick with the gold-coloured sand of its neighbouring hills, under the Pons Sublicius, the sacred bridge constructed of wood, without either bronze or stone, built by Ancus Martius, which remained for many centuries the only bridge on the Tiber. In

## Flora : the Roman Martyr. 149

the distance, near the Meta Græcorum, where the Pyramid of Caius Cestius rose by the wayside, maidens, children, and peasants were trudging on gaily, laden with the produce of the vintage, laughing as they picked up the huge clusters of grapes which dropped from the well filled carts. All was joy and gladness, the very oxen seemed to share in the general glee, as the children decked them with branches from the vine, and sang and danced round them, screaming so lustily, that the very air breathed a holiday. Farther on, in the *fields of the Roman people* were to be heard the sounds of work and hammering: there was shipbuilding going on, on the site of what is now the *Monte Testaccio*, being a hill formed entirely of broken potsherds. Thus, the two streams followed the same direction, the yellow Tiber below, and the human tide above: that bright autumn morning saw many varied scenes; all was not joyful.

On the Aventine side of the Pons Sublicius stood many a sacred shrine: the temple of Piety where the fame of the Roman daughter's memory has survived, converting her father's prison into an edifice, sacred to Filial Devotion; the temple of *Fortuna Virilis* raised by a conqueror in consequence of a vow, to the protecting gods of Rome, rendered more striking from its having. added a page to modern history, for here dwelt the last of the Tribunes, Rienzi, who loved his country, not wisely but too well!

And here, too, stood the temple of Vesta, circular in form; eleven pillars supported the roof, in front was a court surrounded by porticoes, and around it a sacred grove enclosed by walls.

Within these precincts, virgin priestesses guarded the sacred fire, lit at Heaven's rays, which could never be extinguished. They served the Mother of the Gods for thirty years; during the first ten they were novices, then acting priestesses for ten more: the remainder of their time of seclusion they employed in instructing their younger sisters to whom they served as guardians. After this long separation from the world, the hapless votary might return to her former place in society, might seek among her fellow-men a heart that would take hers in exchange, but this was only nominal freedom. Blighted in her youth and early aspirations, after consecrating her life to the perpetration of a falsehood, despoiled of the charms of girlhood, yet feeling herself a woman, what had the poor Vestal virgin to hope for, who returned to her home? had not life become a blank to her, a dreary void, almost as dark as that stony vault in the Campus Sceleratus, which awaited her had she proved unfaithful to her vow!

On this very morning, the space before the temple witnessed a gathering together of patricians, for death had left a void among the maiden priestesses, and lots were to be cast among the fairest and most noble of Rome, for two young girls to fill up the ranks. Interesting as was the sight of those children varying in age from six to twelve, their delicate features and finely formed hands and feet showing their patrician blood, it was a melancholy, heart-rending scene! The little girls, some of whom were too young to understand their doom, had been dressed as priestesses as a sign they aspired to that rank; many a mother, however, had adopted the disguise that it might veil the beauty of her child, and thus preclude her from the awful destiny reserved to her. The parents stood round them in a circle, waiting the arrival of the priests and of the emperor, who, as Supreme Pontiff, was to play a prominent part in the approaching ceremony. One of the mothers present gave free vent to her grief, notwithstanding the remonstrances of her husband, a tribune, who strove to give her courage: "Do not fear," he said, "our girl is the oldest of those present, the lots cannot fall on her."

"She wants but two days of twelve; that is the appointed term, and do you not see how she surpasses all in loveliness; oh! I fear she may be singled out."

"No! I am not alarmed. But why is her beautiful hair displayed on her neck, when the other girls wear it simply braided? that was not prudent; why did you allow it?"

"Poor child! she shuddered when I divided her hair in six tresses as the vestals wear it; she said it looked as if she were doomed. Icilius is in the crowd; she knows his eyes are upon her, and she wishes to wear her hair flowing, like an affianced bride."

A friend came up to the poor mother and took her hand affectionately—it was Siona. "I am sorry you could not be exempted," she said, "I had hoped Volumnia had attained her twelfth year."

"Hail, Lady Siona!" was the courteous salutation of Nemesion the tribune; "I did not think to meet you here."

"I came solely for your sake. My little Flora had heard from Volumnia of this dreaded event, and could talk of nothing else. I wished very much to see you and Paulina; I feel for you."

"But you are a happy mother."

"Yes! happy in this instance, that I am not of Roman birth, so that my child can never be called upon. But your daughter is affianced. They cannot take her from you."

"The gods are cruel!" replied poor Paulina, in a smothered voice.

"Is not Lucilla with you?" asked Flora.

"There she is, close to Volumnia; she clings to her sister who has been so long the light of her sightless eyes. Poor children! they have ever been fondly attached to each other."

"Will you make room for me?" broke in Flora again; "I wish to see them."

The tribune made as if he would raise her in his arms.

"Oh no!" she exclaimed, resenting the offer as an offence to her dignity; "do you think I am a little child?"

"Forgive me, dear one, for I love thee almost as much as thy own father does. Here, thou canst stand upon this pedestal, and be as tall as myself." He made room for her and remained near, holding her up.

She could see all the circle of spectators, and the

young girls in the centre : among them, Volumnia and Lucilla. The latter was stone-blind, and a love, devoted, self-sacrificing on the one side, admiring, full of faith on the other, united those two different natures. Lucilla saw external nature through her sister's eyes; Volumnia's merry laugh had been her sunshine, *her* kind affection the life of her soul, *her* mind and thoughts the vehicle to her own improvement and development. They had gone through life hand in hand, and thus they stood even now; the blind girl leaning on her lovely sister, listening for the approaching footsteps of the priests who were to cast among the young maidens the lot for the service of the goddess. Presently they came from the temple, clothed with long flowing robes, their brows bound with the golden fillet, their hands still reeking from the sacrifice ; they were preceded by Gordian, who performed as Emperor the part of Pontifex Maximus ; he was veiled, as one who has been in mysterious commune with the gods ; his right hand bore the *patena* or small plate, where he was supposed to have collected the vows of men in order to present them to the deity ; his left hand held a small stick immersed in ashes at the hearth of Vesta, wherewith he was to point out the new votary. The youthful Emperor passed into the circle of young girls, and his good heart failed him as he thought of the fate to which he must condemn those bright young creatures, many a one of whom might have graced the throne at his side ; he saw the anxious faces of the parents beyond, all bent on him ; he felt sorry for the power entrusted to him, and turned to the priest, as if he wished him to discharge the office. The latter was occupied in deciphering the scrolls, marked by the Fates; he read out the tribe, then the family, and lastly the very name of the girl on whom the choice of the goddess had fallen; there were two, and one was Volumnia, daughter to the tribune Nemesion. The girl remained erect and unflinching; her blind sister was carried away fainting, her mother came up to her weeping, in an agony of grief, but Volumnia was too concentrated to notice any one; she grew pale as death, and rigid as a stone. Only one voice from the crowd had reached her, a cry from a young man; it was a cry of pain, powerful and deep, like that of a wounded lion. The Emperor stood before her, compassionate and full of sorrow; the priests surrounded her, and began to cut off her beautiful hair. The poor mother had thrown herself at the feet of the young Cæsar, and conjured him, by his father's memory, and his mother's love, to revoke the sentence.

"Alas! that I could," replied the juvenile Augustus; "you know it is the gods, not I, that have pronounced. Rather inspire courage to your daughter, whose firmness at this hour shows her to be worthy of her destiny. Amata," he continued, turning to Volumnia, "for this is to be thy name henceforward, I take thee to be a priestess of Vesta, and to perform the sacred rites, to do all that is for the interest of the Roman people and the Quirites. Remember that the goddess has called thee to the honour of serving her, and show thyself to be a Roman; weak women like thee have gloried in that name, and fulfilled the promises of their birthright. A girl-heroine," and he pointed to the equestrian statue of Clelia, on the opposite bank of the Tiber, "did and dared so much, that she deserved that monument of her country's gratitude, after having made Porsenna wonder at the courage of Rome's daughters. Let her firmness be thine, as will also be her glory. Called to guard the palladium of our country, appointed to watch over the sacred fire to which is attached the salvation of the empire, rejoice, girl, that thy fate is linked with the Immortals, and, rising superior to human weakness, forget the destiny of the Roman matron, to glory in that of Vesta's priestess."

The girl had folded her hands on her bosom; she bowed her head under the veil they put on her, and prepared to follow the priests, when the emperor's *paludamentum* * was grasped by a firm, yet respectful, hand.

"Cæsar!" exclaimed the stifled voice of a man struggling to conceal his emotion. Gordianus turned to recognise the young vestal's father.

"Do not urge useless petitions upon me, Nemesion; I would have sought advice from your wisdom."

"No, Cæsar! a Roman tribune does not need to be reminded of his duty; but, by the long services I have rendered the state, grant me only this: let my child spend this last day with her mother. I promise to consign her myself to the gods this evening."

"Let it be as thou wishest, brave Nemesion; do thou encourage the young heart, and remind the noble girl of

* Imperial mantle.

what Roman virtue inspired to Curtius and to Decius. Less is required of her."

"Nay, Cæsar! far more. They gave only their lives, she immolates her heart. She is an affianced bride, and must now sacrifice, not only her womanly happiness, but the hopes of another who trusted in her."

The Emperor turned away, for his eyes were moist with an emotion he tried to conceal; the tribune felt his hands warm with the royal tears, and rose from his knees.

"Thus have the gods and Rome decreed!" said Gordianus, and veiling his head again, he followed the procession back to the temple.

Volumnia remained, clasped in her mother's embrace. Siona was taking care of the blind girl, when, suddenly, she missed Flora, and looked round for her in alarm.

The little girl had remained standing on the pedestal where her father had placed her; she was not looking on, but trying to calm a young man, known to her as the promised bridegroom of her friend Volumnia.

"You must not give way to passion, Icilius," said the well-taught Christian child; "look at Nemesion, how good he is."

"Hark! what is that?" cried the youth. "They have not taken her away! The high priest is gone! The Emperor too, all gone! They dare not touch her! I do!"

He dashed through all obstacles, pushing aside all who stood in his way, and reaching the spot where Volumnia stood, tore the veil off her head before any one could prevent him, and made as if he would have taken her away, crying out : " This is my affianced bride ! she is mine !"

At the sound of that voice, the only one Volumnia had longed to hear in all that crowd, her firmness forsook her, she turned her lovely face to her betrothed, her features relaxed, her lips quivered, and she burst into a long, low wail.

Her father laid his hand upon the shoulder of Icilius. " For shame !" he said, " respect the gods, thyself, and her. And you, Volumnia, I had expected more firmness from you."

" Behold !" she said, and showed him how, in her strong efforts to control herself, she had clasped her arms so firmly that the nails entered the flesh, and left an impression of livid marks and blood. " Behold ! you told me not to weep, and I obeyed."

The soldier's brow relaxed with pity, then, making a sign to his wife, " This place is too public, let us all go away," he said.

" I will not away," cried Icilius, whose anguish of mind amounted to something like frenzy. " You swore to me before the gods, avengers of perjury, that Volumnia should be mine. I claim your given promise."

" Father," whispered the girl, " let him go home with you, with us ; he will then grow composed."

He complied, took the youth's hand, holding it firmly, gave the girl to her mother, and went on. Siona followed them with Flora, a few steps behind. They proceeded up the Aventine hill where the tribune Nemesion lived.

"Mother," asked Flora, "I see Volumnia is very unhappy, but I do not quite understand why?"

"To leave her parents and give up her betrothed is a great sorrow, my child."

"But if God called me to leave you, and go to martyrdom, much as I love you I should go with joy, but I would never be affianced."

"Because you are called to a higher destiny, my child. Because an Immortal Love has taken possession of your heart, childish though it be. 'Blessed are the pure of heart, for they shall see God.' Poor Volumnia, on the contrary, is condemned to serve false gods who can never console, never reward her. To her, virginity, instead of being as unto the Christian maiden, a pearl of great price, cheaply purchased at the sacrifice of all earth's joys, is but a fearful doom, debarring her from all hopes of happiness in this life, for she has none beyond. Among my people too," here she lowered her voice and spoke as if musing to herself, "it is considered an ignominy to ignore the wife's and the mother's cares; and until She came, She whom all generations shall call Blessed, it was not given to man to understand the ineffable beauty of that single-hearted love, which watcheth alone, like a sparrow on the house-top; it liveth alone, prayeth alone, dieth alone, and yet, joy eternal is its theme, for a mysterious and solemn contract hath been passed between that soul and its God."

Flora looked up wonderingly at her mother, who th

remembered she was speaking in strains too lofty for her little hearer: a poetess by nature, she was sometimes given to express her feelings with the oriental imagery which had been familiar to her from childhood, and the Jewish woman loved to dwell amid the memories of her nation and of the Prophet-King.

They had reached the garden wall which enclosed Nemesion's grounds; slaves were awaiting their masters' return, and came out to meet them: "Prepare the *triclinium* for a banquet," ordered the tribune; "let all our neighbours be hastily summoned, let all our friends come and rejoice!"

The slaves concluded from the presence of Icilius, their young mistress' suitor, this feast was in honour of her approaching nuptials, but they wondered why every countenance wore an expression of grief. Siona endeavoured to draw Icilius to her, but the youth was not recognisable, so fierce was his manner, so stern his demeanour; years seemed to have passed over him in the last few hours, he had grown a man in mind, by one of those revolutions which powerful feelings are apt to bring about, when overworked, particularly at that age, when the intellectual faculties, yet in all their freshness, are more sensitive, when the chords of the young heart vibrate more rapidly, and, like an instrument tightly strung, shiver when weighed down by the pressure of a rude, unskilful hand.

Volumnia had withdrawn with her mother, and Icilius remained deaf to Siona's kind words till Flora, childlike and confident, went up to him, took one of his hands, which was very cold, and, chafing it between hers "Icilius," she said, "speak to my mother who loves you".

The innocent voice, the pressure of that little hand overcame him; he stooped over it, and kissed it respectfully; she looked up at him, and saw tears in his eyes; she led him to her mother's side; the strong boy obeyed, and looked almost bashful in his manly beauty as Siona affectionately chid him.

"This must not be, my son," she said, "forbear adding to the sorrow which has already visited this house."

"But I love her, and she was to be mine in a few days. Oh the cruel fates!"

"You must bear your disappointment as a man, Icilius, nothing can be done!"

"Nothing to prevent, much to revenge."

Again his brow darkened, and again the child's touch dispelled the passing gloom.

"I must see her," he resumed in a stifled voice, "let her come to the garden, let her speak to me once more. Will you be present, lest any blight should fall on her fair name from a farewell interview with her betrothed. But if I am not allowed to speak to her once more, I swear by the infernal gods, you shall never see me again but as a corpse; I shall put an end to my life and my misery this very night."

"Hush, unhappy boy! you deserve your misfortune if you cannot bear it better. Be calm, and I shall give you the only consolation you crave, but you must retract that fearful oath."

Icilius looked up at Siona, wondering at her power

over him. "I shall try to command myself," he said.

She left him, taking away her own child, and soon returned, holding Volumnia by the hand; "I have promised her parents," she said, "that this farewell will be worthy of you both."

"We have known each other as long as we can remember," he said, in a heart-broken voice, but with a struggle to be firm.

There was such anguish in the young Vestal's countenance that he saw it would be cruel and cowardly to torture her with his own sufferings: his noble nature was roused.

"When I followed you here," he said, "it was under the impulse of passion. I meant to ask you to break the bond that binds you to the altar and to fly with me; but now that I see you, I feel my respect for you is as great as my love. Go, Volumnia, to guard the sacred fire, while your youth and beauty waste away: as for me, my life has no scope henceforward."

She saw by intuition the current his thoughts were following, and felt it would depend on her to direct them to a higher channel.

"Brave Icilius, turn all your energies to love our country and promote Rome's glory."

"Our country!" he repeated, and his countenance wore a sinister look as he muttered, "our country is enslaved, and wants an avenger!"

She was too much absorbed in her own efforts to heed his interruption.

"I would have you submit nobly, and with that virtue which heroes display in self-sacrifice. Esteem me happy in that I am chosen to serve the gods. My true friend, Siona, you see I have kept my word to my father; have I not spoken as becomes a soldier's child?"

"Nobly, Volumnia; and now come away, this scene is too much for all of us. Icilius, bid her farewell!"

"Take her," he said, "I cannot see her go!" He put one hand over his eyes, extended the other to her, pressed hers lightly, and tore himself away, running as if pursued.

By this time, numerous guests had gathered together, and the hasty preparations for the feast were completed. A dead calm had fallen over that desolate family, like the lull in a tempest. The lessons on Roman virtue inculcated by Nemesion had sunk into the minds of all, and each prepared to meet stoically the approaching separation. Volumnia sat on her father's right at the banquet, that place of honour she was never more to fill; praises were lavished on her, and the good wishes of all accompanied her, when the shades of night coming on apace, the tribune prepared to escort his daughter himself, as he had promised the Emperor, to the temple of Vesta. A covered *lettiga* was in readiness for her, and all the guests accompanied her to the street door; but Lucilla, her blind sister, clung to her so passionately that it was not without great difficulty she could be induced to relax her hold. Little Flora was the last Volumnia embraced, and in so doing, she whispered to her:

"Wilt thou love Lucilla in my stead?"

"Yes, I promise."

"Wilt thou come often to see her and speak to her of that she cannot see?"

"I will be a sister to her!"

"And one thing more! poor Icilius loves and obeys thy mother; tell her I leave him in her charge."

"Do not fear. Would I could make thee happy."

But Volumnia and her father were gone out of sight, and all the company dispersed towards their different homes.

\* \* \* \* \* \* \* \*

It was a moonlight night, and there was gladness in the heavens, and a sensation of peace stole over all who walked that night. On the Palatine Hill there was a solemn stillness, and the guards who watched the Emperor's palace could hear the echo of their own footsteps fall on the air. Once in the midst of the dead silence, the trees were swayed as if by a sudden rush of wind, and a dark form seemed to be crouching on the grass, but when the sentries challenged it, it vanished. They thought the evil genius of the Emperor must have come there in a spiritual shape, and disappeared, unwilling to be seen by mortal eye; but as they listened, they heard a sound of stones rolling down the hill, and, as it seemed to them, of rushing waters: and a voice whispering, yet deep-toned, echoed round about; it had uttered the word: Revenge!

## CHAPTER X.

ELEVEN years have passed over Claudius, the slave, since we first introduced him to the reader, and again he stands on the brow of the hill of Aricia, on a fine summer evening, as we first saw him looking out on the Campagna and on distant Rome. Eleven years! he recalls the events of that far-off time; the retrospective vision is pleasant; he can look back on a life chequered with good deeds. On such a night, he had opened the way of Divine Truth to the inquiring mind of Siona; shortly after, he had stood sponsor to her innocent child; both mother and daughter were now numbered among the choicest of God's flock. Had he done this, and could he rejoice? Not he, but his Master through him. He bowed his head, folded his hands in prayer, and as he gazed on the sun-gilt clouds, it was almost as if he bid them take his thankfulness to the Almighty Throne! Eleven years! yet his brow was hardly wrinkled, his hair had nothing of the silvery touch of time, his step was elastic yet, his courage was still that of the warrior, subdued by Christian virtue. And, at this hour, his manly frame seemed endowed with something like the vigour of youth, for joy, that renovator of the human faculties, that strengthener alike of the sinking heart and decaying frame—joy, that potent elixir which steeps the mind and body of man in a second youth, the healer and the life-giver, had been poured into the heart of Claudius to overflowing. His master, in acknowledgment of his long and devoted services, had that very day given him his liberty; he was no longer a slave! What wonder, then, that the sky seemed to him more beautiful, and Heaven's canopy more extended? that the atmosphere, balmy with earth's fragrance, seemed to breathe to him like Britain's air of liberty, that he should linger in that sunset, which had been so often the witness of his trials, and whose returning orb was henceforth to rise upon his freedom!

That very morning, a joyous procession had set out from Florentius' house in Rome, towards the Forum, where, according to Roman law, the act of enfranchisement of a slave must be performed before a magistrate. Florentius and Siona were both present, and Claudius, walking before them, wore for the last time the garb of a slave, and the *pileus* or cap of liberty. All the other household slaves followed in order, all rejoicing in his good fortune. Florentius taking him by the hand, declared he manumitted Claudius, who was henceforth to bear the name of his master united to his own. Then a little stroke from the rod of the magistrate had confirmed the sentence, and Claudius Florentius was a free man.

It had been previously arranged by his kind masters that the day of Claudius' enfranchisement was to be held a holiday both in Rome and at their country house in Aricia, an entertainment being given to the slaves in both places; but as Claudius must of necessity be present, he first presided at the slaves' early dinner in town, and then set out for Aricia in his master's open chariot. Laurentius and Flora asked to go out to the country house with their old friend, there to await their parents who were to join them in the evening. The afternoon passed very pleasantly, and they sat down to table as it was growing dusk; there was plenty of good cheer at supper, and Claudius took care that all his old comrades should enjoy themselves within the bounds of order; they loved him, and were so anxious to please him, that they all tried to show him their respect by observing a cheerful decorum. When they had nearly done, he left them, saying he wished to be on the look-out for his master's arrival, and it was just at this juncture that we find him, standing on the hill, where presently Laurentius and Flora came to join him. The little boy, full of fun, stole behind him, pulling down his new toga, the distinctive mark of a Roman citizen which he had that day put on for the first time.

"How handsome you look to-night, Claudius!"

"Oh, Laurentius," interrupted Flora, "Claudius is not a bit changed; he was just as great before God as a slave."

"Dear little mistress, my heart has so clung to you and yours, that the thought of leaving you diminishes my joy at being free."

"And could you not stay, Claudius? you are a Roman now."

"Nay, lady; the Briton never forgets his birthright,

and I have left those in my cottage home who mourn their absent sire and lord."

"But we could send them word to come. My father would dispatch a messenger."

"My home is like the eagle's nest on Albion's high cliffs; the footfall of the stranger must not cross my threshold or discover it."

"But it is so long since you left it, do you think they remember you?"

A pang shot through the man's heart which told upon his features; she was sorry she had caused it, and kindly took his hand.

"All earth's joys are unstable and fleet," he replied, after a moment's pause, "yet there are affections that endure persistingly. The heart that cast its lot with mine in the days of youth has never forgotten me, no more than you, my dear young Domina, can ever pass from the memory of your faithful old slave."

"But will you come back, Claudius?" cried the boy, "that is what I want to know."

"Even as He wills!" was the answer, and Claudius raised his eyes to where the sun was fast sinking in the west, and his own brow grew illumined with the refulgent rays.

"Oh, what can we ever do without you?" continued Laurentius, "you have taught us so many things, and you know such beautiful stories, and you can talk about God just as mama does."

"Then, children, will you remember the humble lessons of the poor slave; will you often repeat a prayer which was the first pronounced over you, Flora, by the Saint and Martyr who answered for your baptismal innocence before God, the last which she uttered when she lay before us in the agonies of a protracted death."

Both the boy and girl clasped their hands in prayer and repeated together: "Fiat cor meum et corpus meum immaculatum ut non confundar".

A cloud of dust on the road, and the noise of chariot wheels, told of the arrival of those they expected; Claudius immediately summoned the slaves from the house to welcome their masters, whom they went to meet in a body. Florentius, pleased with the happy faces and cordial reception he met with on all sides, went on with Laurentius and Flora. Siona beckoned to Claudius to remain behind with her.

"I have been waiting this opportunity," said the lady, "to express to you all my heart-felt gratitude for your many and valued services. Under God, I owe everything to you, Claudius, and you know full well, that had it depended on me alone, you should not have waited so long for your liberty."

"The Lord willed my slavery for His glory; the Lord has this day broken my bonds, I will lift up to Him a sacrifice of praise."

They had now reached the *Lararium*, which still retained that name, although, since the visit of Origen, it had been despoiled of pagan gods; a few busts were there, but simply as objects of honour, not of idolatry; the likeness of the Emperor, and of those teachers of the human mind who ranked most high in Florentius' esteem.

"Let me welcome you as a Roman citizen on the threshold of my house," he said to Claudius, embracing him as he came up, and Laurentius put his arms, too, round the old slave's neck, for the tenth time at least since morning; when the latter, raising his little master from the ground, and, holding him high above his head:

"May every happiness be thine," he cried, "noble heir of this house, mayest thou rise superior to thy fellow-men, not only by exterior greatness, but still more through the intrinsic worth of thy mind and heart; may thy life be honoured, and, when thy career is run, may thy friends have reason to bless Heaven that thou hast lived."

The grateful augury pleased them all; Siona and her daughter, who knew the high purport of his good wishes, exchanged a happy look of intelligence, and they proceeded together to the *aula* or inner court.

"Now," said Florentius to Claudius, "what will you do with your liberty?"

"My master is over-good to express an interest in his valueless slave. I wish I could give the remainder of my days to the service of this noble house, but I have left those in Britain who are ever expecting me, I must go to them. I have found in Rome relations of mine who hold intercourse with the governor of Britain, and I am assured that my wife and son still live."

"Thou shalt go to them then, and thy boy must become a Roman soldier."

"I expect to find him a sturdy Briton, very much

averse from leaving his native land,—but as to myself, I must ask your advice about my journey. I have not thought yet, my lord, of the mode of travelling so far."

"But *I* have," replied Florentius, "for I half suspected thou wouldst pine for thy native land, when free. My friend Adrias is sending next month a ship to Liguria, laden with divers goods; he seeks for one to take charge of his cargo, one who can keep accounts, and transact business in his name. I spoke of thee, of thy talents and trustworthiness; he will gladly employ thee, and, in return for thy services, will recommend thee to another trader who will convey thee to Britain, either by land or sea, for he constantly visits those islands for the commerce of tin."

"My dear master, I could not have expected less from your long-tried bounty, and yet I feel as overjoyed as if this were the first benefit I receive at your hands, instead of the last."

"No! no! we have not done with each other yet, Claudius; we shall meet again. Thou must go to-morrow morning to Adrias, and see with him how thou canst serve him best. Now, go in with the children; I shall take a walk in the garden with the lady Siona."

Florentius took his wife's hand, and led her to the farthest end of the flower-garden; he looked at her a little without speaking, for he was afraid of hurting her feelings by what he meant to propose, and he was warmly attached to her.

"The gods have not sent us a son; I think it is time I should adopt Laurentius."

"My lord and dear husband, I had always looked forward to my little nephew becoming the child of your adoption, and have trained him in the dutiful spirit of an affectionate son."

"Indeed you have! There are not in all Rome two other children like ours, they are as faultless as they are beautiful, they have grown up like brother and sister, and there is a strong family likeness between them. I am sorry to see Laurentius looks rather delicate; he has grown rapidly of late, perhaps that is the cause."

"Yes! but besides that, he has been suffering from intermittent fever, and the best remedy for that is to remove him from Roman air for some time."

Florentius resumed: "Our friend Adrias mentioned to me, only yesterday, that his wife, Paulina, likewise was much debilitated from the effects of the malaria, but she recovered completely from going to pass a season in Liguria. There is a Roman colony called Cimella, which she speaks of as the choicest spot on earth, where a gentle people, highly civilised, dwell in a valley secluded alike from the winter's blast and the sun's rays, where the fruits of the Hesperides grow all the year round, where flowers bloom without culture, and happiness is inhaled with the air they breathe."

"Paulina has been describing the Elysian fields; I cannot believe that such a place exists in reality," replied Siona.

"She is returning there this year, according to her husband's wishes, and one of the duties of Claudius on the journey is to attend to her. Suppose you join them, go with the children to this beautiful Cimella, and I shall come to meet you there later."

"Oh, Florentius! I have never left home yet, I cannot travel without you."

"But I shall follow you soon. A long absence from Rome would injure my interests, for nothing goes on well away from the master's eye. I must moreover look out for another *villicus* now we have lost Claudius; it will be long before I can replace so valuable a servant as he has been."

"I must do as you tell me, Florentius," she answered, "but you never put my obedience to so severe a test before."

"You will please me greatly, Siona, by going; the health of the children and yours will benefit by the change, and, at the same time, I shall enjoy the going to fetch you later. Shall I tell the children and see how they like the idea?"

"They will always like what you choose for them."

The little people were summoned, and expressed their exuberant joy at the good news.

"Oh, how nice!" cried little Laurentius, clapping his hands; "how charming to go on the sea as generals do, and when they come back their names are put on a rostral column."

"Bright little scholar!" exclaimed the delighted father. "You know nothing of life but what you learn out of your books; I want you to open your eyes to what is practical, it is better for you to have a long holiday and to get big and strong."

"Man's strength is here," said the little fellow, touching his forehead; "fortitude is developed in his head and heart."

"Well answered! Who taught thee that clever speech?"

Laurentius turned his loving eyes on his adopted mother, then on Flora, and hesitated.

"I intend to initiate thee myself into philosophy. Let us see whether thou hast any turn that way. What is life?"

"A school in which we learn wisdom; a season during which we sow what we are to reap later."

"Better and better! One would think thy little head carried a system of its own."

"Flora and I often talk of these things," said the child.

"Flora too! well, she would not be her father's child if she had not picked up some notions of philosophy. I must take her in hand too, and make an Aspasia of her. Well, little daughter, canst thou answer me what is death?"

"The hour of man's liberty," replied the girl boldly, preserving in her words, as she had been taught by her mother, the exact distinction between her father's notions and the Christian doctrines. "Death is the end of one life and the opening to another; the soul survives the body."

"Capitally reasoned! I shall take you both to study with me next year; but, for the present, you must have the amusement that suits your age. It is time to go indoors, the dew is falling; run on, children."

He turned to his wife, and said in a low voice: "I thank you, Siona, for making me so happy and proud of those dear ones; all praise is due to your good training. I shall proceed to prepare the act of Laurentius' adoption, so as to sign it before you set out on this journey."

By this time they had reached the house, which they entered together.

## CHAPTER XI.

"AND must it be so, dear Martina, must you leave us, and go to live in your solitary home?"

"Yes, Flora! now that your mother is leaving Rome, I cannot remain under your roof; but trifling circumstances are only links in the chain of events prepared by Providence. I feel warned that my hour is nigh."

"My beloved instructress, do not frighten me!"

"Flora! what do you fear? what have you learned from me if not to rejoice that Christ will be glorified in another martyr; must we not accomplish what is wanting to the Passion of Jesus? Take courage and do not mourn for me, for I must claim your services in that dread hour."

"Oh, tell me! what can I do for you?"

"You were a child, hardly capable of understanding what passed around you, when I took you in my arms to be witness to Cecilia's death; you were signed with her martyr's blood; she foretold to me that you would be my joy in life and my comfort in death. Will you fulfil the latter part of the prediction even as you have the first, Flora?"

"My dear mistress, you speak solemnly, as if we were never to meet again; oh, then, give me some parting advice; I have treasured up all your lessons."

"Pursue your duties, Flora, until the hour when the Bridegroom comes to claim you for His own. Your life will not be fulfilled until you have accomplished all the work your Heavenly Father has given you to do. I need not ask, my child, whether your heart is fixed on God alone for your portion, for I believe He has chosen you, and that your lot is not cast with the children of men. Therefore if you are sought for later——"

"Oh no! no!" interrupted Flora, covering her face with her hands.

"Do not think, dear one, I would wilfully offend your modesty. But I wish to caution you, for, even after I had vowed my virginity to Christ, I was obliged to pain a noble heart that had offered me its affection and would fain have linked its lot with mine. May my prayers and my death profit him! If ever you meet one who inquires after me, tell him that in my last hour I implored for him Heaven's best boon. And you, Flora, watch and pray ever! may the oil of good deeds fill your lamp! may it be preserved from the storms and blasts of the world, from the foulness of sin, from the wavering of temptation, for a voice will be heard in the dead of night, saying: 'He is at hand!' and then it will be your turn to arise and go forth to meet Him, not indeed in joy and festivity, but through suffering, and sorrow, and persecution unto death; you shall go to Him a Martyr Bride!"

She laid her hands on the young head that was bowed before her, and as when Elias covered his servant with his mantle, the spirit of the one passed into the other, Martina left behind her a faithful inheritor of her virtues and good deeds.

Thus they parted, and the orphan patrician maiden returned to the house which she had inhabited alone, since her parents' death, and which she had deserted for the last year to dwell with Siona.

The Emperor was absent from Rome, and the Præfect, usurping a power beyond his authority, having been made aware of the return of the young Christian who excited suspicion by her abundant alms to the poor, ordered her to be arrested and brought before the tribunals. The lonely life she was accustomed to gave her an intrepid assurance which somewhat awed her judges; they did not address her in the usual interrogatory form, her faith was known; they put her to the test at once, ordering her to sacrifice to the gods. Horrified at the impious proposal, she disdained to reply, and, with a gesture of scorn, bid them remove her from the presence of the hated idols.

"Are you then a Christian?" she was asked.

"I am, as my life hitherto hath sufficiently proved."

They condemned her to be tortured with iron hooks driven into her sides. A glow of indignation passed over her patrician features: who was she to be thus ignominiously treated? and then she turned deadly pale; for, as she had previously said of herself, hers was the patience that abideth, not the courage that resisteth. Her woman's gentleness quailed under the fear of torments, and she trembled, even as One had done before her at the approach of death, yet He was mightier than she. It was but a moment! crowds pressed round her, and in their ranks she saw a young girl, conducted by an elderly man; the eyes of both were fixed on her with intense anxiety; she saw, and, stretching out her arms even as He Whom she had chosen as the model of her life, she made use of His words, and said firmly: *In flagellis parata sum.*

They took her away to the torture room, where, after undergoing the shame of flagellation, she lay quivering and moaning on the floor. Suddenly a mysterious strength seemed to be conferred on her, for she arose of herself, put on her robes, and bid them do their worst. She was placed on the rack, iron hooks were again applied to her sides, and they tore her flesh as the wild beast fastens on its prey; but the brave spirit grew stronger with the torment. Her eyes, open to celestial visions, saw nothing of the fiendish forms that surrounded her; a smile lit up her countenance, and, when she fainted away, it seemed to be less from the excruciating pain than because He who stood by her in her agony had disappeared, and her spirit had passed away with Him. They loosened her from her bonds, they took her, senseless as she was, to the Mamertine prison; they let her down from story to story until the lowest depth; there they left her, to die as she would! But it was not so! she awoke! feeling that an invigorating coolness had spread over her heated frame; she thought her wounds had been bathed in a cool stream, and the same pleasant moisture refreshed her throbbing temples . . . . She looked up . . . . above her was

a dark vault, perforated by an opening in the centre, through which she had been let down; by degrees her eyes got acustomed to the darkness, her spirits revived, and she could distinguish the large blocks of travertine forming the well-built walls. She raised herself a little, and found that, close to her head, there gurgled a small fountain, springing from the ground; she recognised it all now, for the place was familiar to her, she had sometimes gone there to visit her suffering brethren, and often to venerate the traces left by the Apostle St. Peter, incarcerated likewise within its dread precincts. How the poor suffering girl rejoiced that she had the glory of being associated with him in the hour of her trial. That spring! she knew it well! it had sprung up at the command of the Saint who had baptized his gaolers with the water. It was an object of great devotion among the Christians, whose piety attributed to it a healing power, even as the Scriptures say "that the very garments of the apostles cured the sick who touched them". She knew too that in the prison above her was a staircase which St. Peter had trod, and when the inhumanity of his gaolers had pushed him down, and made him fall, he had left upon the wall the exact representation of his features sunk into the volcanic tufa, more ably than if engraved by a sculptor's chisel.\*
All these reminiscences passed over her mind like a sweet dream, for she was weak from suffering, her limbs refused to do their office, and, after vainly en-

---

\* To be seen yet in the Mamertine prison.

deavouring to rise, she turned her head a little on one side and lay still.

Returning consciousness had brought back the sense of pain, and she could not sleep. Her eyes remained fixed with an inexplicable persistence on a fissure in the wall where the stones did not meet exactly; she thought she saw the crevice increase . . . . it grew wider and wider . . . . she closed her eyes to remove the delusion . . . . but there it was still . . . . the stone moved . . . . a hand appeared . . . . then another . . . . a small delicate hand this time . . . . she was terrified with a nameless fear, but there were gigantic efforts behind that stone . . . . it yielded . . . . leaving an aperture through which a man's head appeared . . . . the features seemed familiar to her, but she did not look at them long! He withdrew, and she saw what seemed to be a vision . . . . a young girl, crawling on her hands and knees, glided through that opening, a little boy followed her . . . . they came, one on each side of the martyr, stooped over her, and, in accents which thrilled her with joy: "Martina!" they cried, "have we come in time; are you still alive?"

"Flora, Laurentius," she said, in the same suppressed tones, "my dear children, is it indeed you?"

"We have many things to restore you; let us help you."

While the little boy held a glass of wine to the lips of the sufferer, the girl, with gentle hand, washed her wounds and bound her lacerated arms and feet in fine linen cloths; she also applied to her poor friend a perfumed ointment which at once softened the sore festering flesh, and restored vigour to the contracted muscles. When this was done, the man came out of his hiding place; he brought a soft carpet on which they gently laid her, and then Flora, passing her arm under her shoulders, so as to rest her head,

"Are you better?" she asked.

"I am so happy! Oh my poor children . . . . explain to me, how is this?"

"Did you not tell me," said Flora, "that Cecilia, my sainted godmother, foretold I should be your joy in life and your comfort in death? Did I not promise to fulfil the trust?"

"But this prison is so inaccessible! how have you come?"

"I made Claudius be on the watch for the day when you should appear before the tribunals, and I went with him. You saw us."

"I did, and I thanked God; I felt you were praying for me."

"And God heard us. Claudius found you were conveyed here; he told me he knew of a secret passage which had been partially blocked up, but which the early Christians used when they endeavoured to establish a communication with St. Peter in this very prison. The entrance is in a house at the foot of the hill; fortunately, it belongs to Christians, and they keep the secret right well. We are quite safe, and I thank God I have found you, but oh! how changed!"

"From death to life, dear child, and when this poor

body shall have put on immortality, then shall death be swallowed up in victory."

"And what will they do with you, Martina?"

"Perhaps they may leave me to die here; or, if they find me living still, they may take me away again to renew the combat unto death."

"Oh, if you would consent to something!"

"To what?"

"Through that passage, Claudius could convey you away gently and safely; and when your persecutors came, they would find your prison empty, just as it was with St. Peter when an Angel came and broke his chains."

"And when, like unto the apostle rebuked by his Master, I meet my Crucified Lord upon the road, shall I too say to Him *Domine, quo vadis?* Shall I not know rather that He comes to reproach the faithless one who could not wait her doom! Oh, blessed is the faithful servant who, when his Master comes, shall be found watching."

"You know best, dear Martina; I have learned all from you."

"You must not stay longer, dear child, my gaolers might surprise us. Go, think of your parents."

"Claudius is watching, he will call us if he hear any noise."

"I must give you a message before I leave you."

"From whom?"

"You told me that if *one* inquired about you from me ——"

"I remember! Have you seen him? and where?"

"On the Via Appia, we were going to the Catacombs, Claudius, Laurentius, and I; a stranger came up and made himself known as having come to our house a year ago, disguised as a mendicant."

"And then?"

"Poor young man! he spoke of you with anguish and deep feeling. He said he had mingled in the crowd when you were led to the tribunal, had never lost sight of you, remaining outside the torture room, and watching for the sound of your voice. That day, he said, a new life had burst forth within him, the sight of your constancy had opened his understanding to words you had spoken to him long ago; he felt a thirst for truth, he wished to be instructed and to know your God. He has passed the days and nights since your trial on the Via Appia, sleeping in a cave. He asked me to teach him a Christian prayer, and implored of me to procure some one who would instruct and prepare him for baptism."

"Oh my God, my God," cried the young martyr, "Thou hast promised an hundredfold to those who leave all for Thee, and dost Thou reward me, who have as yet done nothing?"

"Then he gave me," continued Flora, "a message for you."

"Do not deliver it, my child, lest it should disturb the calm serenity of this hour."

"Nay, Martina, I have promised! and I must repeat to you his words which were most solemn. He desired me tell you he was quite another man, that a holier love had quenched his early passion, that an image, mysterious as yet, and hardly intelligible, of the God you adore, had taken possession of his heart and effaced all thought of the world. He detached a palm branch from a tree that grew by the roadside, and, cutting it in two, desired me bear you this half, as a presage of the martyr's glory that awaits you, and of that he asks you to obtain for him. 'Thus,' he said, 'will she recognise me when she sees me in another life, bearing a symbol like unto hers and taking my place at her side. There perhaps a union superior to what the heart of man can conceive, absorbing souls in a Divine Essence, may yet blend the spirits of Hippolytus and Martina.'"

The martyr raised her feeble arm to receive the token, and placed it on her heart. "Tell him!" she said, "I have accepted and will bear with me to the last this symbol of a faith which has triumphed over earthly passion. And now, leave me, I entreat of you both. Laurentius, if I have spoken less to you, 'tis because Flora has been more my companion, but God knows, dear child, how I have loved you too; how I have prayed that your impetuous nature may lead you to great deeds, and I have felt, oh, how truly, that my prayer was heard. Go, my dear ones; Claudius, take them away, and, for the good this visit has done me, I thank my God, them, and you."

Again they offered her some nourishment such as she could take in her weak condition, and, promising to return the next day, they left as they had come, by the secret passage, Claudius setting the stone into its proper place, and drawing it after them, so as effectually to avoid detection.

The next day came, but their suffering friend did not require them *there;* men had come and taken her away, and exposed her poor lacerated body to the flames. But God saw she had done enough for His Glory, and His mighty arm stretched over the fire, and bid it leave her scatheless! And it was so! The flames arose, and wreathed round her, and glided over her garments, and covered her with a veil of light; and again they settled over her head, and her brow seemed resplendent with a crown of glory. She lived on, and many of the bystanders falling down, adored her God.

At length the judges accused her of being a sorceress, and of commanding the elements by the arts of magic. They got afraid of her, and ordered her head to be cut off. The sentence was to be executed the next day, for they dreaded some new prodigy, and would not take her life in presence of the people, already won by her beauty, her sufferings and her fortitude. They hurried her back to her prison, but she was left on the upper floor, for the convenience of the executioners. Claudius, according to the desire of his young mistress, had followed the noble Martina in every stage of her passion, reporting all he witnessed. Now, however, he was at fault, he could find no access to Martina, though he offered money to the guards; they had received unusually strict orders which they dared not infringe. The night passed, and found the faithful man watching by those walls, aiding, by his prayers, the soul within, separated from eternity but by a few hours; he was not alone! other brethren came in the shadows of night and mingled their orisons, even as a loving family round the death-bed of an expiring member. Once, Claudius thought he heard a groan near him; it came from a man's breast, and revealed an immense woe! he addressed some words of comfort to the sufferer, who suddenly raised his head. "I recognise your voice," he said, "as all that is connected with her; you guided me to her presence in the garden of Florentius' house, and I met you too on the Via Appia with the lady Flora."

"Yes, that is my dear young mistress, the intimate friend of the holy Martina."

"Will you then finish the good work she began, and teach me how to be a Christian, for, as much as lies in my power, I believe."

And truly the compact was made, and acted upon at once, for in those solemn hours of loving vigil, while the soul of Martina was hovering on eternity, and offering up her sufferings as the incense of intercession, Hippolytus felt the effects of that anticipated sacrifice, that blood which was to be offered for him. In the solemn silence of that night, he hearkened to one who, no longer a slave, was endowed with sufficient instruction to enlighten the young patrician, and liberate his enslaved soul. Hippolytus pressed his lips to the prison walls, not because they enclosed one dear to him, but because the sufferings of Christians had hallowed them, and the redeeming sign of Christ's passion was in many places marked thereon.*

Towards morning, long before sunrise, while most of the Roman citizens were yet asleep, a powerful commotion shook the soil, and made houses tremble to their very foundation. Men started up and asked each other with exceeding great fear what had happened. The faithful who lingered round the Mamertine prison did not feel it; other edifices round about them gave signs of a perilous deviation. Those walls alone which sheltered the martyr remained immovable, and they understood by the prodigy that God had rendered glorious the last hour of their sister, that she had triumphed even in death. Men had willed that her execution should be private, and thus it was revealed to the world! The guards fled frightened, the lictor issued from the scene of his bloody work with all the signs of terrified horror, the gates were left open, and the Christians rushed in. Claudius did not follow them, for he had promised his young mistress he would warn her when it was time to fulfil the last duties to her friend's remains, and he turned his steps homewards. Flora was on the watch, and when she saw him approach, she knew the hour was come, and stole quietly out. Not a word passed between them, they proceeded silently as to the performance of a religious duty. They reached the gloomy abode, she gave her hand to her faithful attendant, and consigning to him a parcel, wrapped in a linen cloth, which she had kept under her *stola*, proceeded down

\* From the Acts of the Martyrs.

the stairs with faltering steps. She trembled violently as she reached the door and saw by the crowd of people kneeling there that she need go no further. Claudius was obliged to support her and bid her take courage to the end. The bystanders moved away, ranging themselves on either side to let her pass; she covered her face with her hands and went in, but for some time she was afraid to look up. By and by, however, the holy calmness that stole over her, the perfume with which she felt the atmosphere impregnated, the impression of the place which partook of the solemnity of a sanctuary, all contributed to soothe her, and still kneeling she opened her eyes. Oh the peaceful majesty of that brow, unruffled by the death-stroke, the rich locks which still encircled the forehead, unrestrained by the fillet, the tranquil beauty of those unclosed eyes, which seemed to await her hand to seal them in death! The neck was severed from the body, but not, as she had feared to see it, bathed in blood. No! for from that corpse, which had lived an unearthly life, never tainted by sin or unholy temptations, gushed a stream unlike that which flows from other dead! That pure body which, long since, had ceased to live for self, emitted a milk-white fluid, spotless as its life had been, emblematical of innocence. Overawed at the portent, Flora gazed long and lovingly at the beloved dead, then called to her aid the Christian women she recognised among those who surrounded her, but she herself wrapped the head in a fine linen cloth, filling it with odoriferous spices, and laid it in the dish she had brought with her, according to the desire expressed long ago by her that was gone. They consulted together whether they could convey the body to the Catacombs, but the concourse of people, the broad daylight, the fear of being followed and of disclosing the Christian place of worship, all seemed to render the transport of the dear remains inadvisable. They resolved to bury her in the garden of her own house. While they were debating there came among the Christians a young man whom no one recognised; he knelt before the martyr, and laid on the body a broken palm branch which he took up again, and carefully wrapped up in the folds of his toga on his breast. He approached Claudius, whispered to him, and those two between them raised the bier on which lay the maiden; they bore her out, while others followed and prayed, strewing flowers as for a triumph. The home she had lived in was close at hand, at the foot of the Capitoline hill; they took her to its small lonely garden, where an obscure grotto had often witnessed her silent meditations and the outpourings of her soul before God, there they effectually concealed her, and laid a heavy stone before the door. By and by, those who had followed her there dispersed, and there remained but a poor man, a young girl, and a youth, who, with bowed head and outstretched arms, uttered and repeated again and again his first Christian prayer.

A considerable time elapsed, and then Claudius told his young mistress they must not stay any longer. The young man heard them, and turning round: "Do not leave me," he said, "you have both done much for me,

I require more from you still. Will you lead me to the priests of your religion? I have loved the world, but at this tomb I vow to it an eternal hatred henceforward; men shall hear of Hippolytus but as of one already dead, one who possessed riches and cast them away, fame and honour, and scorned them. My home, from this day, shall be near the tombs, and living the life of Him Whose Crucified Death you have told me of, I shall prepare, like Him, to rise again; for, henceforward, I believe in the Resurrection of the Dead, and in Life Everlasting. Amen."

They parted as those who have been suddenly linked in a great sorrow and a great love. He went his way, but Claudius sought him again in a few days, and led him to those on whom power had been conferred by the Most High for the salvation of souls. Flora did not recover the shock of Martina's martyrdom; she had nerved herself to the task of assisting her poor friend to the end, but her health suffered in consequence, and Siona was now glad to avail herself of her husband's offer, and made speedy preparations to remove her daughter from the scene of such painful events. They left Rome for Liguria.

## CHAPTER XII.

THERE is in the rush of waters a mysterious influence, akin to a hidden sympathy within the heart of man. It is the voice of nature which harmonizes the most with the human soul, and oh! how it varies and takes the tone of our thoughts. Sometimes a rude hand has touched the chords of our feelings which vibrate to sorrow, and we listen to the long, low wail of the mountain torrent as it swells with the waters of its troubled bosom, even as our hearts with tears. Sometimes it is the voice of hope, which whispers high, and we hearken to the hushed murmur of the surge, as it comes sweeping along the sands, musical in its rising accents, like an evening breeze, and lo! it has broken, and the retiring sound tells of disappointment and vanished dreams! Again, we seek the sea-girt shore when a struggle is at hand, and we feel our weak nature unequal to the contest; the clouds are lowering on the horizon, and there is an under-current which impels the billows, and sends them foaming to our feet; they beat against the rocks, raising their crested heads, and come on like giants of strength moving to the battle! they toss, they fight, until, like defeated warriors, rolling one over the other, they sink on the watery plain, and, expiring, cover the shore with spray. The sun is sinking on the scene, in crimson-coloured clouds, and the electric exhalations, flashing from beneath them, tell of a troubled morrow; yet, there is an invigorating influence in that atmosphere, an irresistible attraction in the wild howling of those waves, terrible as a battle-cry, and the heart that has sought their strange solace does not leave them as it came.

"I hope my dear lady is better," said Claudius, as he followed the steps of Flora along the sea shore, at about two miles from Cimella, where they were staying at present. The good, faithful attendant watched the colour returning to her pale cheek, while her brother, at no great distance, scrambled among the rocks, looking for coral.

"Yes, Claudius, I thank you. I am glad I came out, though I did not like to leave my mother alone."

"My dear mistress, you will forgive me for remarking that I have observed a great sadness steal over you every day at the same hour. I, who have known from my very childhood the salutary effects of sea-air, requested the lady Siona to send you out as much as possible. When your physical strength is restored, the melancholy which has taken so strange a hold of you will give way."

"Claudius, I see you have guessed at the cause of my suffering, which I know to be imagination, but cannot overcome. That scene in the Mamertine prison comes before me each day, at a fixed hour; even now when I looked into the water, I saw it reflected there."

"Oh, how I reproach myself with having allowed you to exert yourself beyond your strength."

"Oh! Claudius, rejoice rather that you helped me to fulfil the charge she herself confided to me. Must I not too prepare to endure more, and greater perhaps? Did she not prophesy to me that my lot will be a happy one, but purchased at the same price as she paid.? Jesus Christ has chosen me for His Martyr Bride."

"Flora, do not brood over the sorrowful past, nor the uncertain future; leave both in the hands of your Heavenly Father, Who knows what is best for us all."

"You are right! but who can be a Roman and not live with the past? There is something in Rome's greatness which depresses the spirits, and makes us for ever mourn the pristine splendour from which she fell! Rome is the Mother of heroes, the Parent of lofty aspirations and great deeds, but to me it seems that youth and innocence would thrive better here. Oh! the overpowering beauty of this land! it must resemble that on which the Creator first smiled, it makes me feel a child of nature, and brings me nearer to my God!" .

She sat down on a rock, and both relapsed into silence: the man thought of his far-off home in Britain, more beautiful to him by far; the girl mused. The scene might have impressed a less meditative mind than Flora's, who was, as we have seen, gifted with the spirit of poetry. The sunny and bright atmosphere of her native land had developed her early girlhood, almost before her childhood was over, but education had done still more: her daily intercourse with Martina had matured and improved her: the histories of the martyrs she loved to hear had inspired her with a lofty enthusiasm, and made her aspire to great deeds. In the same manner, the virtues of the Roman republic were kept up by the fond pride of its children, who would not degenerate from a Regulus and a Camillus.* Flora had grown up, blending the Roman spirit with the woman's gentleness, strengthening by the Christian lessons of self-sacrifice a heart which might have proved too susceptible of human tenderness. Oftentimes, her watchful mother had trembled for the safety of the floweret confided to her care; it seemed to her unfit for the rude blasts of the world, hardly strong enough to thrive on the steep heights of Christian perfection, too inclined perhaps to lean on earth, taking refuge in the genial atmosphere of home affections and domestic happiness: but when she used to consult Martina about their young charge: " Do not fear," was the answer, " do not fear for Flora! she may perhaps linger by the roadside before she climb the narrow path of holiness, but when once she enters it she will go on by strides not by steps; perchance, she may sometimes stoop to gather the brilliant flowers which lure the young along the way of life, but if she press them to her heart and find one thorn among them, she will fling them away for ever. That girl will never wait for her second disappointment: the first will have done its work! if it needs be that she must pass through that ordeal so hard to bear!—but

---

\* Moribus antiquis statres Romana virisque.—*Ennius.*

do not fear! there is a seal upon her brow which shows the Most High has called her, and not in vain."

Time passed, and the prophecy seemed to be moving towards its fulfilment, the dawning virtues of that girl prepared her more and more for her noble mission!

She sat there, with that Roman-built town of Cimella, from which she had strayed that morning, visible on the neighbouring hill. On its brow was a temple standing out in relief against the sky: above it floated the clouds, not watery, nor black, nor threatening, as in other climes, but vapoury and gold-tinged, wafted here and there, like the incense of the earth before its God! and beneath their dreamlike shadow the firmament looked more blue, as if they were only meant to increase its loveliness, for there was in that deep-coloured sky a dazzling radiance and an exhilarating influence, which communicated gladness to the heart.

There was a hill extending all the way from Cimella, and descending in a gentle slope towards the sea shore where the girl stood; at its foot, orange groves were recognisable by their thick verdant foliage, and their golden tribute struck the eye at a distance; above these, a range of olive trees contrasted strangely with the dark pines nearer the summit; but, melancholy as is that greyish verdure, yet how Scriptural is that tree of the silvery aspect, under which Solomon sat, and David sang; it has a mysterious, poetical beauty of its own, ever and anon the wind plays in its branches, and the rustling foliage seems to heave a sigh like the mysterious breathing of the Prophet-King.

Thus Cimella rose in the distance; around it, fair, cultivated hills undulated on the horizon, and, just behind Flora, as she sat on the sea shore, a rocky eminence displayed itself, and there stood another town, and its name was Nicæa.

A citadel on an inexpugnable rock, built by the victorious Phœnicians long ago, and consecrated to Hercules to whom they attributed their success, Nicæa had preserved the name of Victory long after the origin of that name was forgotten. A little further on, Augustus had raised a monument after having conquered Liguria, so that all here told of Roman domination, but Nicæa the victorious seemed to have remained the last bulwark of Cisalpine Gaul. Its rude inhabitants dwelt in fishermen's huts and went out often to sea: their native rock affording no room for cultivation, they would descend to the plain with their flocks, owning as they did a great part of the ground between them and Cimella. Year after year they learned something more from the vicinity of the Roman colony; they acquired a taste for husbandry, already the vine trailed on their sunny shore; they added thereto the cultivation of the olive tree, and, by and by, came the art of making bricks and building. At the time we describe it, Nicæa was yet struggling between the old pride of freedom and the inroads of civilization. Claudius was interested in that town more, perhaps, than in graceful Cimella, too replete for him of Roman memories; the rocky home and its uncouth inhabitants were to the islander a reminiscence of his distant fatherland. He gazed at it long, and asked Flora whether she would like to bend her steps thither.

"It seems to me," she said, "we have been out rather long, and I hardly dare to go where I shall hear no Latin spoken; it is time to go home, but where, oh where is Laurentius?"

They called the boy, but received no answer; Claudius went among the rocks repeating his name till the seagulls shrieked, and flew up frightened from their hiding-places. Flora stepped cautiously on the gravel along the water's edge; she thought her brother might have strayed among the bowers, formed by myrtle trees, which grow very thick near the sea: strong and hardy, they love the marine air and thrive in its sandy soil, but turn away indignant when the breeze visits them too roughly; all their branches then grow inward, and they hide their floral tribute, like a coy maiden retiring from the rude homage of her sailor-lover. Flora went on, stooping under the boughs, which, uncut and uncultivated, spread in wild luxuriance; she heard footsteps, and stopped: they were not her brother's, however; she was too well accustomed to the sound of his boyish tread, so light and joyous, not to recognise it even at a great distance. She remained listening, and could distinguish the light friction of the pebbles by a woman's tunic; another instant of suspense, and she found herself face to face with a young girl of her own age. A blue *stola* was confined by a loose girdle round her waist; on her shoulders, ivory *spiculæ* fastened the folds, leaving her arms bare; a *vestis succincta* covered this, partially gathered up under the girdle as if to facilitate her walking; the sandals she wore were old and worn out, her feet swollen, as if with toil and fatigue. The only foreign addition to this Roman costume was a large hat of plaited straw, such as Greek maidens wear in Ionia; it was fixed with pins on her head, where the hair united in gold-coloured braids formed a diadem over her brow. Her features were cast in the Grecian mould; the complexion was slightly olive, yet so clear that one could see the colour mantle in her cheek with every varying emotion. Her eyes were blue, which was a novelty to Flora; they were full of depth and meaning and fixed now earnestly on the Roman girl, scanning her with a look of smiling inquiry: "Are you Flora?" she inquired.

"I am! but how can I be known to you? Are you a vision?"

"No, indeed! I am a mortal like yourself, looking forward to be your friend, if you will permit me. I have met a boy calling upon your name in sorrow and anxiety;—your brother, I think; my uncle took him by the hand and is helping him in his search among the rocks; I am waiting for them here."

"Then I shall wait with you, lest I should miss them. Sweet stranger, you speak my Latin language well, yet it sounds foreign on your lips; are you a Roman exile?"

"I am a Grecian by birth. My parents were shipwrecked on these coasts; my uncle Pontius and I were saved in that terrible disaster, and we have continued to live in this land where God's Providence delivered us from a watery grave."

"We are sisters, I see, by the mention you have made of His Adorable Name; but what makes you so trustful? How come you to know I am not a Pagan?"

"The boy we met was kneeling under a tree, and invoking the Thrice Hallowed Name! He was afraid of having lost you; that made us so anxious to help him."

"Were your parents Christians?"

"Alas, no! but when the tempest tossed our ship wildly on the waves, and all hope was lost, a Christian mariner seized that awful moment for revealing to us the True God. Saints say there is a special grace attached to that hour, for, though the good man's words were brief, they penetrated many souls, and almost all the Pagans knelt before the few Christians that were in the boat, asking to be baptised. My uncle, who had believed in and practised the One Faith from his youth, poured the Water of Regeneration on my mother's head, and her smile of ineffable peace told of an anticipated heaven in her heart. I knelt by her side, but I was not satisfied, for my father had not joined us, and hesitated still. I flew to him, and conjured him by the Great God my heart already worshipped, by his paternal love, by my own filial devotion, to bow to the sacred rite; but oh! while I was yet speaking, the deck we stood on, already shattered by beating against the rocks, now broke in. He fell over into the sea; instinctively I clung to the mast, and the vigorous arm of a sailor held me up. I looked round, my mother had been swept away; I looked down, my father was struggling with the waves. I held out my arms to him; he saw me, his hand was raised, I thought he was trying to make the Christian sign, and I called on the True God to save him . . . . He sank, with that Hallowed Name on his lips! and oh! how often since have I hoped that fearful death may have proved the baptism of his soul, that the waters which surrounded him may have purified him, for I am sure he desired the Sacrament. Since then I have loved the sea, for I am always seek- my dear ones there, and, when the waves beat high and murmur, it seems to me as if the soul of my father spoke through their voice, saying : ' Reparata, work on and do all the good thou canst, remembering that thou hast, for thee and me, a double work to do'. My uncle conducts me here often, for he goes to instruct the poor Pagans at Nicæa, and he takes me up those rugged steeps, for I love to be the companion of his labours."

"And where do you live, Reparata ?"

A sound of approaching voices interrupted them; Claudius had found Laurentius in company with a venerable man : the moment the boy saw Flora, he ran away from his guide, and, with cries of joy and playful reproach : "Oh sister !" he said, " who was it played the truant this time ?"

" You yourself, naughty boy; where were you ?"

" At first I found such pretty coral on the rocks I thought Claudius would know how to carve it into a necklace for you, then I went on picking up little shells of varied colours; at last I came here and could not find my way back. See! I have discovered a new friend who has taken great care of me," and he fell back a few steps to introduce the stranger Reparata had spoken of as her own uncle. He was rather older than Claudius, or perhaps appeared so on account of his grey hair, which bore the traces rather of study and profound thought than of years. His eye, bright with intellect, was sometimes lit up with a latent spark of mirth, denoting talents which would have graced a comic poet, and such Pontius had been in his younger days, when he learned, in the classic shades of his own land, the plays of Aristophanes. Would he not have graced the world there, in that nursery of genius where his own so fitly shone, while men hung upon his words, where, distinguished in the dramatic art, he would have witnessed his own plays, wielding ably the weapons of satire, and calling forth bursts of applause from his fellow-countrymen, as he pourtrayed to them their foibles with irresistible ridicule? Truly that man was born for fame and the world's applause! And now? A preacher of the gospel to the untutored children of these shores, an apostle of the faith among this people, whose mind opened but slowly to the truth, toiling in the midst of them unceasingly, until he wore out the energies of his mind and vigorous frame in the laborious task. Who is to know this, oh Pontius? who is to register the great deeds of thy seemingly wasted intellect? Thus would men reason, and thy self-devotion would appear to them an utter destruction of all that is noble within thee; but a day will come when the masters of the human mind, the sons of genius and of song will be mouldering in their graves, posterity will have forgotten them, save in those rare exceptions when the sculptor may have traced their features in the undying marble; and then thou, who didst refuse to consort with these superior ones, wilt find thyself elevated far above them in the annals of fame; these Nicæan shores, once witness of thy labours, will bear the echo of thy name to distant ages, these hills will resound with it. When the old Roman founders are forgotten, a shrine shall rise to thy memory, at which earthly potentates will kneel. The Founder of the Carlovingian dynasty will deem it an honour to have slept on his return from Rome within the walls that shelter thy glorious remains, and the Ligurians will reckon it one of the good deeds of Charlemagne that he erected an Abbey in honour of St. Pontius. How little do men know when they are sowing the seeds of their own greatness!

The venerable man cast one penetrating glance on Flora, as if scanning the expression of her mind in her features; he seemed satisfied by what he read there, and turning to his own golden-haired companion: "You have improved the leisure hour I hope, Reparata, and secured a friend to yourself in this young Roman lady".

"We have enjoyed this last quarter-of-an-hour so much, noble stranger," interposed Flora courteously, "that I hope to look forward to many a pleasant day passed in your niece's society."

"Ay, ay, women together make fair sunshine," observed Pontius, and an old, long-forgotton, half-sarcastic smile played on his features, as he adapted to this remark a line from one of his favourite poets.

"Which looks all the brighter when man's shadow comes across it," observed Flora archly, casting her eyes on the ground where the tall form of the stranger was delineated, as he stood with his back to the glowing sunset.

He was pleased with her promptness: an amused expression passed over his face. He looked at Flora again, and met those peculiar eyes of hers, whose mysterious expression no one could fathom, save those who knew that one of her family had conferred with the Most High. Pontius thought he recognised in her the stuff of which superior women are made, and he at once felt attracted to her as to a kindred spirit; his old love of teaching was roused, and he at once conceived the desire to impart knowledge to that young mind.

"Where are your steps directed to, lady?" he asked. "Allow us to show you the way, we know the country so well."

"We live at Cimella," broke in Claudius, who had remained in the background during the whole conversation.

"So do we!" resumed Pontius, and they went on together, the young girls side by side, and the boy giving his hand to Claudius, yet keeping near the stranger.

"How comes it," continued the latter, "we have never met, although we are such near neighbours?"

"It is only a few days since we arrived," explained Flora, "and this is the first time we have come out for a walk."

"I suppose that must excuse my young friend here running wild with excitement," said the old man, patting Laurentius on the head. "You must come to see me, my boy, I can show you many entertaining things."

"Do you live at Cimella, or near it?" asked Flora.

"Farther on in the valley, by the side of the torrent. Christians know my retreat, and often seek me there."

"And where are the assemblies of the faithful held, and when?"

"We have one this very night: will you join us? You could not find out your way, but we can call for you when we set out."

"Will you allow Reparata to come home with me now? I should like her to make acquaintance with my mother. Then, at the appointed hour, we can all go together, and Claudius will take care of us."

"All your relations are Christians, then?"

"No, my dear father is not, but he is in Rome; he will come later in the season to Liguria."

"I am so glad my niece has met you; she has been long deprived of all society, dear girl, save that of her old uncle and the poor people of this strange land . . . . and yet . . . . born to a high destiny! but" . . . . his voice faltered a little, then he resumed: "God's Will be done!"

"My mother will be glad to welcome Reparata," said Flora earnestly. Pontius bid them adieu, for his road lay along the mountain torrent, and the young people, with Claudius, took the steeper pathway up the hill. They had not proceeded far when they met Siona, who, anxious at her children's long absence, had come out on the high road to watch for them. Many questions were on her lips, but she had not time to ask them, all were so anxious to give their news; then Flora, introducing her new friend with the sweet affectionate manner she used to those she was intimate with: " I have promised this Grecian maiden a mother's embrace from you, for Heaven has taken from her her dear ones ".

Thus appealed to, Siona immediately clasped the orphan to her heart, and held her hand in hers, as they proceeded homewards, talking over the events of the day. They reached the house, which was of Roman construction, and surrounded with pleasant grounds, but it was growing too dark to observe anything out of doors; they entered, and found within all the comforts of civilization and Roman luxury. A silver lamp branching into several candelabra was already lit for the evening: its light was reflected in a highly-polished table of a large circumference, carved out of the trunk of a single olive tree; chairs of sculptured bronze, heavy, long, and disposed for reclining upon, were placed round the fresco-painted walls; other sedilia of dark-coloured wood had designs of ivory laid on them in bas-relief; the floor was of mosaic pavement, and many smaller objects in the apartment showed the taste and wealth of the owners. The young stranger's eye ran over the household picture like one experienced in the refinements of life, and pleased to view them. She dropped gracefully into one of the chairs, and, stooping over it, the better to examine its delicate inlaying: "How long," she exclaimed, "since I have rested in an artistic seat like this; I feel as if it were a dream of home once more". An involuntary sigh escaped her.

"I understood from Flora you were not Roman-born, my child," said Siona, gently smoothing her hair.

"No, lady, I am from Greece, the very cradle of art, the parent of all that genius has inspired to man. Ah me! that I should give even a passing regret to such idle things, when everlasting treasures are within my reach."

"Give way to the mood, dear child, it will relieve your heart to open it; think that a mother and sister are by you."

The last words, though uttered low, were overheard by Laurentius, who, young as he was, understood good breeding with the instinct of gentle birth: "When it pleases you to call me, mother," he said, "I shall be with Claudius in the garden," and withdrawing, he left the ladies alone.

Siona and her daughter drew nearer to the orphan, who, overcome by their kindness and her own sad memories, seemed to require all their sympathy. She loosened the pins from her hat, which, falling off, displayed her beautiful hair shining like gold in the lamplight.

"You are evidently a foreigner," said Flora, caressing her. "Roman girls have not locks like yours; and this covering for your head, somewhat like the nimbus * of our statues, only larger, whence comes it?"

"From Ionia: maidens use it to shelter themselves from the sun, which does not hinder us, as you see," here she touched her forehead laughing, "from growing brown as you bronze satyr."

"And you have preserved this memory of your country, woven for you perhaps by a mother's hand."

"No! my mother, though skilled in embroidery, as all women of our country, did not know any common work; she was a princess."

"Poor child!" observed Siona, "how painful you must find the life you lead here!"

"Oh no! duty is a powerful sweetener of the bitter past. My uncle is both father and mother to me now. In ministering to his wants, in following him on his distant excursions, I sometimes feel the hardships to which my childhood was not inured; but I think of my parent gone to his doom with but few good works to present to his God, and I offer up my trials for him, remembering that I have double work to do."

"But how came you all to embark and trust your fortune to that vessel? Where were you bound to?"

"My father was king of a small island in the Ionian sea; he was attacked by a more powerful neighbour, and obliged to flee. The potentate, reviving an insignificant quarrel, had looked with envy on our beautiful island,

* The origin of the Nimbus round the heads of Saints in pictures is derived from a circlet or disk placed on the heads of statues to preserve them from rain.

where the odoriferous trees of the East grew mingled with the cultivated produce of the West. My father made his people happy, and they loved him, but he had neglected to harden them to military life, and, when the invader came, they were too indolent to rise in arms. The few faithful attendants surrounding our palace warned us of the cunning of the invader who had surprised us in the dead of the night. No preparations had forestalled, no resistance awaited the enemy: all was darkness around, when we were told to prepare for flight. Oh! the horrors of that scene, the rapid collecting of our treasures, and the bidding farewell to the court where we had all been so happy. I thought it the most painful hour of my girlish life, but there was yet another, more dreadful still by far."

She covered her face with her hands, and was silent a few moments; tears flowed through the delicate taper fingers, and Flora noticed how the exquisitely formed hands were covered with recent blisters, from work undertaken beyond her strength, while the arms, from the wrists upwards, displayed that roundness of contour and curve of beauty which Grecian sculptors have preserved as the traditional type of antique models. Siona and Flora would not interrupt the momentary solace of tears, but let her weep on in silence. By and by she looked up: "It is so sweet," she said, "to meet with the sympathy of those of my own sex, of which I have been long deprived. I must open my heart to you in its most secret sorrows. A poignant regret has sometimes stolen over me, I have reproached myself with being somewhat the cause of my parents' trouble, and the thought is a painful one. The king who invaded my father's territory had sought me in marriage for his son. I disliked not so much the alliance, as the idea of marriage in itself. Pagan though I was, I had an inexplicable feeling of dread for that state which most girls aspire to; I hated the idea of being a queen, and indulged in a mysterious foreshadowing hope. My heart told me that One would come to me, mightier far than all I saw, and for Him I kept my affections free. My fancy pictured to itself one of the children of men, endowed with earth's choicest gifts. But ah! could I have guessed that I was already chosen by the Immortal Spouse Whose guardian care shielded me from an impending fate. My uncle, long ago enlightened with a superior wisdom, requested my father not to force my inclinations. I fear me, this was the origin of the disastrous quarrel which ended in my father's overthrow. We cannot help," she added, concluding her narration, "wishing for our parents a little portion of earth's happiness, though faith teaches us to aspire higher: suffering is ever painful, though we know it to be good for us."

She rose from the seat she had occupied, and pointing to the silver sconce serving as a lamp which a slave had brought in: "It is night," she said. "If you will come to the Mysteries I shall lead the way, for it is time!"

They were surprised at her abruptness, but the poor girl had thus broken off the conversation to conceal her emotion, for she was accustomed to meet every suffering with renewed energy. They rose at her bidding, and Claudius returned. A few of the slaves, such as were Christians, were informed of what their mistress intended doing, and asked to go with her; they all set out together. Slowly and in silence they looked carefully for the mountain paths which Reparata pointed out, and reached the river in safety. It was, more properly speaking, a torrent, fed at times by the waters which came rolling down the mountains at the approach of spring, when the sun melted the snows; it had made its way through rocks and through the volcanic soil; narrow and bounded as it was on each side in the beginning of its course, its bed became wider as it reached the plain. During the summer it ran almost dry, and pebbles, detached from the rocks, and smoothed by friction, formed a bed, where pedestrians could walk. This was the road generally followed by the Christians, as they directed their steps to the cavern where they held their nightly assemblies. It lay about two miles farther up the source, beyond Cimella. Everything seemed to undergo a change as the traveller, entering the valley, found the air colder, the vegetation more hardy, the rays of the sun excluded by the fir trees, and the very soil, no longer covered with luxuriant pasture, but flinty and stony, reft asunder in some places, as if showing the rocks had undergone a convulsion of nature. The change of temperature was, however, not so discernible at night, but the scene was very beautiful as the moon cast her silvery beams on the cold naked earth. Not a sound was to be heard but the steps of the Christians proceeding on their pious pilgrimage; the conical-shaped shadows of the tall cypresses were reflected on the ground, untouched by the breeze, and from their branches arose the plaintive notes of the bird of mourning and of song; on either side, the rocks looked down like fantastical giants stretching in the moonbeams, records of the past, and silent guardians of that spot of earth; perhaps they had never witnessed a holier sight than these children of the Crucified seeking their God in the darkness of the night.

The party had spoken but little on the way, only to warn each other of any sudden turn or dangerous declivity in the road; at length, Reparata, who acted as guide, said to her companions: "We are very near the cave where our brethren assemble; let each of us light a torch that they may recognise us".

"I cannot see anything," observed Claudius; "where is the entrance?"

"There, behind that palm tree there is a hole in the rock. Lead on your mistress carefully."

The advice was needless, for almost immediately a man bearing a torch came himself from the aperture; it was Reparata's uncle, who had been on the lookout for them, and who now guided them at once to the mouth of the cave.

They were surprised to find it so much larger than they expected, tapers were twinkling from one extremity to the other, and in that light men could be seen kneeling in serried ranks. Obediently to the prescriptions of the Church, the women were partitioned off, and though not as far apart as in the Roman Catacombs, they were as much separated as the limited space would permit. Flowers in profusion had been brought by the simple people to decorate their place of worship, together with offerings for the Agapæ or feasts of charity: most of those present were shepherds, and truly, there was much to recall the grotto of Bethlehem, where the lowly ones of earth had gathered round the Saviour and seen His Glory. When Reparata entered, most of them rose to make way for her, for all knew and reverenced that girl who had converted many of them, and had been to all an Angel of Light, bringing Good News.

She showed Siona her place among the matrons, and modestly retired to her own at the head of the maidens. After praying a short time in silence, she assumed her wonted task of head chorister, and gave the impulse to the juvenile voices which arose, fresh and musical, till they made the echoes of the grotto ring again with the strain. Alas! for how many was that song the preliminary to the final battle cry: how many that now joined in the hymn *Rex gloriose Martyrum* were destined to repeat it in other scenes where it would thrill on their lips in an agonizing death-note. There were no such foreshadowings, however, among the Christians here assembled; they had never known persecution, their faith was in its infancy, Jesus was lately born among them; their religion, not yet inured, as in the Catacombs, to suffering and to death, had more of joyousness and less of heroism; they had been called to Bethlehem's glories, not yet to Calvary's immolation.

Pontius acted as deacon; they had only two priests; the little flock hardly required more, and the Church of Rome could ill spare its labourers. Young Laurentius offered himself to serve as acolyth, for he was well versed in the ritual of the Church. Pontius accepted him willingly, and the boy took the thurifer from his hand, and followed the priest as he went round distributing the mysterious Bread and Wine, in which the faithful adored their Living God.

Unconsciously, Flora's eye wandered over that scene so new to her, yet so familiar, those strange people, so alien to her clime and language, yet her brethren in faith; she felt the powerful link of the One, Unerring Church, and, as her brother took his place near its teachers, she thought, oh how thankful would she be if he were indeed to occupy that place for life. Often and often had she formed for him that high, sanctifying wish, often had she repeated over him the prayer she had been taught as Cecilia's, often implored that, whatever were her fate, Laurentius might be called to the priest's sacred mission. All her childish sacrifices—and a Christian child's life is abundantly stored with those precious trifles—all her girlish sorrows were offered up, with the prayer that they might descend, rich with the priestly unction, on the head of Laurentius. She remembered her many petitions as she saw him standing in the midst of the assembly, the torch he held in his hand lighting up his handsome features, as if with a transparent beauty; she thought of the words in the Acts of the Apostles which relate the Martyrdom of St. Stephen:

"And when they looked at him, his face was like unto that of an angel". Truly thus looked Laurentius now! He knelt down in his turn to receive the Holy Eucharist, and, instead of withdrawing with the rest, he seemed to be seized by an irresistible impulse; his arms outstretched, his face upturned and illumined with a celestial glow, his eyes, with that singular expression which none could read, were now fixed in the ardour of ecstasy on an Invisible Presence! Oh how easy it was to see in the awful sanctity of that face the great destiny the child was called to!

The bystanders moved away, respecting the mystery of his soul's interior converse; he remained alone in the midst, motionless, absorbed, hearing nothing but the voice of Him Who, more than two hundred years before, had spoken to his forefather and not been heard. The neglected Call was now repeated for Laurentius, and his ear drank in the welcome sounds, never more to be forgotten: *Si vis perfectus esse, vende quod habes, et post veni, sequere me.*

The prayers came to an end, and the faithful were beginning to disperse, when Laurentius recovered from his waking vision: the delicate kindness of the brethren who seemed not to notice him, made him hope the favour he had just received would pass unperceived, but he met the inquiring eye of his sister, and saw there she had understood all that had passed between him and his God; pure souls need no interpreter to reveal to them the secrets of Heaven.

The venerable Pontius left the cavern sooner than was

his wont, in order to accompany his new acquaintances on their way home. Siona took the opportunity of asking him as a favour to allow his niece to spend some weeks under her roof: "My daughter has been suffering much of late," she added, "from a melancholy unusual at her age; I see she will cling to Reparata with the ardour of a new and well-merited friendship. On the other hand, your niece is delicate, and requires a mother's fostering care; I shall be so happy to watch over her."

"Your offer is so kind that I cannot refuse, yet I am somewhat loth to consent. Reparata is more to me than if she were my child; the guardian angel of my hermit's home, the ministering apostle to my poor disciples, the friend and companion of my solitary hearth."

"It would be indeed a pity to separate you; therefore noble Pontius, let me ask something more of you. Come yourself with your niece to lodge in my villa, where you can enjoy as much prayer and solitude as on the mountain top. My husband, Florentius, on his arrival from Rome later on in the season, will rejoice that I have provided him with a visitor whom he will be happy to appreciate and converse with. He is a philosopher and loves the Greeks. Do not refuse me, Pontius, I entreat of you, in the name of Reparata. Come, at once, to-morrow, if you can, and bring all that you will require for your studies or daily occupations. May I count upon this arrangement as concluded?"

Thus urged, Pontius gave a willing consent, and bade them good-night, as he had reached that turn in the road which led to his retired home.

## CHAPTER XIII.

SIONA had consulted only her own kind heart in wishing to take under her especial care the motherless young Grecian, and she was amply rewarded by a result the most consoling to her maternal feelings. Flora had been suffering ever since the scene of Martina's martyrdom from depression of spirits: her nerves had been strung to the utmost on that occasion, and her feelings too much worked upon: this had produced a temporary hallucination of mind. Every day, at the identical hour in which her friend had expired, the horrors of the Mamertine prison arose before her, and, flee where she would, the pale face and headless trunk of the martyr were pictured to her imagination. With Reparata's entrance to the house the painful vision disappeared; Flora's mind was diverted by sympathy for another's sorrow, and the playful, winning manners of the young princess effectually strove to occupy her attention at the hour of the daily crisis, or rather, God willed that the Christian charity of that Roman family should turn into a source of happiness for them. Pontius too, struck by Laurentius' pious demeanour and precocious intellect, won, moreover, by the boy's affectionate regard, applied himself, with the love he had in former days given to such things, to unfold to the youth the treasures of Grecian philosophy and literature. Laurentius drank in with avidity his new master's teaching, applied himself to the study of the Attic language, and mastered it rapidly: a few weeks of ardent application under that experienced tuition did the work of years. Siona was overjoyed when her guest and her adopted son, pacing the garden, wrangled in mock dispute, as was the wont of philosophers in Athens; Laurentius would hold forth in juvenile yet not unworthy accents. Poetry, too, was opened to him, and improvisation seemed to be his own peculiar gift. Pontius would often remain listening, hushed and anxious while the pupil poured forth his strains; he was touched by the sweet simplicity of that eloquence to which the boy's Oriental origin imparted a richness of idea peculiar to those versed in Jewish imagery: he would fold in his arms his interesting charge, thanking him for affording him the enjoyment of those intellectual pleasures which he had left untasted for so long. Siona knew she was furthering her husband's wishes by promoting the boy's education, and looked forward to his pleasure and surprise when he should arrive.

Thus the summer season passed away, and the time for culling the olives drew near. Claudius was about to depart: the business he had been required to transact for his employer Adrias had long since drawn to a close, but the ship in which he was to embark for Britain was not yet ready to sail, and his masters rejoiced at the delay. The affection and lingering regret at parting was indeed mutual, the liberated slave clung to those children with an almost fatherly love. The tree, transplanted from its native soil, pines at first in a strange land, yet its roots, too vigorous to waste away, too strong to die, must needs seek for sustenance and for space to expand in, so they fasten to the new earth, which, from a land of exile, becomes a home, and the spreading, verdant branches above tell that early wounds have been healed. Then, in the shade of that goodly tree, young plants grow and prosper, and shoots spring round till they become, as it were, part of its own life. Such had been the intercourse of Claudius with his young masters; he had found in their true affection the requital of his own devotion; their growing comeliness was his pride, their piety, the fruit of his prayers and teaching. He felt indeed that, in retiring from that vineyard, where he had toiled so long for his Master's glory, he left behind him not a single work undone which had been assigned to him. Thus, in the midst of pleasant occupations, in the daily practice of charity, in imparting lessons to young Laurentius of religion and classical lore alternately, the season passed on, and the merry gathering of the olives was at hand. In the sandy soil of Cimella, this produce was the most abundant of all husbandry pursuits, and corresponded to the harvest and vintage of Rome. Reparata, so well known to all the labourers, had been invited to give the first shake to the trees, for as many as knew that girl thought a secret blessing was attached to all she did. Hand in hand with Flora, she visited those plantations whose owners she knew were Christians, accompanied by the slaves of her hostess, who was willing to contribute to the pleasures of the simple people among whom she had of late resided. The young Grecian so arranged the day's work, that the gravity customary among Christian labourers should be mingled with the necessary relaxations and amusements over which she presided. The benediction of God was invoked upon the olives, and, even as Abel had of old offered to Jehovah the first fruits of his flock, so was a part to be reserved for the use of the poor. The youths and maidens were to work in separate bands, until the hour of repast, for which the slaves had prepared kids, roasted whole before rousing fires in the wood, and steeped in wine: "Thus," said the girl, "would the father of poets have regaled his labourers, and thus shall we sit by them, after sharing their toil".

Pontius smiled, and promised to sing one of his almost forgotten Homer songs during the feast; he was pleased at his dear child's thus recalling the classic memories of their favoured land. The maidens then went to spread large linen sheets under the trees, so that the fruit, falling on them, might be perfectly unsullied from contact with the earth, others looked for the olives which had been already shaken off by the wind, and lay hidden in the grass. All agreed that the harvest surpassed by far the produce of previous years: all worked merrily; Laurentius joined the youths, and his sister the maidens, and, from time to time, Reparata enlivened the labour by raising her voice in a song to which each band replied in chorus. Claudius too gave the labourers the benefit of his long experience in cultivation, and resumed, for the day, the task of *villicus* he was about to give up, not without a lingering regret. Siona, who had provided the feast, looked on with pleasure at the gay scene; she went from one group to another, observed the goodly heaps of olives increasing, and being accustomed to take an interest in her husband's property near Rome, she was well acquainted with all that concerned rural pursuits. All rejoiced to see her approach, for she had a kind word for each; and all expressed a hope the Roman family would not leave Cimella before the culling of the orange blossoms, which, in that favoured clime, are cultivated to such an extent as to yield a large annual produce.

"This recalls to me very happy days," observed Claudius, as, following Siona in her ascent up the hill, on which the olive-trees grew, he came by her side, and addressed her respectfully: "Thus, my good mistress, you deigned to visit and examine the labours of your slave at Aricia, making the hours of toil a holiday".

"And thus," she replied smiling, "my slave became my master, and taught me the life-long lesson my heart has loved to dwell upon. Oh, how I bless the courageous boldness with which you opened my eyes to the Truth."

They had reached the brow of the hill, which commanded a view of the valleys beneath; the sea lay in the distance, its waters confounded with the sky above; "I come here every day," she said, "to see whether any vessel be in sight".

"It is yet too soon for my lord Florentius to arrive, and I know his is the only vessel you care to see."

"Oh, but he wrote to me quite lately saying he should soon come." She sighed, and added: "My dear lord! would that I could confide to him the secret of our religion; it is the only thing I have ever concealed from him".

"I think now is the time, my lady."

"How can I! he would never understand Christianity: philosophy is his idol."

"Yet, for the sake of Laurentius, I think it is better that his father know and understand his principles; it is true that my young master is too well confirmed in his faith to fear influence, but he will become the pupil and companion of Florentius, and must needs have a reason to give for not meeting his views or sharing with him in certain acts of idolatrous worship. I perceive he has dropped the *bolla* which Roman youths generally wear till they are fourteen; he is only eleven; how shall we explain to his adopted father this departure from your customs? and, on the day when it will be necessary for him to consecrate that relic of his childhood to the gods, how shall he escape the idolatrous homage?"

"True! my daughter is in my own hands, but the charge of Laurentius must pass to his father; what shall I do?"

"Florentius is such a lover of truth, perhaps a frank and noble acknowledgment that your household is all Christian would not displease him."

"My courage would fail me."

"Let Flora undertake it. She has that daring Roman spirit which her father so much admires, together with that gentleness so peculiarly her own; young as she is, she is gifted with much power, and I have seen many yield to the sweet influence of her words."

"I hope, Claudius, there lies before her a quiet path of duty like mine, that Providence may assign to her the tranquil joys of the mother and the wife, and that her children may rejoice her heart as she does mine."

"Oh, Lady Siona! is that all you see? Do you not notice Flora's precocious wisdom, her ardent piety, the modesty impressed on every feature, the thirsting languor of her eyes, which seem to be ever gazing on an invisible Sacred Presence, do you not understand that a high destiny awaits her? Earthly happiness cannot be her lot, for she belongs to One Who has marked her out for Himself, and she must go to *Him* by the path He calls her ——"

"Claudius, would you then warn me that my beloved child will have to appear one day before wicked men to answer for her faith? Are you predicting for her the doom which has already befallen some of her young friends?"

"Yes, noble Siona! The doom which, in your corrupted Rome, falls upon the innocent, the beautiful, the pure! When Martina, who had watched over your daughter even as you and I have done, observed her dawning virtues, and received the confidence of the young heart she had formed, when she clasped her young charge in a last embrace, then, with the prescience of love, rendered more acute by that prophetic spirit which visits us sometimes on the verge of another life, she foretold to Flora her impending doom. She bid her quit the thoughts of earth for an Eternal Union and prepare to receive the call of the Saviour as a Virgin and a Martyr Bride."

Siona had been listening overawed, she now could not control her emotion and sobbed aloud. For many years she had been accustomed to trust to her slave's simplehearted devotion, and to abide by his conscientious advice.

"Pray for me, Claudius," she said, "as earnestly as in that hour when you first spoke to me of God; pray for me that I may have strength to say over my child: 'Our Father, Thy Will be done'."

"Will you instruct Flora how to make to her father the disclosure you have decided upon?"

"No, Claudius, I leave that to you, you are her sponsor before God, you have the wisdom of age, the sincerity befitting a Christian. I had rather you broach the subject with her, when I am more composed I can speak to her about it too."

"I thank you, my dear mistress, for this last proof of confidence before I leave your service."

"Now let us return to the labourers, for I see they are weary, and are forming into groups to seek shelter and repose. How happy we are in our faith, Claudius, what a priceless gift God has bestowed on us Christians. How glorious it is to look round on these hills and plains, on which the Creator cast His eye in the world's early dawn, and saw that it was good. In that remote time, thou and I, and these untutored children of Liguria, all lived in His Eternal Mind, He pre-ordained all things for us, and loved us with a Mighty Love. And yet," here she clasped her hands, and her accents became mournful, "God is still ignored by the greater part of this people, Rome has brought her idolatry among them, and on that very hill the incense of this beautiful land smokes on the altars of Diana. Alas, that it should be so! Is not Thy Arm sufficiently powerful, O Crucified One, to draw to Thee all things when Thou art raised from earth? is there not a powerful Intercessor, a Spotless Maiden chosen from the daughters of my people, whose image should efface that of the impure heathen divinity? Oh, let Thy Kingdom come! and Thy Name be praised even on these distant shores! May She whom all generations shall call Blessed be honoured publicly in future ages on this hill, and the praises of the Immaculate Mary be sung aloud in Cimella by the pure of heart." \*

These last words were a prayer, and Claudius, respecting the deep feeling with which they were spoken, fell back a little distance, and then silently followed his mistress back to the plain where the labourers were assembled. They awaited her to open the harvest feast which closed the day of labour, and the remaining hours

---

\* The Church of Cimella, near Nice, is built on the ruins of a temple of Diana.

of twilight were spent in innocent diversion, after which they retired to their respective homes.

About a week after this, as the family rose from their morning prayers which Siona daily said aloud in their rural residence, where she felt more free than at Rome, Claudius came in to announce that a distant sail was in sight, and he was going to the port of Nicæa to watch for his dear master's arrival. A burst of joy welcomed the glad news, all surrounded him in a moment, and the ladies and slaves, together with Pontius, expressed themselves eager to follow Claudius. Siona proposed that the whole household should set out forthwith, and each slave immediately fetched a palm branch, or collected fresh flowers which they bore in their hands as a sign of gladness, then ranged themselves in rank and file, with Claudius at their head, prepared to go and meet the master they all loved so much. Siona declined the lettiga they brought her; she preferred walking, she said, with her two dear girls; she felt exercise was necessary to calm the excitement of joyful expectation: even Pontius set out with a firm step, while Laurentius kept close by him, ready to offer himself as a support. Never was there a happier party! The road between Cimella and Nicæa was not more than two miles, but they had much farther to go, round the bay, in order to reach the port where vessels put in. When they arrived they found the shore already lined with persons who had disembarked, and among them they immediately recognised Florentius. A loud cheer burst, almost unwittingly, from the grateful band of slaves. Florentius sprang forward, and before the traveller was aware of the welcome that awaited him, his adopted son had gently drawn him aside to meet his wife and daughter at a little distance from the intruding crowd.

How sweet is the hour of reunion! Perhaps there is no joy in life so intense as that first glance we give on a face we had loved, lost, and which we now meet again. Each parting is, as it were, a death! for, alas! the pang of separation is like the closing of a tomb! What matter that the dear form we clasp in our farewell embrace be not consigned to dust? for us, it lives no more if it must pass away from us: if the eyes we have so long gazed upon look upon ours no more, then, indeed, the pain is to us the same as if death had already closed them, and our grief is not to be comforted, save when the hope of reunion remains, whispering consolation to our anguish, and beguiling us with the invitation to gaze into futurity. How stricken, indeed, must be the heart which cannot look forward to that comfort! hapless the soul which cannot say to itself: *Resurgam!* The very shortest separation is not without its pang, the ceasing of it is accompanied by a corresponding joy. As Florentius looked round on the dear faces about him, he thought a change of years had been wrought in each, and had added charms to them. Laurentius had grown taller, his childish brow bore the impress of thought, study, and high resolve. Flora, more gay and light-hearted than when she had left Rome, inherited all the winning beauty which had distinguished her mother at that age. The very slaves were radiant with joy, and the good father and kind master, feeling himself beloved, turned to the dear partner of his life, his eyes glistening with honest, manly tears.

"I have a new friend to present to my lord," said Siona, "one whom I am sure you will be glad to meet, a stranger from Greece; he has been very kind to our Laurentius, who has profited much by his lessons."

A few words explained the circumstances which had brought Pontius in contact with his hosts, and Florentius was as pleased as his wife could wish, that she had invited so noble a guest under her roof.

It was now time to think of going homewards, and the happy family turned their steps thither, lingering on the road in cheerful converse: the slaves preceded them at a quicker pace, in order to prepare the banquet which Siona had already ordered and disposed for her lord's return. Friends and neighbours had been invited, and a goodly company awaited Florentius on his threshold.

Paulina, the wife of Adrias, was there, with her little children; he saluted her on the part of her husband, whom he had left in Rome. Of those who welcomed him, many were fellow-citizens who had come to Liguria for business or health, and others were neighbours residing at Cimella, but all were friends, as they testified by the reception they gave him. A joyous and numerous assembly sat down in the triclinium of the villa, and they did not break up till an advanced hour.

When Flora wished her father good-night before retiring to rest, he gave her a letter from her young friends in Rome. She withdrew to a small room which

Reparata and she had fitted up as a private oratory, and found her friend waiting for her to say their night prayers together. That duty performed, they always gave a last half hour to intimate and confidential conversation.

Flora now drew out the folded parchment, and read aloud:

"Rufina, Secunda, Lucia, to Flora, daughter of Florentius, greetings and salutations in the name of all her sisters.

"The time has appeared to us very long since you left, and we miss you much at our meetings; no one fills your place near us at the Mysteries. We like to go to Mount Aventine to look at your garden and talk about you: your father has kindly invited us to go there as often as we like, just as we did when you were here, and whenever he receives a letter from Liguria, he rejoices us by giving us news of your improved health. Doubtless, Flora, your mind also dwells with your absent friends, and you will be anxious to know what Providence has done for each of us since we parted. We three are all well, and our days have passed peacefully, occupied with our various duties at home, to which we have added the care of the poor and the infirm for whom you used to work. We often go to see your friend Lucilla as you desired us; we take her out to walk and try to amuse her with the recital of many anecdotes, but she is ever inconsolable for the loss of her sister. It is dreadful to see her, feeling with outstretched arms in those places where she used formerly to find Volumnia, and now only embraces a shadow: sometimes we are by her, and as she does not see us, and fancies herself alone, she breaks out into lamentations for her lost sister. Poor girl! I fear she cannot long outlive such violent grief; the one for whom she mourns was the light of her eyes, and the joy of her life. Sometimes we meet Volumnia with the Grand Vestal; she looks as if she were turned into stone. We smile at her, but she does not seem to see us. We have heard from our brothers that Icilius has become a maniac; he shuns the society of men, raves incoherently when he speaks at all, for he generally keeps a moody silence. He wanders night and day along the Tiber, or among the trees at the foot of the Palatine Hill; his hair is matted, and his skin brown like that of one who has been exposed to storms; he gnashes his teeth like one possessed. Oh, that the Light from on high might shine on his benighted soul!

"Hippolytus, who was converted at the death of Martina, is the most fervent of penitents; he lives in a disused cave, on the Via Appia, which he only leaves to go to the Catacombs. Your old nurse, Concordia, came to see us the other day to enquire about you. I think she has some suspicions about Barbara being a Christian, for she seems almost vexed at her daughter being so good, and tries her a good deal, but the poor child finds her comfort in prayer. Concordia seems to be much attached to you; she says she always regrets you, and could never expect to find again such kind masters as your father and mother. Her present charge, the young Hippolytus, has much grown, and is about to engage in the military service: he is very young to go to the wars, but he looks quite a soldier already.

"Your good father having told us he was going to join you in Liguria, and that he would take charge of our messages for you, we three have put our hands to this letter, which we now conclude, requesting you, dear sister, to remember us before God, and may the peace which surpasseth all understanding be ever yours."

"Why, Flora!" exclaimed Reparata, as she concluded reading the epistle, "how many friends you have! I shall get quite jealous, and almost afraid to be ranked among them. How can you be faithful to all?"

"Why not? As I have no sister, it is kind of Providence to have given me so many others, by adoption, and the more love we put into our hearts, the more they will contain."

"Oh," said Reparata, laughing, "why don't you write poetry, when you can analyse tender feelings so well?"

"Do I? I was not aware I was poetising. I am so accustomed to think *viva voce* with you."

"And I do the same: now forgive me for saying that it must be pleasant, not to say dangerous, to be so universally loved as you are, Flora."

The young girl half tossed her head with a pretty expression of disdain, but the habitual self-command of the Christian repressed immediately the feminine vanity, and she replied humbly: "If God has put into the hearts of others much charity towards me, shall I be vain and ascribe it to myself? Oh no!"

"No one is ever vain of attracting friendship, that is almost sacred, but it is dangerous to be sought after and admired."

"Have not you tasted of that, and found it bitter?"

"I! oh I was only courted as a princess; my rank brought me flatterers, that was all. That prince who wanted to marry me excited nothing but my aversion: it is strange how our female hearts revolt against those who would woo us against our own will."

"And to me it seems, on the contrary, that a natural feeling of gratitude springs up in the heart of one who feels herself loved; it is difficult to repress, yet, if not guarded against in the beginning, it may steal into the threshold we have forgotten to close, and take up its abode there, unbidden and unwilled."

"Oh, Flora!" cried her friend with a merry laugh, but seeing a deep blush suffuse her cheek, she stopped, fearing there existed in that heart some hidden chord which delicacy forbade her to touch.

It was not so, however, but Flora was naturally keenly sensitive to the feelings she excited in others. A passage in the letter she had read recalled to her one to whom she knew she was not indifferent. She had met the younger Hippolytus in the public walks, or at places of entertainment,—for though Christian maidens sought as much as possible to live retired, they were obliged to conform to their parents' wishes in all that was consistent with their own religious principles. Thus, Hippolytus had known Flora when they were both children—his mother and Siona had been great friends, but, since the death of the former, the intercourse between the two families had dropped. Flora now felt a pang of self-reproach at her peace of mind being somewhat troubled by the remembrance of her old playmate.

Shall we blame the innocent girl that something of womanly weakness was mingled with the lofty aspiring thoughts of her pure soul? No! for who that belongs to earth has not felt its dust cling to him at times, through the long path we tread, which proves so often, alas! a barren desert; how often does the scorching wind pass over the freshness of youthful souls and disturb the mirage of early dreams! The training of the heart is not achieved in a day; the warrior is not clad for a life-long combat at the first call! God's saints are sent on earth with His image in their souls, but sent to strive, to fight and conquer: theirs is the glory! to be won with long and earnest struggling, through bodily torture and mental agony, through men's persecutions and the wiles of an enemy; worse perhaps than all these, the temptations of their own soul, the instigations of the Evil One, who has never slumbered since the day he spoke to the first woman in the garden, who can only be conquered by the words of Him, the Promised Seed, the Fruit of that Immaculate Maiden who, alone of all mortals, was placed beyond his reach. His power was tried too upon the Son of God, clothed in mortal garb; shall we then wonder that our frail nature succumbs at times in the contest?

"Good-night, Reparata," said Flora at length, after a long pause, during which each had indulged unconstrained in her own thoughts, and they exchanged a sisterly kiss, but the young Grecian felt the cheek that touched hers was hot and a little moistened. She forbore any remark, and soon sleep stole over her, but Flora continued to sit up, and was very thoughtful.

She felt that a charge had been entrusted to her by her mother, the weight of which oppressed her. Siona had told her she thought the time had come when the secret of their religion must be confided to Florentius; she provided her with all the arguments she could suggest, and bade her choose a propitious moment, for she had decided that this task was to be entrusted to herself alone. Her devotion to her father, and his great confidence in her, would facilitate the disclosure, and if Florentius' feelings were roused, he would give vent to them with his own child more unrestrainedly than with others. Flora thought over the difficulties of this delicate task, as she sat, still dressed, in the cubiculum, while her friend slumbered peacefully. She became so agitated that she felt the want of fresh air, and went to seek it on an open terrace. The moon was resplendently bright; she looked out into the garden, and saw by that light the figure of Florentius walking up and down the gravel walks; her heart was on her lips, and she called out without intending it: "My father".

Though little more than a whisper, the sound of that voice reached him in the solemn stillness of the night.

He turned towards her with outstretched arms. Moved by an irresistible impulse, the girl left her chamber at once, ran down-stairs, found the porter standing by the open gate, rushed past him, and found herself clasped in her father's embrace.

"Fie! puella," he said, "what makes you keep such vigils?"

"You had given me a letter," she said, stooping and kissing his hand. "I read it, and that prevented me retiring to rest. And yourself, my dear father, why do you not go to bed?"

"I am a surly old philosopher, Flora, who watch while others sleep, for night is, with the sages, the most favourable time for acquiring wisdom. I am very fond of the stars too, and I love to examine them. And what brought you down, my dear child; would you like to study with me?"

"Yes, father, I should like to know all that is an object of interest to you, so as to be able to converse with you."

"*Dulcissima filia*, I believe you would do anything to please me. I fully appreciate your devotion to your parents."

He had taken her arm within his and felt it tremble: "You are cold," he said.

"Oh no! the night is so beautiful! let me walk with you, I have something to say to you."

Her manner was so pressing that he complied at once.

"Not here," she continued, "let us go out of this

garden; take me out on the hill, where none can hear us. I have a great secret to tell you."

"Flora," he said, in a tone of anxious, tremulous enquiry, " you cannot surely have done anything wrong?" and he paused as he gazed at her fair forehead, rendered at that moment ghastly pale by the moonlight.

" Dear father, could I look at you thus in the face, if I were not the same Flora you have fondled in your arms as a little child ? "

Her calm tone and loving eyes reassured him, he went out at the garden gate with her, and they wandered on the hill, he several times asking her whether it were time to stop, and she always replied: "No! let us go farther on".

They reached the amphitheatre, a mimic representation of the Coliseum of Rome, and built likewise by Roman hands, for the colony established here sought out varied amusements for themselves, as they had been accustomed to do in the capital of the civilised world. They passed under the solemn arches into the arena, and the girl gazed into the blue expanse, where myriads of twinkling stars looked down on her, like so many silent witnesses of her faith, and of her God's glory. Would it be given her thus one day to stand in broad daylight in the arena, to brave public shame and declare herself boldly for God's holy cause, would an increase of strength be given her in that hour? Yea! even as now when she had to speak the truth, braving her father's anger.

" Will you take me to sit down ? " she said, " I am exhausted."

He wrapped his cloak kindly round her, raised her in his arms, went up with her the little steps leading to the seats of the spectators, and then, sitting by her side, "Now tell me, child," he said, "what is it agitates you?"

"Alas!" she said, "do not fold me in your arms while I confess to you what may appear wrong in your eyes, but God Who sees my heart knows it to be pure."

She knelt before him and laid her head on his knees, saying: "Have I been a good daughter to you, father?"

"Yes, girl! and may the choicest rewards filial piety deserves fall upon your head!"

"Do you esteem my beloved mother? Does Laurentius answer to your wishes? Have you found in Claudius an honest, faithful slave?"

"Whence these questions? As for myself, I acknowledge gratefully that my own household is a paragon of moral virtue."

"Father, deign to forgive my mother who, wishing to form children worthy of you, imbued them with principles of truth, justice, and universal love. Forgive Siona that, seeking to make my brother and me virtuous, she made us Christians, and embraced herself the precepts of that faith."

Florentius rose suddenly; a cry of horror escaped him, and he relaxed his hold of his daughter, who, falling on the stone steps, remained stunned and motionless. His paternal feelings instantly rose above his anger, and bending over her, he asked: "Are you hurt?"

She did not hear him; he raised her and chafed her hands; she was not insensible, but so frightened that she could not speak, till tears came to her relief. He repeated his question.

"I am hurt, indeed," she answered, "if you be offended."

"Child! the revelation you have made to me has certainly called forth my deepest anger. You a Christian, and my wife likewise! my boy too, my adopted son!"

"Would you have him adore the pretended divinities of stone and wood which you yourself despise?"

"We cannot desert the gods of Rome!"

"Do you believe in them, father? will you answer me in this hour when there are none by to hear us, but the Uncreated God?"

"Ha! One God! Is that what Christians teach? Plato thought that too, and so did Socrates, yet, at the last hour, he ordered a cock to be sacrificed to Æsculapius."

"There is but One God, father!" and the girl, encouraged by her parent's kindness, ceased to weep, stood up on the stone step where she had been resting, and, with her outstretched arm pointing to the clear heavens above, gave way to the sudden impulse which moved her to speak.

"There is but One God," she said, slowly and solemnly, "and He reigns there. We are all of us, naturally, so convinced of this, that when we implore a superior Power, we look up to Heaven, and we expect all good to come to us from above. Yet He that made all things is everywhere, He surrounds us; this world, created by Him, is full of His Presence; He that gave us a high intelligence is superior to His own works, and our very minds are contained in His. A Divine Essence fills the universe; and we, half of earth, half of heaven, must struggle day by day to become more virtuous, more worthy of that great end for which we were made. When, purified by our own exertions, and by His help, Who is ever by us, we seem to men to die, it is then only we begin to live anew in another world, where sorrow shall be no more, and virtue obtain its reward."

"Something of what you say, girl, figures also in the teaching of the sages of Greece, and, were I young as you, then I might be tempted to study the doctrines you describe; but a man must abide by the convictions of his ancestors, and if I permit you to practise a religion you love, as I must infer from your words and the tenor of your life, Laurentius must worship with me the gods of Rome."

"Oh father, he could not act against his conscience; do not ask him to obey you on that point, for if he yielded even exteriorly, it would only be feigning to adore that which his heart detests. Is it not enough that a forced dissimulation has hitherto kept his religion a mystery from you? The secret has, I am sure, weighed on his heart as on mine, but now, that in the fulness of my reason, and freedom of my will, I come to confide to you what we hold most dear, our religion, do not force him to abjure it, do not abuse our confidence; be not to us an enemy more to be feared than the Roman Prefect, because your influence would be that of love, but be to us a wise, indulgent, forgiving father."

"Will Laurentius fulfil all the duties of a Roman citizen, if I cede to your request?"

"He will!" exclaimed the girl triumphantly, seeing she was gaining ground; "he will be to you all your heart could wish. I pledge my word that Laurentius will leave behind him such a name as both his country and you will glory in."

"I do think," continued the philosopher musing, "your doctrine is not far removed from Plato's."

"I can only say this, that to all who are wise and good, a first great cause appears to be a primary necessity."

"If Christians reason thus, and do not commit crimes?" . . .

"They do not!"

"But their secret meetings, their murders in the dark, the child given as a midnight repast."

"All these assertions are false, as false as the pagan gods. We assemble to pray in secret; we hide, because it is not right to expose ourselves in vain. Murder is with us a heinous crime, unexpiable but by long years of penance. In the repast you allude to, which I may one day explain to you perhaps, we receive bread which we break together; our feasts are assemblies of a religious nature, they almost all include a distribution of alms to the poor."

"I must needs believe what my child affirms, for I have never known you to speak anything but the truth, and this concealment has been the first act of deceit I ever knew you to practise."

"It was unavoidable, father. My fidelity to my God enjoined that I should dread all exposure that might in the slightest degree make me swerve from His service; but now, how glad I am to think that you know all. May I assure my mother of your forgiveness?"

"You may tell her," and he clasped her to his arms, "that the religion which has formed a heart like yours has my approbation; but let it remain as hitherto, secret. Let no one know that Christianity has penetrated the household of Florentius, lest he should become an object of reproach in Rome. And now, dear child, the moon has described much of her orbit since we left the house together, we must return. This has been a solemn hour to us both; I rejoice to have read into your heart, for, pure as I know that sanctuary to be, it ought never to have been closed to a father's gaze."

She could only kiss his hands and repeat: "Forgive me!" for she was more moved than he was.

They went down, through the wood and the olive groves, undisturbed but by the silvery leaf which fell in the grass slowly, and almost at stated intervals, like a measure of time, telling the progress of the night: now a plaintive note arose from the nightingale, and Flora thought of the mysteriousness of life, cheered yet for her by the hopes and passing joys which never desert the young. What would be her path through it? dark and hidden like this her passing through the trees, yet directed to a certain, unerring goal, and through its course she would rest on the arm of God even as now on her father's.

## CHAPTER XIV.

"VALE, my noble master; vale, my little lord, may you become the pride and joy of your parents! Vale, my beloved mistress, when we meet above, may I be permitted to recognise in you the first soul it was given me to bring to God. Flora, my lady and my child! it is hard to say good bye to you, for the tie which links you to your old slave is not an ordinary one, my own offspring has hardly a greater claim on me than you; I promised for you that you would be faithful to the baptismal vows registered above. I shall precede you to the dread account, for years have already stricken me. May it be my reward to await you in the Eternal Mansions! and oh how great will be my joy"— here his voice sank to a whisper, lest the bystanders should hear—"if I see you there, wearing the white stole of those who follow the Spotless Lamb, if the crown of martyrdom sit on your brow, if the prophecy of Martina be fulfilled, and Flora enter Heaven a Martyr Bride!"

"Amen!" said the girl, and, taking within her small patrician hands the strong muscular fingers which had grown hard on the battle-field and in toil, she stooped over them, and he felt them moistened with her hot tears. "*Valete*, all my brother slaves," he continued, "be faithful to our master Florentius, and to the Great

Master some of us have served together: to all of you, Claudius bids a grateful farewell!"

The mariners called aloud, repeating again and again their shrill whistle, the signal of departure, the slave once more waved his hands, then, raising them on high, commended all those he left to a Superior Power. Again they would have pressed round him, but he was gone!

How mournful, yet how soothing to our sorrow, is the sight of a vessel which bears away a friend: it remains so long in sight, that we can scarce tell which has been the exact moment of its disappearance or of our parting. There is the sea between us; yet we hardly feel we are separated, so long as the fleeting ship still appears above the waves, and the very waters, as they come to our feet, seem in their rushing sounds, and stifled language, to bring us messages from the absent one, fast disappearing to sight. All the family of Florentius remained long on the beach, watching the sails which bore away the British slave to his island home. He had been a friend to all, and it was with real sorrow both masters and fellow-servants deplored his departure. The fact of his having been the first to introduce Christianity into the household was still concealed from Florentius, and he regarded him as a faithful domestic who could never be replaced. They went away, speaking of him and of his great worth.

"Thus will it be for us, Reparata," said Flora to her friend, " when you and I part: in a few days, that same sea will bear me away from these Ligurian shores. Oh, how happy I have been here! It has been to me a season of complete forgetfulness: I feel as if the seriousness of life must be resumed when we leave Cimella."

"Why do you speak in such a tone of despondency, oh girl of little faith?"

"When I return to my country," continued the young Roman, "I shall miss so much that I loved in it; Martina, my beloved preceptress, is gone, and now Claudius."

"Listen to me, Flora," resumed the other in a tone of admonition, as they walked together, lingering somewhat behind the rest. "You have been too much accustomed to lean on others, henceforward seek rather to be in your turn a support; you will find your strength increase, and your cheerfulness return. True, you will be required to practise self-abnegation, but with it fortitude will be given you. When I was in my father's court, flattered, loved, happy, I thought myself incapable of performing any of the duties which I saw done by women of a lowlier condition; and now see," she said laughing, stretching out her arms, "who would say these were the hands of a princess?"

"*I* do," exclaimed Flora, taking them within hers and caressing them. "You have not, dearest, fallen from your rank; your Grecian brow bears still, in my eyes, the diadem it was made for, and I console myself by thinking another more glorious crown awaits it."

"Do you think so? Oh, I am not worthy, and besides, totally unprepared."

"So Martina used to say of herself, and yet when her hour came how great was her courage."

"But persecution can never visit this distant land."

"I think that when the Pro-consul discovers how much Christianity has spread in Liguria, the first edict which is issued will have due course here!"

"And then, the first victim would be my uncle. I hope I shall be able to induce him to conceal himself in another part of the country, for we ought never of ourselves to expose ourselves to trials, which it belongs to God alone to carry us through."

"I believe my father has asked the noble Pontius to return with us to Rome, they enjoy each other's society so much, almost as much as you and I."

"My uncle has not mentioned the subject to me. Are you aware of what his answer was?"

"He said he would be glad to accept for your sake, as it is painful to him to see you lead a life of poverty, devoid of that mental culture to which you were accustomed, but for himself, he considers that his post is here. I cannot help thinking that a little persuasion on your part would bring him round; do you try and persuade him, Reparata, to come and stay with us in Rome, at least for a little time. It is just the place for him, he will meet there with men of superior minds, who will understand him, but of course we must not tell him that. I like to watch him when he does not perceive it, and see his old enthusiasm for knowledge fire up at the least spark of science my father strikes. It does them good to be together; try to extract a promise from him that we shall all go together to Rome."

"I shall! for certainly I will not separate from him."

A few days after this the two girls stood again on the brow of the hill looking down on the peaceful valley below and the sea beyond.

A miniature Rome was there, with its temple to Diana, another to Apollo, its Thermæ, its Coliseum, its walls of powerful construction, and bricks, baked and cemented, as if in Rome; but it was not this attracted the young friends, the face of nature was to them a greater holiday.

"You are sad," observed Flora to Reparata; "do you regret leaving Liguria to come to Rome with us?"

"Oh no! that is delightful, and my uncle likes the idea so much. But that sea! I can never look at it without an expectant feeling, as if it were to give me up my dead; when I hearken to its murmur, I imagine I hear the groans of my dear ones moaning over their Purgatory under its watery billows."

"Come away, *dulcissima*, I know by experience how wrong it is to give way to melancholy fancies."

"Nay! I love to dwell in spirit with the departed; those waves which closed over them may have cleansed their souls from sin, if, as I hope, they repented in that hour, and desired eternal life. I love the sea and its gurgling sound, its beating, sighing, foaming waters! To me it repeats the battle cry of life; it tells me, in the name of my lost ones, gone unprepared to meet their Judge, that I have for them, and for myself, a double work to do."

"I suppose that is your motive for persevering in the hard life you have embraced here, and the principle of the good you do, young as you are. Do not fear, Reparata, that the hour of the final trial find you unprepared."

"I dreamt last night it had come."

"Do not give heed to dreams! The designs of God are not revealed to us in sleep, as to the patriarchs of old."

"But this looked so real," pursued the girl, "it haunts me yet. Methought I knelt in an arena like our Coliseum up there, only much larger. I did not find myself transported there at once, as we generally are in sleep, but was led thither slowly, by lictors. I passed through a great Forum, then out of that on a broad, straight road, then under an arch, and I can still call to mind all I saw around me: within that arch were sculptured figures, seemingly taken from Scripture, a seven-branched candlestick, and conquerors bearing away spoils from a temple. I went on, I came before a *meta sudans* with clear, sparkling water issuing from its orifice, falling over statues, and bubbling at the surface of its white basin; I was very thirsty, and longed for a drink of that beautiful water, but my guards refused it me; again we passed under deep archways and covered passages, and I could hear the confused sound of many voices, like unto that of a vast population assembled, and then they united in one great overpowering burst of applause. I understood the Emperor had entered the amphitheatre, for the spectators rose to salute him with the cry: '*Populi Imperator, Dominus es, primus es omnium! Felicissimus vincis, ab œvo vinces!*'"

"All you say is strange, Reparata, more than strange! Have you ever been in Rome, even as a little child?"

"No! I never left Greece, but to come here."

"Then I cannot understand how you can describe so accurately the Roman Forum, the Via Triumphalis, the Coliseum, unless that, as my father says, the mind is independent of the body, and can traverse realms of space at will; but my dear father's opinion may not perhaps be sanctioned by the Church; in that case, I ought not to emit it. But go on, can you remember more?"

"Only the flashing of steel before me, and the cold contact of a sword at my neck, that awoke me, and, as you may suppose, I was much agitated."

"Did you hear the name of the Emperor, when the people applauded him?"

"No! but it was inscribed on trophies before me; where shall I trace the Latin characters I saw? Ah, come here!"

She went to a low wall, which was built along the road on the hill for the safety of foot-passengers, took from her shoulder the sharp *fibula* which fastened her *stola*, and, reflecting a little, as if trying to recall something she had seen, she traced slowly the letters which form the name of D E C I U S.*

"Can you read that?" she asked her companion; "I am unpractised in Latin characters."

"It is indeed a Roman name, but not the Emperor's;

* On a wall at the summit of the hill of St. Pons, near Nice, is the name of Decius, engraved as above described, in very ancient characters.

never did a Decius reign over the Empire, which proves to you, Reparata, we ought not to put faith in dreams."

"But our hour is not yet come: perhaps this one may yet reign, and his accession be the signal of our being called away."

"Do not be so fanciful: these are idle, dreamy words."

"Perhaps so! but they *will* dwell with me, and when the tide of my life flows on, I shall look back to this obscure part of it, full of doubts, and fears, and presentiments, even as that stream at our feet has issued from a rocky cave, and hewn out its own road, with a force stronger than the secular granite. Have you been to the source? it is a beautiful spot, one you ought to visit before you leave the country."

"I have only been to those places you led me to, and heartily admired them; will you take me to this source, as you call it?"

"We must have some of your father's slaves to accompany us with torches, for it is a narrow, lonely valley, growing almost dark, the more we penetrate into its depths."

"I shall send word to Laurentius to get every one and everything ready, he enjoys all that savours of a discovery; let us go and ask my mother if the excursion be not too much for her."

She beckoned to a slave, by whom she sent her message home; she and her friend following leisurely.

"What a change has come over your brother of late," observed Reparata as they went on together; "when first

I met him in the wood calling you and distressed at having lost his way, he was but a child."

"The change is always rapid," replied Flora; "have you not felt it, that moment which does the work of years, breaking the bonds of childhood, and making us men and women before our time? With me, it was the sight of Martina's death worked in me that strange revolution, and I saw it in Laurentius, the first night we assisted at the Mysteries with you. I think he had a vision, wherein his future life was unfolded to him. Perhaps, in that hour, he experienced the effects of a sentence spoken once to the head of our race, but certainly his thoughts and manner have assumed since that night a more solemn tone."

"And it will be your work, Flora, to complete what the Divine Word has begun in your brother: apply to that all the energies of your mind, and you will find it strengthened and made happier. If God has already permitted you to do so much for that boy, by watching over his early infancy, be sure that a greater task is reserved to you. Perhaps it will be yours to stand by him in those hours when man's failing strength needs the restoring, gentle help of a sister. Perhaps the martyr's palm may not be awarded him, unless you prepare him to cull it; perhaps, poor Flora, your heart may have to suffer as many deaths as there will be dear ones taken from you. But, if the prescience of friendship speak true, then indeed I foresee for you a great triumph. Absorbed in your self-sacrificing love for those committed to your care, you will be clothed in an invisible armour, which will repel the shafts hurled by God's enemies, and screen you alike from the assault of earthly affections. Do not blush, Flora, your heart cannot be stronger than that of other mortals, you can never become cold or indifferent, for you are more sensitive than others of your age; but a mighty strength shall be given you, when you devote yourself to be the strength of those around you, and a mighty reward will be yours."

They had reached the house by this time, and stood outside, still conversing. Flora grasped her friend's hand: "I am so glad to have you," she said, "you seem to know by instinct all that will do me good".

Laurentius interrupted them, by bounding over the threshold, with a glee he had not shown for some time: "I am so glad!" he cried, "and quite ready to join you, sister; I have been studying so hard that my father and Pontius said I must have some relaxation, so your message came just in time; shall we go?"

"Not till I have asked leave of our parents," replied the girl, "and inquired of them whether they will favour us with their company."

"I have asked them that already, but they prefer staying at home. My father has begun a wrangle with Pontius as to whether the earth were first formed of fire or water, and that dispute seems likely to last till the consummation of the world; our mother is making preparations for our journey to Rome, so desired me tell you not to wait for her. Shall we go?"

"In a moment," she replied, entering the house, from which she soon again issued, and the slaves that usually waited on their masters when they walked out, having gathered round them, she took the lead with her friend.

On they went, till the orange groves were passed; above them rose olive trees. They left these behind too, till, rising higher on the hill, they found a region quite different from the smiling plain below.

"We are going to enter the Obscure Valley," said Reparata, "and the country people say that they can see the stars shining at noon, when standing in its depths. Of course this is only a fable, but it is not without its moral: as if the light of Heaven, so often eclipsed to us in the noon-day of life, when the world shines brightly and smiles upon us must needs illumine the pilgrim sunk in the depths of adversity."

"But you seem to believe in the fable, Reparata, for you desired us bring torches."

"Only to guide us through certain caverns: see, here is one!"

There was a hole in the rock before them, which they would never have noticed, had it not been pointed out. Reparata crouched down, glided through, and was out of sight in an instant. Flora shrieked with terror, thinking she had fallen into a pit, and ordered the slaves to hurry to her assistance; a merry laugh from within reassured her, and great was her surprise to see all those who had stood round her a moment before, disappear one after the other, as they, each and all, entered the orifice; she wished to follow their example, and asked her brother to help her. She found the passage an easy one: a beautiful sight burst on her view; a subterranean palace seemed to unfold itself, its vaults supported by stalactite columns, in which the lights were reflected with prismatic colours, the walls fantastically sculptured, and displaying a long row of arches; graceful festoons, glittering like so many chandeliers, concealed the rough rocks, and a simultaneous cry of admiration burst from all.

"See more," cried Reparata exultingly, and taking a torch in her hand stood up, on a huge pedestal, and held the light to an aperture whence many vaults and long colonnades of similar structure were visible.

"How beautiful!" exclaimed Flora. "How my father would like this! I wish he had come."

"And that would have settled the point they are always arguing about," exclaimed Laurentius. "Pontius will have it that water was the first element of the world, and my father says fire. I should have liked them to gaze on this beautiful production of dropping waters."

"What treasures the earth enfolds in her bosom!" said Reparata. "I wonder how long this has taken to form."

"Perhaps since the universal deluge," resumed Flora musing; "if so, how impressive to find God's word and threats mining the soil, and leaving here and there the stamp of His sovereignty."

"I shall bring both my father and our visitor here to-morrow," repeated Laurentius; "what a prodigious place! I shall come here every day, as long as we remain at Cimella; I wish I had known of this grotto before."

"Oh, but we must not stay very long," observed Reparata; "remember we have not yet reached the valley I spoke to you about. Come away!"

They lingered a little longer to see the sparkling walls recede, as the slaves moved backwards, making their torches play before the crystal surface, then ascended the gradual slope, formed by the accumulation of a watery sediment, which had trickled down the aperture; and thus they returned to the light of day.

"That place would make a catacomb," said Flora, as they resumed the narrow path forming the dried-up bed of the river whose track they had been following some time; "what large tables for our feasts, chairs and altars already carved out, and all so beautiful, it is quite ready for an assembly of the faithful."

"But the bodies of our dear martyrs!" observed Laurentius.

"Surely a crystal tomb like that is as befitting for them as our native tufa," said Flora.

"No, no!" he cried, shaking his head, "a Roman prefers his own tufa bed; the soil he has lived on, toiled on, through life, must needs be mingled with his dust! Dear Rome! there was a great one that, stung by his countrymen's ingratitude, forbade thee, *alma patria*, to receive his bones, but such is not the Christian's disinterested affection for thee. Others may revere thee, in that thou wert the mother of heroes, but we cling to thee as to the standing bulwark of our faith; we glory in thee, because of Peter's teaching, we love thee, great Mother, at whose breasts we imbibed the sweetness of Christianity, and if a thought of earth may mingle with those desires which have well-nigh filled our hearts with Christ, I for my part hope that this my body may rest in Roman soil till the day of resurrection. I can understand that, for those who have no hope beyond the grave, there is a pang more bitter than death, and that is, exile from their country, but even then, when their eyes must close without seeing it again, it arises before their memory at the last hour. *Moritur, et moriens, dulces reminiscitur Argos.*"

The boy had spoken with that enthusiasm which was wont to steal over him at times, and more so of late since he had been stuyding the classics with the learned Pontius. He stopped short; for Reparata, impressed with the beauty of his words and the remembrance of her own country, had covered her face with her hands, and was striving to conceal her tears ; he felt sorry, and walked on quickly, leaving the ladies together. Flora spoke to her with sisterly sympathy, and then effectually diverted her attention to the change of scenery, and windings of the road, which was getting narrower and narrower as they proceeded. Soon they were obliged to walk one by one, while on either side of them the huge rocks rose almost perpendicular, being a channel through which the mountain torrent had been forcing its way for years. It was very striking to see how that silent stream had done its work, slowly, resolutely, surmounting the giant force opposed to it, until it had issued, purified and clear, from the rocks it had cleft through.

"And thus," said the young girls, as they communicated their reflections to each other, "thus shall our woman's will, gentle, but firm and unyielding, triumph over the strength of our persecutors, thus shall we surmount all obstacles and pass on."

"Yes," added Laurentius, who had been waiting for them on the road, for they had reached the end of the valley and were turning back: "yes! it shall be so with you both, and I hope with me too. Beyond lies the sea, where the stream finishes its course, even as the Immensity of God will receive our souls to be absorbed for ever in His Divine Essence; and there we shall, during all eternity, reflect one image, that of the Eternal Sun of Justice."

The orb of day was fast sinking behind the hill; they remembered the long walk that lay before them, and proceeded homewards with hurried steps.

## CHAPTER XV.

THERE is a wind on the sea which has been howling all night with an unearthly sound. On dry land, trees have been torn up from the roots, roofs of houses blown off, men have risen from their beds in the night and asked each other whether the earth were shaken to its foundations. Soothsayers and astrologers explained that a sudden collision had brought the earth in contact with the sun, but the more wise shook their heads, and reckoned on an approaching misfortune. This was the day fixed for a sacrifice in the temple of Jupiter Capitolinus. The Emperor Gordianus, before setting out on an expedition to Persia, was anxious to ascertain the will of the gods.

During the course of the morning, Adrias, the husband of Paulina (whom we have left spending the winter at Nicæa with Siona), called on his friend Nemesion. Hearing from the porter that the tribune was at home, he entered with the freedom of an old acquaintance, and went at once to the *triclinium* where the family were assembled.

" Ha, friend ! " cried the master of the house. " It is a long time since we have seen you ; do you come to share our repast ? Sit down and welcome."

## Flora: the Roman Martyr.

"No! I cannot touch anything to-day, I am too anxious."

"What is the matter?"

"I am expecting my wife and children to return; they must be out at sea in this fearful weather."

"The gods preserve them, for no human aid can reach them."

"I came to you because I knew you would share my anxiety, and besides I want to have prayers offered up for the safety of my dear ones; I wish to offer a sacrifice to Vesta through the hands of your daughter-priestess."

"Vain hope!" exclaimed a girl sitting at the table, whose eyes showed by their changeless expression that their life was gone. "Vain hope! the gods are cruel, and mock us."

"Do not use such impious language, Lucilla!" he replied.

"She is much altered," explained her mother, apologetically. "She used to be pious, contented, even happy, in her misfortune; we ourselves hardly recognise her."

"Why did you take her from me?" retorted the girl in a smothered voice.

"She is ever lamenting her sister," explained Nemesion.

"What weather!" resumed Adrias, returning to his own subject of anxiety. "It is a goodly ship, well stored, that I expect; but that matters little, I would sacrifice twice its cargo to ensure the safety of my wife, my children, besides our common friend, Florentius, and his family."

"Is Flora with them?" asked the blind girl.

"Whom do you mean? Florentius' daughter is with him, of course, and so are my dear little ones."

"Flora in danger!" shrieked Lucilla, and rising from her place she came groping in the direction from which Adrias' voice proceeded, and laying her hand on his arm, she grasped it as with a clasp of steel, whispering audibly: "I will not leave you till you have promised to take me to her."

"But all those I speak of are on the sea, dear child."

"Then how can you be here when those you love are in danger? Ah, had I my eyes, nothing should separate me from Volumnia; I would be every day at the door of the temple she serves, to receive her morning smile and her evening greeting. I could live on that remembrance, oh how long! Take me, oh take me, to the shore where you expect them, to the banks of the Tiber, where I can hear the sound of the water and wind; let me but hear, and I will tell you whether they are safe. You ask for prayers to propitiate the gods; if they will listen to the cry of a broken heart, here is mine!"

"Adrias," said her father, "it is seldom in my power to gratify any of her wishes; but as she is so vehement about this, I wish you would take her with you, to await the arrival of the ship you expect. I know you will care for her, as for your own child."

"That I will!" replied the visitor, and receiving her

as a sacred charge, he put a fold of his cloak over her to shelter her from the tempest, and led her gently from the house. Her mother would have followed, but Lucilla with a gentle, though firm touch, put her back.

"It must not be," she said, "the weather is too stormy, no one can brave it but such a one as myself, who see not the world without but my own world within: do not come, mother, leave me to the care of my father's friend."

She went out, and that storm, coming from the deserts of Lybia, blew into her face with a scorching breath; she did not heed it.

They went together to the banks of the Tiber, and stood there all day till sunset, now strolling up and down, now returning to the same spot and waiting. The girl beguiled the time with varied songs, some tremulous and fitful like the breeze, others wild like the sea-gull's cry: there was more of inspiration than of melody in her strain; and when her companion asked her where she learned all she sang: "Do you not know," she replied, "that sorrow teaches us to sing? Cruel men deprive the nightingale of her sight that she may sing the more, according to the measure of her affliction. When Volumnia was by me I never sang, for she was the voice of my soul, but now I call up my own thoughts to fill up the void."

The storm continued to rage for three days, as is customary for the wind that comes from the desert. Each day that man and that girl were at their post watching: others came to join them, till there grew to be a crowd on the Tiber's banks, watching for the ship that was expected from Liguria; by and by the wind abated, and their hopes rose.

The sacrifice which had been appointed to take place in the temple of Jupiter Capitolinus was delayed on account of the weather, but on this morning the sun rose brightly in a cloudless sky, nature was clothed in verdure and freshness: the branches torn from the trees of the Palatine hill and uprooted shrubs bore witness to the late conflict of the elements, while the laurels at the Emperor's door were cloven to the very centre: a fearful omen! the tree of Daphne had never yet been known to be scathed by the god of fire, and now it was scorched by lightning!

A procession of priests, all veiled, came to fetch the Emperor Pontiff and escort him to the temple. Young Gordian issued from the palace, clothed in his sacerdotal robes; the sacrificators leading the milk-white heifer he was to offer to Juno awaited him at the foot of the hill; the procession formed. Just as they were falling into their ranks, a strange, hollow laugh was heard, which seemed to come from the very earth at the Emperor's feet; he turned deadly pale. An Augur was at his side: "Let not the divine Augustus be surprised," he said, "if the spirits of the Palatine be heard, for it was they sent the storm; but, fear not! the genius of Gordian will prevail".

Then the Emperor and his retinue wended their way down the hill, and disappeared.

At the same hour, the muddy waters of the Tiber

flowed on, under a bright sun: "How peaceful that sound is!" said Lucilla, "it brings good news!" Again she listened, and this time a messenger came in sight; her quick ear had detected the sound of his footsteps. Adrias had stationed some of his men at different places along the river, and these now came to announce that the long-expected ship had been stopped at some miles' distance from Rome, it could not proceed further, owing to the Tiber having overflowed its banks.

"Let us go and meet it!" cried Lucilla at once; "I can ride with you. Do not leave me behind, I entreat you; remember that my father allowed me to stay with you, till they arrive; I cannot endure any longer suspense, I must know whether they are safe!"

Adrias, as anxious for her sake as for his own, ordered his slaves to go for the small chariot which he was in the habit of using when he went of a morning to the country to inspect his farms; he took Lucilla by the hand, and walked on, until they met the vehicle, which he mounted at once, alone with her. There was no room for more, and the good merchant drove himself. Both were perfectly silent during the drive; fear and anxiety seemed to stifle their very breath. What if the vessel had been carried away by the rapid overflow of the waters? what if it were stranded on the banks?

Presently they came to a place where a great crowd were assembled: people on the river-side were calling out to each other! . . . were those cries of danger? No! they seemed to be the expression of sympathy and rejoicing with their fellow creatures who had escaped from peril.

Adrias alighted, and helped the blind girl out. The crowd opened: familiar voices called out "Father". Another moment, and Adrias pressed his wife in his arms, while their little children hung about them.

"How had they fared?" he asked, "what had happened? had they been in danger?" But they were so happy, they could not answer these questions, or even hear them, till Florentius, coming up, greeted his old friend heartily, and explained how they had been obliged to disembark in this spot, the ship having been stranded on sands which had accumulated in the river owing to the number of trees that had been torn up in the tempest and impeded the current. "But all your merchandise is safe, Adrias!" he added.

"Then I shall devote the greater part of my profits to a sacrifice of thanksgiving to the gods, in honour of your safe arrival. I was beginning to fear we should not all of us meet again."

"And I had the like misgiving, but my daughter Flora kept up our spirits; she seemed so certain that no harm would befall us."

Meanwhile, Flora had thrown her arms round her poor blind friend, holding her in a fond embrace; the meeting was one of thrilling emotion to both. Since Lucilla had lost her sister, she had become the especial charge of Flora, who endeavoured to hold the place of her that was gone, and the girl, with that concentrated affection peculiar to those who do not live in the exterior world, had clung to her young benefactress with an intensity which had rendered the pain of separation almost too acute to bear. Poor girl! she listened to every tone of her voice, and, feeling her face all over, and smoothing her hair: "You are changed, Flora, your cheeks have filled up, you are stronger, your voice is clearer, and it sounds more happy. Oh, now I am glad you went away, for I see it was for your good. But what has altered you so?"

"I think this kind friend is the cause of my change for the better," replied Flora, as, leaving her for an instant, she went back to the group assembled round Adrias, and, leading out a young girl whose hand she laid in Lucilla's: "This," she said, "is a friend I met in Liguria; she is to be our guest for some time, and I trust you too, dear Lucilla, will find a friend in her; her name is Reparata."

A passing shadow of anxiety was discernible on Lucilla's countenance; she shrank at first from contact with a stranger; but the young Greek took her hand soothingly, caressingly, and spoke to her so sweetly, that the bruised spirit felt the healing influence of girlish genuine friendship.

"You must be fair," she observed inquiringly, "for there is music in your voice."

"Indeed! I do not know," replied the other laughing; "lay your hand on my face, and judge for yourself."

Lucilla did so and was satisfied: "May the gift of beauty," she said, and her voice grew stifled with the emotion of a painful recollection, "prove less fatal to you, stranger, than it has to many. I allude, in particular, to one whom I love, who has become to me as dead."

Reparata had not time to ask for an explanation, for while they had been talking preparations were being made for conveying the weary travellers to Rome. *Lettigas* were now ready, each of the ladies ascended her own, and slaves supported the poles, which were run through rings fastened at the sides. A goodly train surrounded them, for by this time slaves, clients and parasites, belonging to the separate families of Adrias and Florentius, all had heard the good news, and came to congratulate their masters. They all marched in order to the Ostian gate, where, to their surprise, they found a guard of soldiers more numerous than usual, all drawn up and under arms. Nemesion was too much accustomed to military command not to discern something very determined in the sentries' mien; he went up to the tribune at their head, and asked in a whisper: "What has occurred during my absence? surely there are no signs of insurrection, I hope?"

"No! but when our Lord and Emperor ascended the steps of the temple to offer sacrifice to Jupiter Capitolinus, an attempt was made against his august life. In the confusion, the criminal escaped, and we are guarding the gates lest he should leave Rome."

Nemesion uttered a suppressed cry of horror: "Is the sacred person of Gordianus wounded?" he asked.

"Only slightly! The dagger, men say, was wielded by the hand of a maniac, and consequently the blow was ill-directed."

"Who? what!" stammered Nemesion, "if the criminal has not been taken, how do you know him?"

The centurion took him into the guard-house, which was empty.

"If you want to hear more, remain here," he said, "and bid your party go in through the gate; they have my permission to enter Rome."

Nemesion followed the suggestion, and consigning his daughter to the care of Adrias, he returned to the appointed place; he looked uneasy and pale.

"Noble Nemesion," began the centurion, "it grieves me to afflict you, but you had better hear the truth from me who have so much reason to be devoted to you, and whom I know you will trust. Return to your home by a short cut across the fields, and do not let yourself or yours be seen in the streets for some days, lest suspicion should attach to you. He who sought your daughter's hand and was disappointed in his suit, Icilius who went mad when Volumnia became a Vestal, has been often met wandering in a wild mood at the foot of Mount Palatine, uttering threats which no one heeded at the time; they were considered the ravings of a madman, but now, this attack on our Lord the Emperor is supposed to proceed from him—the more so, that he is not to be found anywhere."

Nemesion veiled his head with a part of his toga to conceal his emotion, and his heaving breast told his indignation.

After some silence: "It is only a suspicion," he observed, "it may be ill-founded".

"*Vox populi, vox Dei*," replied the other, "I am afraid that in this instance the saying is but too true; the maniac was always to be seen in every public show that drew a crowd together; this day he has suddenly disappeared, and the popular outcry repeats his name."

"Ah! the fates are cruel to me and mine. I have ever gloried in being a Roman. To-day, for the first time, my birthright weighs upon me."

"Hide yourself, Nemesion, for it is well known this wretched youth was about to marry your daughter, and some of his disgrace may be fastened upon you."

"Alas! had their innocent affection been respected, how much better it would have been for all of us. The shivering to pieces of that poor boy's heart produced the smouldering fire of revenge. But how did the dreadful act take place?"

"The procession was slowly ascending to the temple of Jupiter Capitolinus, the young Emperor, his head veiled, and temples bound with the sacerdotal fillet, followed the milk-white heifer which was to be sacrificed to Juno. Before entering the sacred edifice, he stopped and turned round, perhaps to gaze on a dark cloud of sinister shape. It looked like a winged eagle with talons, hovering over the Mount Palatine. All present saw the omen, and some would have turned Gordian away, but his piety prevailed. He went to the altar where incense was smoking, took himself the golden knife which was to immolate the victim; but, with a compassion becoming his youthful age, turned away his head. The heifer fell under the stroke of the high priest, and its entrails and heart were immediately taken out to be examined; an unaccountable deformity was noticeable in the animal's liver, though nothing could exceed its spotless beauty, as the people had noticed, when it passed in their midst with gilded horns and crowned head. The priests showed the Emperor the signs of a great misfortune, perhaps his own approaching doom, foretold by the gods; he turned away shuddering. He did not leave the altar hurriedly, however, but knelt down and prayed. It was this act of piety that saved his life; for, just as he dropped on his knees, a hand directed against him missed its aim, and inflicted but a slight wound. Gordian did not stagger, but rose to his feet with a strength and dignity that would have befitted a Cæsar advanced in years. He looked round in the direction from which the blow had come, but the crowd had closed upon our beloved Emperor. No one had seen the assassin, some had heard a strange laugh which they ascribed to spirits, but others remembered that sound of hollow merriment was familiar to the unfortunate Icilius; popular indignation immediately fixed itself on the maniac of Mount Palatine, and every one is on the look-out for him."

"Friend," resumed Nemesion, in a tone of calm energy, "I thank you for having told me all, but I shall not seek concealment. A soldier and a Roman, I have no reason to stand aloof from my sovereign, even if calumny should malign my name. I will go to him this moment, ready to give up my command if he suspect me, but, at any rate, anxious to show him how free I esteem myself from suspicion."

"Do as you will, Nemesion; men such as you have

seldom to fear for their own faults, but often suffer for those of others."

The centurion pressed the hand of his friend, bid him farewell, and directed his steps, as he had said he would, towards the palace of the Cæsars.

Meanwhile the slaves went on, bearing the *lettigas* to their respective homes. When Adrias had seen Lucilla's father engaged in conversation at the Ostian gate, he had left his own party to take charge of the blind girl, and walked by her side. Her sense of hearing was so acute, that she could discern his presence from his breathing alone, and said: "You have taken my father's place; why has he remained behind?"

"To give orders to the soldiers at the gate, I suppose; do not be uneasy, Lucilla."

"No! I am happy to-day and will give way to the mood, which is a new one to me. I have not yet saluted the lady Paulina, so confused and hurried was our meeting. And your children, how are they, have they grown?"

"Yes! but I too may say I have hardly had time to see them, in the joy of recovering those who I feared were lost."

"The air is getting more light and expanded; I think we have reached an open space. I hear the sound of the flowing Tiber. I feel we are in the vicinity of Vesta's temple, something tells me so. Is it not true?"

"Yes! what a strange instinct is yours."

"Tell them to set me down here, I must breathe the same air as Volumnia, were it only for a little while."

"Lucilla, you have shown great courage during the last few days you have been under my charge, you must not give way to your feelings now."

"I shall not falter, I shall remain perfectly quiet; only let me stay here for a very few minutes, do gratify me. I ask it in the name of your little ones, you cannot refuse that appeal."

Adrias knew too well the depth of feeling which lay in that simple request; he could not, indeed, refuse the poor girl, so, requesting Florentius to escort the other ladies, he desired the bearers of Lucilla's *lettiga* to stop, lifted her out, and then, taking her hand to lead her: "What do you wish for now, self-willed girl?" he said kindly.

"That you take me to the temple where my sister is imprisoned, and though I cannot visit her now, as my mother must always be present at our interviews, at least I can feel those walls, and imprint a kiss on them. Ah! if you knew the love which unites Volumnia and myself, you would understand how her spirit will be gladdened, if I only pass here, although she do not see me."

"Poor child! living secluded in the solitary world of your own heart you imagine strange things."

He took her as she had desired to one of the columns that supported the temple of Vesta; they were eleven in number, she knew them well, and went round counting them. There was, attached to the temple, a building where the priestesses dwelt, when not on active service. Lucilla knew that too, and felt her way along the wall in that direction; there was a narrow passage, roofed over, leading from that to the sacred edifice, into which air and light were admitted by means of small windows, covered with iron gratings. Lucilla applied her ear to one of these; she listened, and gradually consternation became visible in her countenance, she seized the hand of Adrias and whispered: "There is a man concealed here".

"What are you dreaming of, Lucilla? do not even hint at such a thing."

"I know perfectly how dangerous it is to make a discovery of this kind, but, nevertheless, I hear a man's breathing, it is half-suppressed, almost smothered; do you look in and see whether I am mistaken."

Adrias was startled at her decided manner, yet terrified at the idea of being implicated in a sacrilege; he looked in at the window where she had been listening, and there saw a human form crouching, concealed under a toga, which was soiled and torn. The face was covered, but long locks of matted hair were visible; a fearful suspicion crossed his mind. "Profane intruder," he cried, "what dost thou seek in the holiest sanctuary of Rome? Begone! or the gods will crush thee, and men will slay."

The figure rose, came to the window, uttered a low demon-like laugh. Lucilla heard, and suppressing a shriek of anguish, stretched out her hands: "Begone!" she cried, "madman and unworthy, would you lose my sister?"

"I lost her long ago," he answered, in a tone which

had not its usual wildness. "I come here to save her."

"Come away!" cried the blind girl vehemently; "tear him away, brave Adrias, you are stronger than he is. Or, wait! let me first try gentleness. Be good, Icilius," she resumed, adopting the tone she thought might soothe him, "try and find out the place you entered at, and come away, come!"

"Do you see that iron grating yonder? I tore it down with a strength I have long been preparing in secret. Ha! ha! the maniac is clever!" and he chuckled.

"Come to me, Icilius, or we must call the guards."

"They are seeking for me! they will soon find me; blood has a strong scent! Ha! smell my hands, Lucilla, they are perfumed with an enemy's blood! but I did not strike deep enough, I did not wound his heart as he did mine!" Here the madman grew thoughtful, and it was fearful to see the sudden change in him.

A low, solemn chant was now heard, the vestals were going to the shrine; an inner door opened, and a blaze of light illumined the narrow, covered passage. They were only six in number, besides the Grand Vestal; the youngest walked first, carrying the wood to renew the sacred fire. The unfortunate Icilius, instead of escaping, as he had been urged to do, turned round to face the priestesses; he recognised Volumnia . . . no incoherent exclamation escaped him, but before any one could prevent him, he knelt down, touched the long flowing *suffibulum* or veil she wore, and kissed it respectfully.

A low murmur of indignation was uttered by the young girls, who knew not whether to advance or retreat.

"Sacrilegious and accursed!" cried the Grand Vestal, "how comest thou here? dare not to pollute that sacred veil with thy touch. Didst thou come to rob the sanctuary? Fly! lest the vengeance of Heaven and men pursue thee."

Icilius was now weeping: for a long time his overwrought passions had dried up the source of his tears, but now they fell abundantly, and his unsettled reason seemed to be regaining its ascendancy: he was calm and subdued.

"I have sinned!" he cried, "but do not let my fault be visited on her; she did not know of my coming."

Lucilla had remained clinging to the iron bars of the little window during this scene, nor could all the efforts of Adrias tear her away. Now, the guards who continually watched in the vicinity of the temple came up, and rudely ordered her away. Immediately the Grand Vestal appeared at the door of the temple, and, calling the lictors, committed to their charge the intruder who had been found in that inner part of the temple where no one but the High Priest could ever penetrate. They immediately closed round him, while the unhappy Volumnia called on the goddess she served, on the Vestals her sisters, to bear witness to the purity of her life. All loved her, but they hardly knew how to console her, for they knew how full of danger was the least suspicion that fell on Vesta's priestess.

Bystanders had congregated round the sacred edifice; some came from idle curiosity, but the compassion of others was attracted by the evident sufferings of Lucilla, who lay, gasping for breath, in the arms of Adrias; they took her to the nearest house, and restored her sufficiently to be placed in a *lettiga* and conveyed away.

At the same time, a tramping of horses announced the arrival of the Prætorian guard; they rode right into the middle of the crowd. What was their errand?

"They came," they said, "to seek for the parricide who had attempted the life of their Emperor, he was supposed to have fled in this direction."

A strange feeling of presentiment ran through the crowd, and it was soon realised. Icilius, already in the hands of the lictors, now raised his voice, which was calm and firm: "Seek no more!" he said, "I confess my guilt, in the hope that it may explain my taking refuge in this sanctuary, to which let no other suspicion be attached. I attempted the Emperor's life, out of a motive of private revenge. I had sworn to do so, on the day that my promised bride was consecrated by him to Vesta. This very morning I resolved to carry out my project, but failed. Knowing that my life was at stake, and led by a secret instinct which prevailed over my wandering mind, I sought this asylum, the most sacred of Rome. Had I simply clung to the altar of the goddess, my life might have been spared, but the yearnings of my distracted heart led me to the inner sanctuary, where no profane person can enter. I have seen once more the consecrated maiden who was mine, before the gods took her: since the day she entered this temple, I had never crossed her path. I attest that she is as pure as the day she left her mother's arms to become a Vestal. The very sight of her and the agonising fear lest her good name suffer from my folly have sufficed to restore my reason. I conjure you all to believe me, and confirm my attestation of Volumnia's innocence."

He held out his hands for the links that were to bind him, but, before doing so, waved them in token of farewell towards the goddess. The Grand Vestal hastened from the temple, bearing away the youngest virgin, who had swooned.

## CHAPTER XVI.

THE shades of evening were gathering around, with that rapidity, peculiar to southern climates, where there is hardly any interval between sunset and nightfall. Flora sat with her mother, in the *impluvium* of their villa, on the Aventine Hill, where they watched the last glimpses of daylight, falling on Siona's many coloured weaving. The loom rose and fell, while Flora mechanically passed the shuttle, but her thoughts were far away, and her mother had more than once to remind her she must change the shade of the wool. After repeated mistakes: "Give up trying to help me, dear child," said Siona, "you only set me wrong. Persons are differently constituted; when I am depressed with sad thoughts I labour and work them off; you, on the contrary, fall into an uncontrollable fit of dreaminess."

"Yes, dear mother, forgive me, but I cannot help thinking of them; I fancy I see poor Volumnia's white robes in every cloud that passes, and as the shadows grow more distinct, when night comes on, I feel afraid to be alone."

"Flora! this is a return of the complaint you suffered from at the death of Martina: you must gather up your energies, remembering you have many duties assigned to you. Do not allow womanly weakness to betray you into useless and morbid sensibility."

The girl kissed her mother's hand, and, as it was growing dark, they left the *impluvium*, carrying their work implements to the *aula*, the most important apartment on the ground floor of every Roman house, and generally decorated with taste. They found Reparata there, singing to a lyre she held in her hand. An adept in the fine arts familiar to her own land, she had found in Florentius' house much of the music that had belonged to Cecilia, and resumed with joy her long-forgotten instrument. The young Greek had become so dear to Siona and her daughter, that they had extracted a promise from her uncle that she was to be their guest for a long time to come. Pontius himself was not averse from the opportunity thus afforded him of finding intellectual enjoyment in the society of the litterati of Rome. His mind, long debarred from the pleasure of learning, now drank in with delight the refreshing draught, from which he knew with Christian discernment how to subtract the deleterious poison of Pagan philosophy.

"Have you any new strains, dear one," inquired Siona of her interesting young charge, "wherewith to enliven our disconsolate Flora?"

"Indeed, lady, I can sing of nothing but woe to-day; and am watching for the return of your lord Florentius to know how fares our good Emperor."

"Strange!" said Siona, "that a blow so ill-directed should have caused a wound that has become so serious! No one thought anything of it at first. Oh, if we lose Gordian, woe to the Empire!"

"And woe to those who interest us," added Flora.

"The unfortunate Icilius might have hoped for pardon from the intercession of a clement minister, but my father says that Gordianus is irritated against the hapless youth, still more for his impiety, in desecrating the temple, than for his attempt at assassination."

A diversion was occasioned in their conversation by the entrance of Laurentius, who came in with several rolls of vellum bound together by a thong, and strapped over his shoulder. He had just returned from school, and in his girdle was still the bunch of reeds he used for pens. The bloom of health was on his cheek, and a glow of manly beauty on his features; a pleasant smile was on his lips, and his vigorous frame stood out well defined in the dim twilight. Flora's thoughts reverted to the time when this stripling had come to their home, in early infancy; how her sisterly care had developed him; how his mind had unfolded, and how much it contained now! There was the innocence of childhood on that brow, and in that young heart, which had imbibed the spirit of self-sacrifice in the sweet atmosphere of home influence, there were noble inclinations, high resolves, and a magnanimous capability for virtue.

"What has kept you at school so long beyond the usual time, my son?" asked Siona.

"I played the truant, mother, on my way home, and wandered about the forum to collect news. Our Emperor is still a great sufferer. Misitheus hardly ever leaves his bedside, and Philip, præfect of the guards, transmits the royal orders to the world outside the palace. I do not like the wily Arab: he has already risen very high in favour at court. There are certain natures whose ambition prompts them to crush those who have been instrumental in raising them."

"Did you hear anything of poor Icilius?" asked Flora.

"Yes! at your request, our father has been much concerned for him, and got an excellent lawyer to plead for him before the tribunal, but the popular indignation was so strong they would not listen to the defence, and he has been condemned."

"Oh God! and what is his sentence?"

"The pain of parricide!"

Both Siona and her daughter uttered a cry of anguish.

"Oh, what has the poor madman done," said Siona, "to incur such a doom?"

"The Emperor is the father of every Roman; an attempt against his life is considered as a parricide."

"But he has not killed the Emperor."

"He tried to do so."

Here Flora sobbed aloud. "Oh why!" she said, "why did I neglect the trust Volumnia left me? The day she went away, she told me to comfort and advise Icilius! Alas! had I done so, perhaps this would never have happened!"

Her emotion was so uncontrollable, that Reparata led her out to the garden, where the fresh air somewhat calmed and invigorated her. Her friend's soothing words brought her round, and they spoke more tranquilly on the painful subject.

"Do you think," asked Flora, "we could find any means of saving Icilius?"

"Impossible! besides you have nothing to reproach yourself with. What influence could you possibly have exercised over a declared maniac? His parents themselves could not control him, when he chose to run wild night and day on the Mount Palatine, perhaps meditating in his delirium the act he has since performed."

"Yes! he must have been planning his revenge against the Emperor ever since the day that Volumnia was consecrated a Vestal. He made Gordianus responsible for that. Do you think the attempt is a sin in poor Icilius' frame of mind?"

"We cannot judge. God is more merciful than man. But if the poor madman be not accountable for the act itself, there must have been a long chain of wicked, angry feelings which culminated in this point; and as to all the failings of his misguided, erring Pagan life, who can say, Flora, what account he has to render?"

"Poor fellow! noble as he is, to die such an ignominious death! Gifted with a soul, just as you and I, he has to bear it before the judgment seat of God, laden perhaps with heavy sins; and in this very hour, when his reason has returned, he is alone, face to face with the horrors of his approaching doom! Not one voice near him to awake the pang of remorse, or call up one good feeling!"

"Where is he?"

"In the Mamertine prison. I went there once before with Laurentius to visit Martina!"

"Flora," cried her friend energetically, "I see what you are thinking of, you must not entertain any such wild project. I shall oppose you by every means in my power."

"Do not say that!" replied the other with a stern calmness which had succeeded to her previous agitation. "You were not a witness, as I was, to the parting scene between those unhappy young people, whose very nuptial day was close at hand. I still remember the forced resignation of Volumnia, the rigidity her features assumed, as if she were gradually turning into a marble statue. I can never forget, to my dying day, the wild despair of Icilius; and then, when all was over, she called me to her, saying: 'Thou wilt probably see him again; when thou meetest him, speak to him kindly; bid him take courage and act nobly; console him if thou canst.' Do you not understand, Reparata, that those words implied a duty which I have not fulfilled!"

"And now what is it you wish to do towards it?"

"To visit him, if possible, as I did Martina when she was imprisoned where he now is, console him as I did her, speak to him as no one else can or will, since his own parents have abandoned him. And, if I dared, I would ask him to believe in the Master condemned, like him, to an ignominious death, Who, in that last hour of loving sacrifice, pardoned the condemned criminal, and called him to Heaven by His side."

"Flora, these are noble thoughts, but perfectly unreasonable to indulge in, because it is impossible to carry them out."

"Here comes Laurentius to fetch us. We are staying out too late, the dew is falling. I must tell him what we were just speaking about. Laurentius, I should like very much to visit Icilius in the Mamertine prison; you and I know the way to get to it, do you remember Claudius taking us along a subterranean passage?"

"Dear sister, I fear that is impossible! The unfortunate Icilius is watched night and day, lest he should attempt his own life."

"How do you know that?"

"I was told so by the young Hippolytus, whose father has the command of the guard at the Mamertine. I met him on my way home from school, we are great friends, although he is a few years older than I am; I asked him about Icilius. He was rather surprised at my being interested in the poor criminal, but when I explained that it was on account of Volumnia being your friend, he offered to go himself and see poor Icilius; then he will call on us, to give us an exact account of him."

"That was very thoughtful of Hippolytus," observed Reparata, "he must be a good young man."

"I think," said Flora hesitatingly, "I ought to refer all this to our mother; I ought to have expressed my desire first to her."

"That is true," interposed Reparata earnestly; "whatever is right can only be so within the limits of your mother's sanction."

"Come into the house now," said Laurentius, "our father has returned home."

That very night, before retiring to rest, Flora spoke privately, and at full length, to her mother, expressing to her the strange desire which had taken possession of her whole soul, and which seemed to point out an urgent duty. Siona appreciated her daughter's motives, but from still weightier ones of maternal prudence, opposed her, and the girl yielded. The next morning, however, Hippolytus sought Laurentius early, to give him the desired information as to the prisoner; the boy went to ask his mother's leave to introduce his friend. Flora was with her in the *aula*, and Siona admitted the young stranger at once to give an account of the unhappy prisoner who interested them all so much. Hippolytus was taller than Laurentius, but not as good-looking; he had not, like him, that gentleness of manner which bespeaks one bred in all the refinement of home training; he had been, on the contrary, inured to the hardships of a soldier's life, which was to be his career as it had been his father's. Already had the tight-fitting garment replaced the *vestis succincta*, which Roman boys generally left off at the age of fourteen, to assume the more manly toga; soldier's buskins cased his feet, thereby adding to his height; his sun-burnt brow became him, and dark curls clustered under the light helmet which he wore. As his father had the sole command of the Mamertine prison, where persons of note and political offenders were often consigned, he could give ample information about Icilius. "His frantic fits had quite ceased," he said, "and he was now in a state of great despondency. Is there anything you would wish to have conveyed to him?" he continued. "Laurentius spoke of a message from your friend the Vestal, but that would be very dangerous."

"Could you, Hippolytus," asked Siona, "obtain permission from your father for my children to see the prisoner?"

"His orders are very strict," replied the youth, "and what motive can I adduce for such an unwonted request?"

"The friendship which existed between your mother and myself is a sufficient pledge that I would not compromise any one connected with her, by soliciting an undue privilege, were I not influenced by the purest motives. I think it right to try and console poor Icilius, to bring him to a sense of duty, to arouse him to repentance and regret for his attempt against the Emperor, so that he may meet death in a proper spirit, with becoming fortitude and peace of mind."

"How strange, dear lady, that you should compassionate one whom all Rome shuns and abhors, for his attempt against our sovereign's life. And yet, your views are so noble that I cannot but admire them, new and incomprehensible though they seem. I think my father will consent to your proposal, if Laurentius present the matter to him in the light you see it in, but do not ask me to plead, I am no orator."

"Time presses," observed Laurentius, "and every day brings the unhappy Icilius nearer to his doom. Mother, allow me to go at once with Hippolytus; if the noble centurion, his father, think proper to refuse our suit, we shall have the satisfaction of having made the trial."

"Yes go! my son, and explain with all deference why

I solicit this permission for both yourself and your sister. When Volumnia left us to become a Vestal, she begged of Flora as a parting request, to try and do all the good she could to Icilius. This is the first time an opportunity offers for the fulfilling of that promise, which is certainly a sacred duty."

The young men were not long absent, and they returned the more joyfully, that they brought back the desired permission, with but one condition annexed to it. The centurion required that a trusty person, belonging to his own household, should be present at the interview between the young people, and he had chosen to this effect Concordia, who he knew had formerly occupied a post of confidence in the family of Florentius.

This worthy woman, who had served as nurse to Flora and to Hippolytus, was now a Christian, having been converted by the example of her daughter Barbara, who had imbibed the faith in early childhood from her foster-sister, Flora.

The faithful old nurse was overjoyed at this opportunity of rendering a service to her former mistress. She proposed that both she and Flora should wear thick veils, and a plain mourning garb, so as to look like relations, going to bid farewell to the condemned criminal. She promised Siona to watch over her dear young charge, not suffering her to do anything imprudent, nor to overtax her strength. She also bound herself to put a stop to the interview if she saw Icilius was not capable of understanding the suggestions of his friends.

All four then set out together, the youths going first,

in order to select the best part of the road for their companions. When they approached the Mamertine, they cautiously guided them up the steep flight of steps, known as the *Centum Gradus*.

They reached the prison door, and Hippolytus showed the sentries his pass, and introduced his friends into the upper storey.

It was a lonesome place, which Christians venerated as sanctified by the captivity of Peter. Here Martina had been imprisoned; here so many Christians had left an atmosphere of holiness impregnated with the memory of their sufferings and prayers.

Hippolytus made the gaolers place a ladder ready, for there were no steps leading to the inferior floor. He helped Flora to descend with the greatest care; then, telling the sentries who kept Icilius in sight, that orders had been sent for them to relax their strict watch, he himself withdrew.

It was some time before they got accustomed to the darkness; and, even then, they could hardly find him they sought, for he was crouched in a corner, his head on his knees, and his face entirely covered by his matted hair. Flora called him by name, and he started.

"I know your voice," he said, "but you are not Volumnia."

"No! but I am her friend, and I wish to be yours. Men have been cruel to you; sorrow and despair have driven you to madness. I come to console you by telling you of a love which has clung to you through your many trials."

"Is it hers?" he asked.

"No! we must not speak of her, but as one dead; you must not think of her any more."

"Have the cruel gods killed her then?"

"No! there are no gods. You cannot believe, Icilius, that you are obliged to reverence the cruel Vesta, who robbed you of your bride, the wicked Jupiter who profaned the duties of a husband and a father, the shameful Venus whose very name is sufficient to corrupt the air, breathed by innocent maidens. Can that religion be pure in which each vice is deified? We come to tell you of One Who reigns alone, the Creator of the beautiful world Who made each one of us, out of the immensity of His love: it is He who incites us to do good, and Who rewards us when we obey. He has His Eye on our most trifling actions, knows of our sorrows, and will comfort us Himself. It is He Who has sent us to speak to you this day, for He penetrates the gloom of this prison, and even here He embraces Icilius in the arms of His Mighty Love."

The poor prisoner looked round, as if seeking the Presence of which she spoke, then put his hands upon his breast and breathed more freely.

"This thought is an overwhelming one, is it not, Icilius?" continued Laurentius, pursuing the same strain of ideas as his sister, and adopting her soothing persuasive tone; "but we cannot remain with you long. Men have condemned you: there is a God above Who forgives. They will sentence you to a cruel death: He will receive you to an eternal glory. Will you accept the alternative, Icilius?"

The prisoner shook his head. " It is very difficult to understand," he observed.

Flora knelt beside him, clasped her hands, and prayed in silence. He roused himself all of a sudden : " I have seen people die," he said, " such as call themselves Christians, and they seemed to be more triumphant than their judges."

" So they are, Icilius, because they believe in a God Who is Holiness Itself," explained Laurentius ; " and the God they have served faithfully supports them, and rewards their sufferings. They are pure in His sight, and they go to Him."

" But I am not pure," replied the culprit mournfully ; " I am guilty of much wickedness, such as I never understood before."

" He of Whom we have been speaking to you, the One True God, foresaw all your thoughts and feelings ; He will accept you for His son, if you repent : will you belong to Him, even understanding Him so very little ? "

" You say there is a God Who loves me ; one God Who lives in Heaven, and you tell me He loves me ; I find it very beautiful to believe, very sweet for my heart to rest on."

" And can you, will you love Him in return ? A little child can hardly comprehend its father, yet it stretches out its arms to him, as an act of love," interposed Flora.

Tears came to the eyes of Icilius, and trickled slowly down his face. " Tell me more about this Father-God!" he said.

" Time presses, and we can only tell you, without explaining at length, that this good God, in order to expiate your transgressions and those of all men, offered up a Sacrifice, and this was His own Only-begotten Son, God like Himself; we Christians participate in the merits of this Sacrifice. God became like unto us, suffered for us, died for us, shed all His Precious Blood for us, and in that Blood He washed away our guilt. When we become Christians, water is poured on us exteriorly, a symbol of the internal regeneration of our souls."

"I want to become a child of that God-Father, I want to be purified!"

"Men made Him suffer and die; before dying He forgave them!" observed Laurentius significantly.

"Why so! revenge is a duty with us."

"But not with the Christian, and such you are about to become. Icilius, if you would be a child of our God, you must learn to forgive."

"Then let Him change my heart, for with my own I cannot."

They knelt down together, and Flora prayed aloud. From the depths of her innocent heart, she poured forth such soul-stirring expressions of Christian faith, that the poor youth's hardly recovered intelligence drank in the wholesome draught and revived, even as one whose sources of life have been parched up within him.

"I wish to go to my Father, God," he exclaimed, "I wish to see Him; if I must die first, I am willing to die . . . . I was wrong in seeking to be avenged of the Emperor! . . . . I see it all now, understand all

". . . . Gordianus did not rob me of my bride . . . he was sorry to take her to be a Vestal . . . . the false gods alone are the cause of my misfortunes . . . . I renounce them! I wish to be a Christian!"

"Have you learned so soon!" exclaimed Flora, weeping for very pity and tenderness. "Oh great goodness of God! Oh mysterious power of prayer: has the Light of Faith already burst upon your soul? If the minister of our religion cannot come here to instruct and confer baptism upon you, only desire it, and the desire will be accounted to you for your purification. Offer to Him Who came down on earth and suffered for us, offer Him your bitter death, and you will pass from this life to a happy one, where all those who have loved and forgiven meet again."

"I never felt like this before," he said, "I am so tranquil and happy. Will you speak to Volumnia as you have done to me, Flora; will you tell her about the Father-God of the Christians?"

A new spirit had been infused into the once passionate fiery youth: he did not linger over the memory of her he had idolized; his thoughts were elsewhere, he had learned to pray for the first time!

They left him, and returning to the ladder they were to ascend, called upon Hippolytus, who, according to previous agreement, was waiting to help them up. Soon they passed out from those walls, and resumed their walk through the streets, in the same order in which they had come, but all were silently absorbed in their own reflections.

Oh, thought Hippolytus, if this could be his lot through life, to walk in the same path as Flora. He dared not speak to her, for she was so rapt up in the holy duty she had performed, that she seemed to be surrounded by an invisible panoply which, as Reparata had foreseen, screened her from all thoughts of harm or earthly temptation; she looked so beautiful and pure, that Hippolytus felt an intense admiration for virtue arise in his heart, and thought, if ever she became his, how noble and great would he strive to be; how easy he would find it to become a hero by the side of Flora. His manner, imbued with this feeling, grew reserved and respectful: he conducted his friends to the foot of the Aventine Hill. There they parted, Laurentius and Flora turning towards their own home, leaving Concordia with Hippolytus. They thanked him warmly for the assistance he had rendered them in the execution of their self-imposed task, which they simply stated had been happily accomplished.

"I am happy to hear you have had that satisfaction," he replied; "if ever it be in my power to render you any service, command me. I count upon Laurentius for calling upon me without fail."

They then exchanged an affectionate farewell with their old nurse Concordia, asking her to come and spend a day with them whenever she got a holiday.

"Thank you, my dear young masters," she replied; "how happy I am to have such dear good foster children!"

"I hope I have a share in that compliment, nurse!"

chimed in Hippolytus, playfully; "and now, farewell, dear friends, Concordia will give a good account of her mission to my father."

A glance from the faithful domestic testified as to the prudence with which she would speak of what she had witnessed, and she respectfully fell back, following the young soldier, who walked on, thoughtful and happy. His sensations were like those of one who, having borne a load of flowers, feels impregnated with the perfume even when they have passed away. He felt that the passing interview of that day had not left him as it found him: and that, if ever he obtained Flora's hand, she would work a change in his nature, she would exalt him, raising him to her standard.

Go thy way, noble youth! that boy-worship thou hast vowed to a fair girl, that sentiment, deeper still, which lies in thy breast as it has throbbed in the heart of every son of Adam, that affection has not been given to thee in vain! it will lead thee upwards, higher than all thy hopes! The union thou dreamest of may never be, but another will be revealed to thee, more precious by far. It is not on earth that thy destiny will be joined to Flora's, but she will unfold to thee a world thou knowest not of! a kingdom of glory, where she has chosen to enter undefiled, where thou wilt precede her, and where, when her arduous career is run, she will come to sit at the feet of her Lord, thy Master and hers, and thou wilt welcome her to her heavenly home, a Martyr Bride.

## CHAPTER XVII.

"BUT why now, my child? we can go to-morrow evening with the faithful."

"Mother! I cannot wait. You have accustomed me whenever I was in trouble, to go and pray on the tomb of Cecilia, who always comforts me. May I go to her now?"

"I will take you there, my child, if you so much wish it."

"Thank you, mother, I shall then call Reparata."

She returned shortly after with her young friend, who was a welcome sharer in all Flora's pastimes and pursuits. The latter had many companions, with whom she exercised in secret the practices of the Christian religion, but she was linked to Reparata by the ties of hospitality, and that friendship which always springs up between those who have known each other in days of sorrow. Flora, still mourning for the loss of Martina, had found in the young Greek the sympathy she required, and an affection which cured the anguish of her bereavement.

Oh, the blessedness of sincerity and trustfulness which exist in early youth, never perhaps to be found again! One of the reasons why we all love children, and cling to the memory of our own early days, is that in those hearts, as once in ours, there lives the first freshness of perfect truth. A child's soul is a fair garden, unvisited as yet by the spoiler; a world in itself, just issued from the hands of the Creator, on which He has gazed, and pronounced it good. Each age has its gift! There are the wisdom of gray hairs, the vigour of manhood, the intellectual joys of a riper age, but over these the breath of the world has passed, and it is a destroyer which leaves nothing as it found; innocent hopes cannot survive its blasting influence; the fountain of innate poetry dries up at its approach; the flowers of fancy, reared by an imaginative mind, fade away under its withering scorn, and a dreary desert arises, with nothing but a deceitful mirage to take the place of what was good and true!

Siona thought of these things as she laid her hand on her daughter's brow, ruffled by thoughts and cares beyond her years, but bearing also traces of calm self-control, and she resolved that, as much as it lay in her power, that girl's trustfulness should never be deceived. They were just crossing the threshold to go out, when they were accosted by a tall graceful girl, somewhat older than Flora, and followed by a female slave. Both mother and daughter greeted her with affection, and were about to re-enter the house with her, but she said she would prefer accompanying them, and dismissed her attendant.

"We are going far," observed Siona, "perhaps too far for you,—to the catacomb of Pope Calixtus."

"Oh, I am glad to hear it, it is so long since Flora

and I have been together to honour the tomb of our dear friend and teacher Cecilia."

" I am so pleased that you should join us," continued Flora, passing her arm within that of her old friend. " I have so much to tell you, and we have hardly had any time to talk since I came home."

Lucia was the eldest of those blessed little ones, brought up under Cecilia's care, and taught by her in their infancy lessons to which they proved hereafter, oh how faithfully true! She had passed from the holy martyr's school to the pious care of her mother, who concentrated in this child the pride of a noble house, and clung to her, perhaps, with too human a love. The girl's appearance bespoke at once the patrician race from which she sprang. Her refined features were striking, less from any singular beauty than from a certain loftiness of expression, which would have degenerated into haughtiness, had she been a Pagan; her face had that regularity of contour so peculiarly Roman which has remained a characteristic down to the present day, so much so, that sculptors declare it impossible to find a Roman woman in whom there is not some beautiful feature worthy of serving as a model. Endowed with fortune, Lucia had persuaded her mother to allow her to dispose of a great share of her wealth in favour of the Christian poor, and the days of that girl were filled with good deeds. She had had many suitors to her hand, but most of them understood, from her coldness, they were not welcome, and if any ventured further, pleading their cause in open terms, the disdain which curled her lip revealed an innate pride in which she forebore to indulge. Accustomed to take, in her own household, the place of her mother, whose delicate state of health confined her almost continually to her couch, Lucia had grown into a woman, while yet a girl; she had more of that dignified manner which commands respect and admiration than of the winning attractiveness of girlhood.

All around her loved her; her younger friends looked up to her for advice and protection, her companions in age all tacitly acknowledged her superiority, and were ruled by her; her very mother leaned on her with a proud, loving confidence, and Lucia would sometimes express the fear that her own life was too happy. There is a tide, however, in the stream of human existence, and it set in for the young girl.

Providence sheltered her from the dangers she would have encountered, had her life glided smoothly on; her gifted mind was such as would have secured to her the world's applause; she was withdrawn from its influence by having to attend on her parent, during a long and painful illness. The sick room and daily watchings were wholesome restraints for the high-spirited girl, and the energetic mind found scope for its moral strength in the discipline of self-denial. Lucia had bowed to the will of her Heavenly Father, and understood that what He willed was for her good.

She responded to the confidence with which Flora clung to her, and, looking at her with something of that protecting affection which was her wont, said: " I know you too well, of old, not to see by your face that you have some trouble on your mind. How did you fare in Liguria? Your voyage back was, I hear, a dangerous one."

"Yes, indeed!" interposed Siona, "I thought we should never have reached land again. Yet all things work together for the good of those who love God! We, Christians, rejoiced in the very fearfulness of the storm, for my husband, seeing how God heard our prayers, has respected our religion ever since."

"You were then many Christians?"

"No! only our family, besides two noble Greek strangers who will favour us by abiding under our roof for some months in Rome. Allow me to introduce to you Reparata, who has proved a kind friend to Flora."

Lucia exchanged a cordial greeting with the stranger, and said playfully, "I hope you have not stolen my place, I mean as Flora's friend? I have known her every thought since we were five years old."

"And look at her now," replied Reparata smiling; "she has loads of secrets to tell you. Do walk on together, while I speak with my noble hostess."

She fell back a few steps with Siona.

"Well! I must tell you," began Flora at once to her companion, "that I am not going simply to honour the tomb and memory of Cecilia, but to seek light and grace."

"There you are, just as of old, always in perplexities. Wait, before you tell me, I must take you to the cave inhabited by Hippolytus, we are close to it now. He inquired so often about you while you were away."

"Hippolytus!" repeated Flora, very much astonished.

"Surely you must remember him. I told you in my letter that he who had sought Martina in marriage was now a fervent Christian, living on the Appian Way to be near the Catacombs."

"Oh yes! I shall be very glad to see him; I had forgotten, because I am so anxious about something that happened yesterday."

She then told her friend about her visit to the Mamertine prison and its results.

She was very desirous for Icilius to receive sufficient instruction, so as to be baptized before his execution, if possible, but she foresaw insuperable obstacles in the way, and feared, lest by disclosing the Christian religion to him too prematurely, she had increased his responsibility.

"I do not see," replied Lucia, "what cause you have for self-reproach; are we not always advised to do good when we can, either by word or example, and you have certainly aroused the better nature of Icilius, and made him long for God. By informing a priest, you may obtain that a deacon be sent to him to finish the good work you have begun. Thus he will be prepared to meet death. Poor youth! it seems hard that he should be condemned for an act which was committed when his reason was disturbed. God at least will not punish him; He is the more merciful when men are unjust."

"I do not think," resumed Flora, "the Emperor will suffer him to die; his reign has been one of clemency and justice, and if his life has been spared on the occasion of Icilius' mad attempt, may it not be that the Almighty God has willed to reward visibly one who spared the flock of Christ ?"

"If his good heart were appealed to, we might hope! but truth seldom reaches the ear of kings. Gordianus will be told that Icilius' attempt was the consequence of previous guilt, and thereby they would cast a stain on poor Volumnia. Oh, paganism is so blind and cruel; like its own god, Saturn, devouring his children."

"Oh that I could approach our sovereign," exclaimed Flora.

"You who are so bashful! Why, what would you do if you could approach Gordianus ?"

"I should feel courage in presence of the good Emperor, who has inherited the wisdom of Augustus and the virtues of Trajan, the sight of him would kindle me up, and I should kneel to him, and ask for the life of my friend Volumnia, whose innocence I would attest, and" . . .

"You! you never could! Besides, why should we talk of what can never happen? Let us keep to the present! We must turn up this side path which leads to the cave of Hippolytus; I shall go on and tell him you are coming; will you ask your mother to follow ?"

There was a huge mausoleum on the left side, raised to the memory of a conqueror, who had triumphed in the East, and whose tomb bore witness to the riches accumulated in the spoils of victory. The pyramid, divided into three gradations, rested on a base of granite, bearing a sphinx at each angle; each of the blocks of different marble showed fine bas-reliefs, some of which, even now that the hand of time has destroyed the edifice, excite the admiration of the antiquarian as he sees these relics of the past, buried in the dust. The ladies passed under the wall, formed by this gigantic tomb, and soon trod the soft grass, so long and flexible that their footsteps marked a path in it as they walked. There is, in all Roman soil, a surface of light dry earth, so pure that if cast on a white toga, the garment would remain unsullied by the contact. It is this which, when moistened, forms the Roman cement whose solidity is hardly inferior to that of stone itself. Extremely useful at all times, it was indispensable in those days when the Romans gloried quite as much in the durability of their edifices as in their victories abroad. Excavations for this earth were sometimes carried to such an extent, that long vaulted galleries were formed from cavern to cavern, as the workmen extended their labours. From this circumstance an erroneous idea has arisen, which a short survey suffices to eradicate : it has been supposed that the Catacombs might have been excavated for the same purpose, and consequently not be the work of the primitive Christians, but a convincing proof of the incorrectness of this statement is, that this earth was only found at the surface, whereas the Catacombs are hewn out of the granitic tufa underlying the soil, and the marks of the pick-axe which have left traces in the vaults, bear witness to the hard labour of the *fossores*, to the daily, solitary toil of those who, circumscribed within those narrow walls, worked out a tomb for the martyrs of the Lord! There is a vast difference between the dormitories of the dead, as the Christians loved to call them, and the spacious, roomy galleries cut into that light soil which required arches to support them. It was towards one of these *arenaria*, rather smaller than the rest, and whose orifice was somewhat concealed by the long grass, that Lucia directed her steps. She stopped, uttering a salutation in a loud voice, which was answered from within; she made a sign to her companions to follow, and then went on, stopping again at the entrance to an underground passage, which sloped downwards. Here she struck the ground with a stone three times, then proceeded to walk down cautiously. She had not gone more than a few steps further, when the salutation they had previously heard was repeated, and a man, followed by two little children, came to meet them. The latter recognised Flora, and clung to her, repeating her name with delight, but it was so dark she could not see them: "Let us go on," said Lucia, "to that part of your cavern, good Hippolytus, where we can have light, for I bring you many friends."

"My eyes, accustomed to the darkness, distinguish them already," he replied; "let me guide you, Flora," and he took her hand. "The last time we met," he continued, "I told you that men should only hear of Hippolytus as of one already dead, have I not kept my word?"

He stood under an orifice in the vault which let in light and air from above; a ray of sun had penetrated, and fell on his emaciated features, still bearing the stamp of patrician birth; his head was bald, not from age, but from the inclemency of the weather, and the insufficient repose he took on the hard rock, thereby wasting away prematurely his once vigorous frame; his hands, formerly soft and perfumed, were callous to the touch, as Flora found, and the change wrought in him was so great, that she could hardly speak, from the depth of her emotion. The children roused her from her silent astonishment, embracing and caressing her.

"What! you here!" she cried, "Eone and Maia, how is this?"

"We came to see our uncle," they said, "our dear good uncle Hippolytus: our mother sent us."

"What then!" inquired Siona of Hippolytus, "does Paulina know?"

"Oh, yes, she knows about her brother the philosopher, as they call me, supposing I have imitated Diogenes, and thrown away the cup of earthly joys, but ah! they little know all I have found instead. The dear children like their ugly old uncle, with the dirty beard. I caress them and encourage their innocent prattle, for I well know how the Master loved such as these. Soon I shall endeavour to give them more substantial food. From what I hear, they have already derived much benefit from their stay in Liguria, thanks to God and you!"

"We spent indeed a peaceful, blessed time there: faith is undisturbed and no corruption of civilization has as yet reached those shores. Yet Paulina never penetrated the mystery of our secret meetings, I am a little afraid of her; she is good and well-disposed, but I fear of a weak character."

"Is not that the case with all of us, till the Strengthener and Great Consoler take possession of our poor hearts? What are we of ourselves, but withered branches detached from the Tree of Life!" He raised his hand to the wall where hung, from a nail, a broken palm branch; a sign full of meaning to all Christians, but which struck Flora as being connected with a dim memory of the past: "You do not recognise it," he said to her, "it is a fragment of that which Martina bore with her to her last triumph, and which I asked you to restore to me, hallowed by her contact; it is the sign whereby she and I shall know each other when we meet above!"

A solemn silence fell on them all: he spoke calmly, not as mortals do of one they have loved and lost, but as of a blessed death which had been to him the opening to a new life.

"I have often inquired for you, Flora," he continued, "often desired your return, for you know my conversion is your work, and that of your slave Claudius. What has become of him?"

"He left us," replied Siona, "to return to his country and friends, but if the heart speaks true, methinks we shall see him again. Who knows whether Britain will be to him in his old age the Alma Mater of his early love? I hope for his sake his wife and children may have survived the long separation; yet I trust he will pine for Rome again."

"And your husband, lady Siona, my old friend Florentius who used to preach philosophy to me? how differently I could preach to him now!"

"His hour is not yet come: pray for him!" she replied.

"And have you come on purpose to see me, noble ladies? the hermit of the cave is but little used to such honour."

"We are on our way to the Catacombs, and Lucia wished to show us your habitation; she said you had often expressed a wish to see Flora."

"I have!" he answered, "and, thank God, I see her again, pure and good as when her childish features first taught me what virtue was like. I wished to show you, maiden, the barren home and dreary palace chosen by the late Sybarite of Rome. Who among my former companions would believe that I bathe with tears of joy the stony couch on which I take each night a few hours of rest, interrupted by prayer? The poor of the wayside are my friends, the Catacombs my constant resort. My conversion was the first fruit of a saint's martyrdom, and thus I love to consider myself as a victim set apart for a sacrifice. My happiness does not end here. I have been called to the office of deacon, and I can look forward to the day when, attaining to the plenitude of the priesthood, I shall be allowed to offer the Divine Mysteries, and draw others to the knowledge of eternal truth. It is a sufficiently great privilege that I am allowed to baptize!"

"Thank God!" they all exclaimed, but Flora's thanksgiving was not spoken in words; with clasped hands, she raised her eloquent eyes to the speaker's face, and her cheeks were tinged with the flush of subdued joy. He looked at her surprised. Just then the little children proposed to the visitors to go farther within and see more of the hermitage. Lucia took them away, leaving Hippolytus to speak more at his ease with the ladies. He observed to Siona: "If I am to judge by your daughter's countenance, you have something very interesting to communicate to me".

"Yes! we have much to tell and to ask of you. I know what is uppermost in Flora's mind, but let me present my petition first. Will you allow me to send my adopted son, Laurentius, to you?"

"I remember him as a frail, interesting child, too delicate to live, at least so I thought; I am glad to hear he has grown up."

"He has, *by* God's help, and *for* God. Called like you to be a special servant of the Most High, will you accept him for your scholar?"

"Joyfully. What next?"

"Perhaps you live too remote from human society to have learned what has been the last few days the talk of every Roman, the attempt against our good Emperor's life."

"The brethren whose charity provides me with food brought me that news, but Providence watched over him and saved him."

"Do you know who was the assassin?" asked Siona.

"No!"

She whispered: "Poor Icilius," at which he was deeply pained.

She explained to him, as rapidly as she could, all the circumstances we are acquainted with.

"And now," said Flora, "that you have the power to baptize, perhaps God destines you to finish what my brother and I have begun for Icilius. Will you undertake to refer all my mother has told you to a higher authority, for I am so troubled and confused, I hardly know whether I have acted right or wrong in speaking of religion to Icilius?"

"A cloud sometimes comes over our intellect, lest vain glory should swallow up the merits of our good deeds; yet, do not fear, Flora, you undertook this for the sake of your Heavenly Father, and He will reward you. But how can I reach the poor youth?"

"I know not," replied Siona. "I obtained permission for my children with some difficulty from the governor of the Mamertine, but I dare not apply again."

"Well! let us unite in prayer to this effect! Perhaps when the time of poor Icilius' execution draws near, something of the strict custody may be relaxed. I shall wait, and, at the same time, enquire and profit by the first moment I can see him. To those who have sorrowed as I have Providence grants a mysterious compensation, the gift of consoling others in their turn. I wish I could do something for you, Flora, to repay you for the faithful, strong, unremitting devotion you bore Martina to the end. When we had both of us seen her laid in that tomb, which, like that of her Master, will be one day glorious, I felt she had left me a bright example to follow, and when my pagan heart grew chastened by Christian feelings, I longed to take up every good work she had begun. I felt as if you, more than others, had an especial claim to my prayers, and to my poor services such as they may be."

"Most willingly do I accept the proffered aid; in many circumstances I cannot seek advice from my father. I have lost Claudius, who was far more teacher than slave to me. Do *you* then be my mother's friend and mine."

"Let us help each other," he replied, "in the path those great ones have trod before us; let us remember how short the combat and how great the reward. It was you, Flora, taught me my first Christian prayer."

"Was it?"

"Yes. I followed the Christians on the Appian Way, and, not being able to discover where they assembled, I took refuge here, and like Him, Who, falling into an agony at Gethsemani, prayed the longer, I fell prostrate on the ground, repeating the whole night through that prayer I had learned from you. When I went forth, the great trial was over, and my soul felt the effects of that baptism of blood which Martina had perhaps offered up for me. But I ought not with you, her companion and her friend, to dwell upon these sad memories. To me they are a stimulus; pardon me for forgetting the respect due to a sorrow so persisting as yours. Farewell, Flora, if ever any circumstance arise in which you wish to call upon me for help, remember that it will be the joy of my solitude to become to you what you were to Martina, a friend in life and a consoler in death."

Flora had restrained her feelings so long, that she now could bear up no longer, and wept bitterly. Hippolytus, alarmed at the emotion he himself had called forth, summoned his nephew and niece to divert her thoughts, and requested her mother to take her out into the open air.

## CHAPTER XVIII.

THE first breath of spring is again wafted over the Latian campagna, leaving impressed on the air the perfume of the climes through which it has passed; it plays in the gentle undulations of the breeze, creating sounds of strange harmony, which seem to the meditative mind to bring messages from another world. It touches the old withered trees with the new creating kiss of a mother's love, and invigorating youth is restored to them; it glides over the sterile naked fields, and they are reclothed in pristine beauty. It is now hushed, now refreshing, now soothing to the overworked mind of the public man who has left the haunts of cities, to come and take refuge in solitude : Nature and her charms bring excitement to the young, and to the old, repose.

On one of the Latian hills, first cradle of the Roman people, where the name of Æneas is, to this very day, often quoted by common labourers, as if the Trojan hero, by landing on those shores, had imparted something of his greatness to the very soil; in the vicinity of Alba the Long, founded by Anchises' son, lie mouldering in the dust of centuries, the bones of young Astyanax, the hope of Troy. History has often recorded such contrasts, showing us nations and heroes finding, after a long interval, their cradle and their grave, side by side. There is a lake known in the history of the Republic as having been designated by the Delphic oracle as a gauge of the fortunes of Rome, for, according as it overflowed its banks or not, victory or defeat would ensue to the empire. It lies under the shade of the Alban hill, which was consecrated by Tarquin the Ancient to Latial Jove, and which became the centre of the Latin league conspiring against the Eternal City. In no other district of the Roman campagna is there to be found such richness of vegetation. The hills terminating so abruptly are striking in their magnificent primæval roughness, as if the Fiat which created them had been breathed over them but of late: most of them are extinct volcanoes which have imparted great fertility to the soil. The trees are of enormous size, their leafy shelter being as widespread and secure as a tent; the forests are dense and luxuriantly cool. Many of Rome's statesmen delighted in their shade. It was here Pompey loved to play the gardener, and preside over the building of his villa, while his rival's hatred pursued him. Strange retribution! when Cæsar was murdered in the senate house, he fell at the foot of Pompey's statue; the slain triumvir seemed to rise from his grave at that hour " in all the austere form of sacred majesty ".

When he had passed away, and the scythe of time had mowed down the flowers that he loved, and the laurels he had planted, there came one to Alba whose name history has handed down to us with execration. Perhaps the hatred he met with, fit reward of his evil deeds, made him fear to consort with his fellow-men, for he resolved to build to himself a magnificent solitude, and chose the borders of the Alban lake where Pompey had dwelt. The magnificent ruins, enriched with choice sculptures, show that Domitian had called round him all the talent of the empire, to embellish his villa at Alba. Yet here, as in most of the works of Imperial Rome, beauty pourtrayed itself on a colossal scale; the crypto-porticoes were temples, in each of which dwelt giant gods. The Emperor Pontiff was very devout to his heathen divinities, fit types of his own wickedness, and there still exists a circular temple in which he offered sacrifices to Minerva. But the most remarkable feature of the palace of the Cæsars, is a series of hanging gardens, several miles in length, consisting of three distinct galleries: of these, the highest borders the lake, being secured from any possible deviation in the soil, and supported by constructions similar to those we admire on the old Roman roads. These again served as walls to the second gallery, which was less extensive, and opened out on the grounds. The third, situated on the declivity of the hill, was the most pleasant, as the last rays of the setting sun lingered there; it was divided into several porticoes, before each of which the trees had been cut away, so as to leave an empty space for the eye to rest upon the view of distant Rome. At the hour we are describing, it was morning, the sun shone only in the east, and the deep shade of the leafy bowers gave a certain solemnity to the scene; the songsters of the grove had scarcely yet awakened to harmony, and the paths of the forest, moist with the heavy dew of the night, were yet untrodden, when two persons entered the lower gallery, the one leaning on the other for support, and both walking slowly. One was aged, the other youthful, but the latter had none of the elasticity of agile years; care sat on his young brow, and he moved with pain. The elder man seemed to be the stronger of the two; endowed with a vigorous constitution and an intellectual mind, he was serious, but free from that weight of anxiety which was visible in his companion's countenance. The youth was evidently not his son, for the look he cast on him from time to time was one of affectionate respect. There was much love between them; but, gentle as was the younger one's manner, there was about him that involuntary haughtiness, unavoidable in those who have learned to command early; his features were delicate, yet strongly marked with the characteristic outlines of Trajan. He was suffering from a wound in the leg, and, after some painful efforts to walk, he flung both his arms round his guide, saying in a faint voice: "Good Misitheus, I can try no longer!"

The man held him fast, to prevent his falling, then lifted him up kindly, gently, as a mother would have done, conveying him to one of the porticoes where cushioned seats awaited him: "My lord and gracious master must recline for some time yet; we had miscalculated your strength".

"I am always strong when I lean on you, dear friend and minister; the gods treated me kindly when they placed my inexperienced youth in your charge."

"Great Augustus! it has been an easy task to direct such a mind as yours. Would that I could as surely have shielded your sacred person from harm."

"Oh, it is only a scratch! I am ashamed of bearing it so ill. An Emperor that is going to the wars ought to have more courage."

"My noble master, you make too light of it, and by this you endeavour to palliate the crime that had well-nigh plunged the Roman empire into mourning. Oh, how the people love you! how great has been their affliction!"

"Well! as the gods have spared our life, we must spare that of the poor maniac. But have you examined why the unfortunate youth took refuge in Vesta's temple? We are Sovereign Pontiff, and if it be sweet to pardon our own wrongs, it would be impious to leave unpunished an offence against the gods."

"There is only a suspicion in the case, Augustus, but that has fallen on the Vestal Volumnia."

"I grieve to hear it, for it was the first painful act of my pontificate to separate that maiden from her affianced husband. She showed such virtue on that occasion; her calmness and resignation were surprising. I grieve to hear she has given rise to any suspicion." He leaned his head on his hand, sighed heavily, then, looking up at his minister, said inquiringly: "She must be put to the test, good Misitheus, for a Vestal may not be suspected".

"Augustus, I have myself examined Volumnia, I have spoken with her at full length: my experience is that of one who knows human nature. The girl is pure as the driven snow."

"Then the gods will attest her innocence, she must bear in her hands a sieve full of water from the Tiber."

The minister, wiser than his young charge, was forced to smile; but the young Emperor had spoken with such simplicity of conviction, he would not contradict him, and changed the subject.

"My beloved Sovereign, you are now no longer my pupil. The people whose hearts are yours, wish to see the name of Gordianus descend to one born of you. It is time you should think of forming some alliance which may consolidate your throne, and ensure your domestic happiness."

Gordianus did not answer for a while; he seemed not to attach any importance to his minister's words, but turned them off playfully.

"Do you think me, then, very unsteady? Why do you want to settle me down?"

"Nay, my lord Emperor. I have watched over you with the reverence of a subject, guarding a precious treasure for the welfare of Rome, with the love of a father clinging to the last scion of a noble house. I can bear witness to your blameless life and noble virtues; but remember, great prince, you belong not to yourself, but to Rome."

"Well, suppose I love Rome so much, that I will love her alone, nor share my allegiance with any one."

"Seriously speaking, may I ask whether you have thought already on the subject?"

"Well, to speak the truth, when I made my sacrifice the other day at the temple, you know how unfavourable the prognostics were; I was more impressed by them than I chose to appear; the augurs spoke of an impending danger, and I feel it is at hand! An interior spirit whispers to me that my days are numbered, and my life will be short."

He spoke calmly, as the young often do when they allude to death; that death which causes the aged such a pang; as if the great journey were easier to those whose bark has just been launched, and glides on swiftly, its sails filled by the breezes of hope, while golden clouds at the horizon bid it speed on in its bright track, to realms of promise beyond.

"My beloved Sovereign," said the minister tenderly, "why do you speak thus to me, whose years already incline me to the tomb?"

"Yet I shall precede you, Misitheus, or follow you very closely. The spirits of the Gordians beckon to me from the Elysian fields; even now methinks I hear them, and shall join them soon."

A dead silence fell on them both. The youth looked out on the panorama before him, over which the sun had risen rapidly. The shadows of the trees were very long, and in their interstices were glancing golden rays, as if lambent light played round the heads of the Emperor and his minister.

The latter observed the blushing tints of the morning sun rest on the pale features of Gordianus. "A happy omen," he said, "great Augustus, the sun of glory courts you."

"We will go to meet it in the Eastern wars, when I recover, and see what fate awaits me there. Meanwhile, I was reading another page in the skies."

"Where, my Sovereign?"

"See how the leaves, dancing in the air, trace characters against the blue firmament, like unto the sentences of a volume written in the skies. Observe," he continued, following with his finger the imaginary letters, "how clear they are—there they sketch images; here they are dark and closely written, like the pages of a book. Now, look beyond—there is a rent in the foliage, and it forms a fanciful profile against the golden sky. Methinks I recognise there the features of my beautiful mother. How I loved her—that dear lost one! How the fleecy clouds wave; even as the spotless robe she wore, which has lingered in my childish memory, indelibly connected with her form and the tones of her sweet voice! How good were her lessons! how sacred her farewell! How, when my lips pressed her cold hand, already stiffened in the embrace of death, she bid me be worthy of my father and of the memory of the great Trajan!" . . . He stopped speaking, as if the scene were passing before him now; he bowed his head, oppressed with the memory he had evoked.

"And well and nobly," continued the minister, "have you fulfilled the behest of the parent you regret; Rome has found you worthy of her."

Gordianus looked up again: "See there," he continued,

"the tiny leaves are quivering; they form a page; it is short, but the characters are closely put together. Perhaps it is the history of my reign, that I see written there; the story of my life, which must be well filled because its span will be short. Misitheus, I hope thou mayest remain near me to the end."

The grateful minister pressed affectionately the delicate young hand which the boy-Emperor extended to him; and then raising him from his reclining position: "You are suffering," he said, "more from the effects of seclusion than from illness. Your spirits have been depressed by long confinement to a sick chamber, and this morning's walk, which I hoped would have revived you, has saddened you still more. But I must not let you return to your couch within doors. Come, Augustus, I shall order the slaves to bring hither your *lettiga*, they will carry you about, that you may breathe freely the mountain air."

"I do hate to be thus borne," exclaimed Gordianus, "it is so unmanly, yet I cannot walk. At least, let no escort come round us, good Misitheus; for I do not wish to be seen reclining like a sick girl. An Emperor ought to die standing."

He submitted, however, to stretch himself in the *lettiga*, which was brought up by attendants, and as they bore him out of the dark avenue, he seemed to revive. They passed on to the very borders of the lake, and he sat up to gaze on its blue waters, so mirror-like and undisturbed in the early morning.

"How calm!" he observed to the minister, who

walked by his side, "and yet, 'tis said that a volcano raged there once, and those clear sparkling waters once hissed with burning fires. How time changes all things!"

"'Tis the history of many a heart," replied the other smiling; "how many have, in early youth, felt the interior working of ambition, the aspiring flame of genius, the turmoil of human passions, which make the soul overflow; and then has come the soothing influence of age; the tears of a later sorrow have quenched the living fires. Disappointment and bitterness, wounded pride, forsaken love, and sad experience have flowed down into the crater, like so many streamlets from the hill-side, and the volcano has been extinguished. Happy he, who standing on the borders of the crystal lake, can say: 'Thus passed my life! There may be much below, but all is forgotten now, for the calm and peace of age has filled the void!' And you, my Sovereign, may the course of your career be more uniform! may the streamlets descend into a heart already pure, and, when you have filled the same number of years as I, and look back, you will feel what a boon it is to have passed your youth in innocence."

Gordianus raised his eyes to the heavens where he had said that morning he could read his early death, shook his head, and then endeavoured to speak more cheerfully.

"I will visit the Emissarium, and then go down to the Nymphæum."

They bore him on among the rocks thrown up by volcanic eruptions, which had survived the lapse of centuries: there, in conformity with the oracle which declared to the Romans they could not take the town of Veii till the waters of the Alban lake should have been drained off towards the sea, the Sovereign People had decreed a work so stupendous, that its very ruins excite the wonder of all beholder to this day. Titus Livius declares this marvellous construction to have been terminated in one year, and this short space of time is no less a marvel. The canal was cut through grey granite, often interrupted by masses of lava; it was 7,500 feet long, 6 feet high, and $4\tfrac{1}{2}$ feet wide. This space admitted only of four workmen at a time; and it seems impossible to reconcile this small number of labourers with the short time allotted to them, but a discovery has been made which explains away the difficulty. Vertical wells have been found which, situated at regular intervals, were calculated to sub-divide the work, and, at the same time, served as an exit for those who worked within, enabling them to throw out and carry away stones and rubbish. These wells were situated at the distance of 120 feet from each other; they were 62 in number, as we can easily calculate by what remains. Strokes of the chisel about an inch deep, are plainly discernible in the granite. We can calculate that each man cutting a foot deep of stone per day, and each well being 200 feet deep, it must have required 200 days to open the 62 wells, and bring them to the level of the Emissarium or canal. We must add 120 days more for the space comprised between them, which, giving a total of 320 days, proves the veracity of Livy, who gives the year 356, A.U.C., as having witnessed the commencement of this work, and the year 357 its completion. At a later period, the declivity given to the waters, having been found too rapid, it was raised by means of a solid construction for the length of 400 feet. Later again, at the opening of the canal, a vaulted chamber was built in solid quadrilateral blocks of grey granite, so as to resist the first impetus, and break the rush of the water, which afterwards passed into the canal.

The young Emperor left his couch, and leaning on his much-loved minister, proceeded to examine anew a construction which he knew well, but which was replete with interest to his active enquiring mind. "And I too," he said, after terminating his inspection, "would fain leave behind me something by which I may be remembered. Good Misitheus, inspire me with the thought of some great public edifice, by which I may benefit my country, so that, when others come, treading the soil I have trod, they may admire, even as I do here, and say: 'This was the work of Gordian!'"

The minister folded his arms, reflected a little in silence, then, placing his hand on the breast of his royal pupil, with a gesture of paternal fondness, he said solemnly:—

"It is here, my beloved Sovereign, in your own heart, that you will find your noblest victory and your greatest achievement. You can do no greater work for Rome than to show her the example of great virtues. If you cultivate the precocious wisdom with which you are gifted; if you remain pure in the midst of corruption; modest, while occupying the first throne in the world; clement and just, while wielding the sceptre of universal dominion, then, verily, will Trajan live again in Gordian, and your name and your glory will lie enshrined in the memory of your people."

The young Emperor bowed his head under the solemn words: "I hope you have spoken prophetically, my indulgent friend; if there has been anything good in my past life, it has been owing to your wise advice. Now, will you point out to the slaves the path that leads to the Nymphæum? I have never been there."

Again they swung him on their shoulders, and began to descend into what once had been the crater of a volcano. Willow trees, which had grown to a prodigious size, throve well in the moist soil, and their branches, which were so long as almost to touch the ground, brushed Gordian's face as he was carried under them. The servants would have lopped them off, and cleared the road, but the young Cesar forbade them doing so. "It is so pleasant," he said, "to forget I am an Emperor, and to play with the unruly trees, which have not sworn allegiance to me; let them be!"

On he went, enjoying the sight of that luxuriant vegetation, uncontrolled by the hand of man; the birds seemed to his delighted ear to sing a carol to liberty, and the first bright coloured insects of spring came buzzing round Gordian, as if courting him in their very vagrancy. After a walk of a short mile, the party came to a halt; they had reached the water's edge, and found themselves in a delightful enclosure, where the pink oleander bloomed, and orange trees, thickly planted, diffused a fragrant odour. A natural grotto had been transformed by the care of the Emperor Domitian into a beautiful Nymphæum, whose walls, covered over with marble, added the beauty of art to the picturesque of nature. The original structure had not been altered, and was consequently irregular; the vaulted part formed a recess divided off by columns; the lower, which was sunk beneath the level of the soil, received the waters which came in eddying from a stream beyond, and formed a miniature lake, in which was reflected, as in a mirror, the panorama of the green hills around. The young Emperor lingered over this scene of complete repose; he looked up at Mons Albanus, the giant of the chain of the Apennines that lay near; he thought of the scenes of Roman history, in which it had acted so prominent a part, and now, its shadow fell upon those waters, as an old warrior, weary with glory, seeks in the shades of his native valley forgetfulness and content.

"My Sovereign is very thoughtful to-day," observed the minister.

"I am listening to the rippling of the waters, Misitheus, the rushing sound of the wind in the leaves is full of music. How eloquent is the silence of nature, it is the voice of our Great Mother! Yet I am not sad now, as I was this morning. To hear of our subjects' woes is the greatest pain a Cæsar can know, and the image of that Vestal girl haunts me. I hope sincerely, though, that she may be found innocent; the gods will protect her, and prove her virtue, when she passes through her trial."

"I am not so sanguine, Augustus; but let us not dwell on this sad subject. Are you inclined to return homewards?"

"No. I have a strange fancy for wandering this morning. I have never been so far as Diana's wood. Good Misitheus, can you spare another hour from business, and go with me thus far?"

"And neglected despatches, my royal master, and messages from Rome, perhaps?"

"They can wait a little longer. Come, it is our holiday! When I recover, you shall see what a man of business I will become."

The winning gracefulness with which the request was spoken, made the old man smile his consent; he put his hand in the Emperor's, and walked on by the side of his lettiga, under the shady avenues once more, all along the border of the lake, till they got quite beyond it. Farther on the pathway led through the beautiful valley, to which the Latin people gave a name of peace it preserved during centuries: the Vallis Aurea separated the promontory of Aricia from the territory of Alba the Long. They ascended the hill, and stopped to rest. The scene which lay outstretched before them was that which we have described in the beginning of our story; save that now, the morning sun, almost reaching the hour of noon, flooded the widespread plain in a brilliant atmosphere of dazzling light. The green fields were variegated with a long tissue of gold colour, as the proud buttercups raised their heads, waving their shining corollas above the grass; in contrast with these, the ripening corn-fields were visible beyond. There was no uniform monotony in all that scene, though it lay so hushed and tranquil in the sun; for, where the forest ended, other groves began, of a brighter and more tender green. The very sea which bounded the horizon was not blue or grey, as is its wont, but its hue varied, as there it sparkled under the sun, here it was darkened by a cloud passing over it, there again a long bright yellow stripe showed the course of the vigorous Tiber, as it rolled on in solitary majesty, unmingled with the waves through which it flowed, like a great destiny which passes through the tumult of ordinary life unheeded and alone.

The Emperor's party had now reached the temple of Diana Aricina, the tutelar divinity of the neighbouring forest; she had guarded Aricia ever since the days of Porsenna, who besieged it.

"Let me alight," said Gordian, "I wish to offer a sacrifice to the goddess, she must needs protect the Imperial household, for the mother of Julius Cæsar was born here. Let the priests, guardians of the temple, be told that I am in their precincts."

The good news spread immediately through the village, up the hill, and down the valley. In a few minutes, the royal suite was surrounded by a joyful, noisy, yet respectful crowd. The goodness of the Emperor was keenly appreciated by those who had suffered from the tyranny of the last reigns, and this had secured to Gordian a deserved popularity. All the country people left their labours, donned their festive garments, and came forward, with green boughs in their hands, all joining in one cry: "*Ave Imperator!*"

He was evidently moved, and made a sign to them to come near.

"How do you know me?" he asked, "I have come among you without guards, or any signs of royalty. Few of you can have ever seen me."

"*Ave Imperator,*" repeated the crowd, "*vives in æternum!*"

"Thank you for the wish, good people, but I cannot live eternally,—on this earth at least. The gods are immortal; let us honour them. I have come to offer a sacrifice to Diana, and, while the preparations are being made, I shall withdraw to the Thermæ, which I see are near at hand."

"They offer but poor accommodation, noble Sovereign," interposed one of the most prominent personages in the group, a wealthy land-owner, "Aricia is but ill-prepared for the honour done to it this day."

Gordian smiled, and quoted a line from Horace—

> "Egressum magna me excepit Aricia Româ
> Hospitio modico."

"Is that what you are alluding to, my friend?" he continued. "Yet the kind greeting of these good people is so welcome to us, that we exchange willingly the luxury of our palace, on the hill at Alba, for an hour's rest at Aricia. Give us your name. Our nomenclator* is a stranger here."

"My name is Florentius, and I kneel in homage to the divine Gordian. I am from Rome, and I recognised on the road the features of our idolized Sovereign; it was I who had the honour of announcing your arrival amongst us."

"Thanks, Florentius; then, will you lead us to the Thermæ? I am ashamed to acknowledge," he added, in a low voice, "that I cannot bear much fatigue since my late indisposition, and I need very much the refreshment of the bath."

Gordianus made himself popular by following the dictates of his own heart, and showing his people he trusted them. As he passed on, now leaning on the arm of the proud and happy Florentius, he walked slowly, and with difficulty; shouts of joy rent the air, mingled with expressions of sorrow at the good Cæsar being so disabled.

"How pleasant it is to be loved!" exclaimed Gordian, and, turning to Misitheus: "See, I told you this would be a holiday to me!"

His attendants alone followed him to the Thermæ, and, while he rested there, preparations were made in great haste for the sacrifice which the Emperor had proposed to offer in the temple of Diana Aricina. A

---

* *Nomenclator* was the name given to a slave who, ever by his master's side, acquainted him with the names of all those he met, that he might make himself popular, in greeting them by name.

black heifer was produced, which the priests had put apart some days previously, owing to its colour rendering it a fit offering for the queen of night; a white crescent on its forehead seemed to designate it as marked more particularly for the goddess of the silver bow; youths and maidens led it, holding it with chains of flowers. The procession formed, and went to meet Gordian, as he came forth, quite refreshed, from the bath. He accepted from the priest's hands a sacerdotal garment, and took the lead, with the pious demeanour which was habitual to him. The tripods were smoking at the foot of the steps leading to the temple, and the religious rite began with the usual ceremonies. When the young Emperor, after separating from the rest, issued from the temple—where, according to custom, he had withdrawn alone, to hold mysterious commune with the gods—he found that a still greater number of loving subjects awaited him. He looked around for Florentius, who was there indeed, but not alone, for he had profited by Gordian's short absence to go and fetch his wife and daughter, together with all his slaves, who now formed a goodly retinue, bearing fruits and flowers in their hands.

"Is this your household?" asked the Emperor, with a gracious smile.

"These are my slaves, divine Augustus, who have seized hastily on the first produce of my gardens, as a rural offering to be laid at your feet."

"I accept them as first fruits due to Ceres; let them be sent to her altars in Rome. And this noble lady?"

Florentius presented Siona, who did homage to the

Cæsar, and then, taking Flora's hand in his: "This is our daughter, our beloved child, she has a petition to present to you; she wished me to do so in her name, but I told her that Gordian is as good as he is mighty, and a child of Rome may speak to him without fear."

"An Emperor is bound to hear the petitions of his subjects at all times, and I feel sure that this maiden can ask for nothing but what is right and good."

There was a slight tremulousness in his voice, and his manner was even kinder than usual, as he met the strange eyes of the girl fixed on him with that expression which we have often noticed, as if another person than he she spoke to were before her, a Being visible to herself only. She was quite calm and self-possessed, and stood for a moment recollected, as if revolving within herself what she had to say, then kneeling:—

"Have mercy, Cæsar," she implored, "on the madman who attempted your life; have mercy, in acknowledgment to that superior Power that watched over you."

"The pardon thou implorest has already been granted of our own free-will; he whom the gods had bereft of reason is more deserving of compassion than anger. Rise, daughter of Florentius, do not kneel to thy Sovereign as a culprit. I never exact, like my predecessors, the meed of adulation or idolatry."

"I must yet kneel as a suppliant, offering up another prayer. I have a friend whom I have loved as a sister from early childhood. The destiny of Volumnia the Vestal is known to many, but few know her virtues as

I do. Suspicion has fallen upon her. Most just and clement Cæsar, deign to believe in her innocence!"

"The gods must prove it."

"Spare her the trial, my Sovereign, the laws of nature will have their course; water must flow through a sieve; do not trust to such an inevitable issue the life or death of my poor friend."

"I cannot violate the laws, puella, I cannot infringe upon what wiser minds than mine have decreed. Volumnia must abide the test."

Flora was silent, but remained kneeling with her hands clasped, while her upturned eyes implored more than her words.

"This much I can grant," he said, in answer to her mute prayer, "I shall order all enquiry about this subject to be postponed for a given time; that delay I can prolong at will, and, meanwhile, every liberty shall be allowed the Vestal to plead her cause and clear herself."

She sprang to her feet with exultation, first kissing the hem of the Emperor's toga: "May a reward be conferred on thee, O Cæsar," she cried, "proportioned to the desires of thy good heart; may the remembrance of thy mercy give thee peace, and bring thee joy every day of thy life!"

She withdrew to the side of her father, who cried: "*Vivet Imperator*". The cry was taken up, and repeated a hundred times. Gordian remained standing, absorbed in thought. Florentius felt a little anxious lest Flora had dared too much; therefore, consigning her quickly to her mother, to whom he whispered it was time to retire, he drew near to the Emperor alone, and said: "May I ask the divine Augustus to forgive the over-confidence of my daughter. Unaccustomed to the manners of a court, or to intercourse with the world, she felt unabashed in the presence of one who is best known by the love he has won to himself in the hearts of his people; and she addressed our august Sovereign with the same simplicity with which she appeals to her parents."

"No homage could have proved more touching to me, good Florentius. I have but one ambition, that of becoming one day in very deed the Father of my people, if my life be spared." He paused, looked round at the crowd, then resumed: "We must now bid you farewell, and I request of you, noble Florentius, to dispose of a sum I leave to the faithful people of Aricia. Let it be spent in some way that may tend to their pleasure and advantage, in some public work which may remain to them as a memory of Gordian."

He waved his hand, promising to come back to see them again, and shouts rent the air as they had done on his arrival. The Emperor was well-nigh exhausted; he had gone through a great deal of exertion for one in his feeble state of health, and though he would have preferred not to be carried in his lettiga in sight of the people, he found he could not walk a step further, so allowed it to be brought up. He remained sitting up on it, to look at the people, still returning their salutations, while the slaves bore him away. Crowds accompanied him to a considerable distance. Misitheus had resumed his place by his Sovereign's side, who asked him, in a low voice, whether Florentius were yet in sight.

"He is at the head of this loyal procession," was the answer.

"Then bid him come to me."

All who saw the worthy Roman approach his Sovereign, supposed it was to receive more ample instructions with regard to his generous Sovereign's munificent donation, but it was not so. Gordian only took a ring of Etruscan workmanship off his finger, and, giving it to Florentius: "Take this to your daughter," he said, "she implored a favour of me; she must be able to prove I have answered her appeal; tell her this signet will always admit her to our presence, if ever she require our aid."

He fell back in a reclining position, and a hectic flush of excitement passed over his features, remaining there so long that his attendants hoped it was the bloom of returning health. By and by, he saw the eye of Misitheus fixed upon him with a look of smiling enquiry.

"You want to know whether I am pleased with my day? Yes. I now wish ardently to recover."

"To do great things for Rome, Augustus, is it not so?"

"Yes! to make others happy, and myself too."

"Perhaps you will then be disposed to consider more favourably what I hinted at this morning; if, as I hope, a long life is before you, you must think of sharing your throne with an Empress Augusta."

"I begin to think it is a duty, Misitheus, but the choice. . . . Must I think of Rome before myself in a matter which so nearly concerns me?"

"Your happiness and that of Rome need not clash, my once royal pupil, now my cherished Sovereign; consult the high principles which have guided your life hitherto."

"The Romans would not like a foreign princess; Titus was obliged to give up Berenice, you know."

"True!" rejoined the minister, with a half-suppressed smile. "The mother of Julius Cæsar was from Aricia, and who can sufficiently extol the blessings she brought on the empire? Choose a Roman lady, and you are sure to choose well."

"But I should not like to force the inclinations of any of my subjects."

"Why!" exclaimed Misitheus, "after piety to the gods, adoration of the sacred emperors is a citizen's first duty."

"I do not want to be adored, but to be loved."

"Well, command what you please."

"No," replied Gordian thoughtfully, "servile adulation and forced obedience may satisfy those who have reached an advanced age; for those who have done with life and its hopes, a shadow may take the place of reality; but with my youth, Misitheus, with all the freshness of early dreams about me, I must have that boon which is not denied to the poorest plebeians in the land; to them a wife is the solace of their labours. I must have a sharer in my troublesome pleasures; I must be cared for, not because I am an emperor, but because I am Gordian."

"Well spoken! but this morning you would hear of nothing but living alone."

"I was depressed, and gave way to gloomy forebodings. Or, to be more truthful, for I can conceal nothing from you, my counsellor, friend, and confidant, I have been much struck with the daughter of Florentius; but I will not give way to a first impression, I wish to know more of her. How can that be done?"

The minister kissed with paternal fondness the hand which the youthful Emperor extended to him, and mused over his words, looking up at the Latial mountain which we have already described. He seemed to be struck with a sudden idea: "Order," he said, "the public games in honour of Latial Jove, as is customary with the Cæsars before engaging on a military expedition; say that you intend on your recovery to proceed to the East, and that you mean to implore beforehand the protection of the gods. Then will maidens, both Latin and Roman, flock to join in the pious pastime, and Gordian can choose, according to his own heart and judgment, her whom he thinks worthy to be the Mother of the Roman people."

"Thanks, you are ever my wise friend, both in things of moment and youthful fancies. I shall follow your suggestion; let the orders be issued to that effect."

They were now entering the thicket which led to the beautiful leaf-covered galleries. Misitheus left his Sovereign to the care of his attendants, and returned to the palace by a shorter road.

## CHAPTER XIX.

THERE was a gathering of young girls in a garden on the Aventine hill, where they had so often met in childish days. Years had passed over those fair young brows, death had thinned their ranks. Christ had selected His own among them, the first-fruits of His flock. And of those who remained, which could say her life was a certain tenure? Yet, Christian as they were, and condemned to an early death by the very fact, the gloomy future did not seem to impart to them the darkness of suspicion or the vague uncertainty of fear; it had only added to their demeanour the calm majesty of later years; a modest serenity was the distinctive feature of the Christian virgins, who, watchful yet confident, seemed to be ever waiting the bidding of the Heavenly Spouse, *Estote paratæ*. They looked round at each other, remarking how many events had passed since last they had all met together, they wondered—
"Of which of them would be said first: 'She is gone!'"

"I thank you, dear friends," began Flora, in whose house they had assembled, as of yore, "I thank you for so promptly answering my invitation; we must plan together how we can best manage to avoid detection. Sabina, you, whose father is a public man, can best inform us what you have heard about the regulations for this approaching feast."

"The games in honour of Latial Jove," replied the girl thus appealed to, "used in the commencement of the Republic to be solemnized every year, but when the simplicity of those days gave way to the corruption of the empire, it became customary for victors alone to order them, either in fulfilment of a vow, or in order to implore the protection of the gods. Our Emperor has resolved upon undertaking an expedition to the East, and this is the occasion of the feast, which it is specially enjoined must be a mingling of Romans and Latins."

"It is somewhat new to us," observed Flora; "I suppose it is meant to commemorate the rural sports of our forefathers."

"But I wish they would leave us out," observed another.

"They have, on the contrary, thought particularly of our amusement," continued Sabina, "my father tells me that more than one *altalena* will be set up on the camp of Hannibal, for we young people are supposed to find particular attraction in a *festum in oscillo*."

"We should not object to a feast, if swinging were the only object," remarked Rufina, laughing, "but we cannot join in idolatrous practices."

"I think I might obtain from my father," resumed Sabina, "a dispensation from joining in the procession; would that save us, do you think?"

"Yes, if properly managed that would save us from detection, and save our consciences, for we are always told not to expose ourselves unnecessarily."

"Then I must explain to my father that I have a certain number of companions who are extremely fond of amusement, and I must add they cannot afford to take any time from play to give to the gods."

"And we, to corroborate your statement, must swing each other most unmercifully."

"Agreed!" they cried in chorus; "would that it were always as easy to avoid sin."

"We must interest your father too to protect us, for your sake, Flora; I think you told us you had confided the secret of your religion to him."

"Yes, while in Liguria, and he has been kind and considerate to me ever since. If our abstaining from anything idolatrous be remarked, he will endeavour to smooth it down with the Emperor, who, you must have heard, favoured him greatly on his visit to Aricia."

"And you, too, made a right good use of the opportunity," observed Lucia. "How strange, Flora, that what you were saying to me the other day should so soon have come to pass. I thought you were dreaming when you expressed so earnest a desire to see the Emperor and implore his clemency for Icilius and Volumnia."

"It was indeed very strange. And the courage I felt was no less so, for I had not planned how to express my petition. I may almost say I was alone, for my father only presented me and drew back."

"I am glad I was not there," remarked Reparata, "I should have felt so anxious for you, whereas, when thrown on your own resources, you find you have much more courage than you supposed."

"Well," said Lucia, "I thought you were inseparable, I must confess to being a little jealous."

"In a sisterly way, I hope," replied Reparata, laughing. "I seldom quit our kind hosts, but my uncle has returned to Liguria, and on that very day I was helping him to make preparations for his journey, so we were both of us prevented going to Aricia. The noble Siona has kindly invited me to spend another winter under her hospitable roof, and my good uncle has urged upon me to remain, as he is anxious about my health, but I was very loth to let him go without me. You must forgive me, dear companions, if I steal away some part of Flora's heart from you, but indeed I think it is quite large enough to contain us all."

"I may say we all feel the same towards you, Reparata," rejoined Flora, with a touch of emotion in her voice; "all of us who enjoy our parents' love feel we cannot do too much to show our sympathy in your sorrows."

"Now, let us talk of something else," interposed the young Greek, with a strong effort to master her feelings. "Give our young friends an account of your interview with the Emperor; they have only had a very imperfect version from me."

"Oh, do, do!" they all repeated; "but the sun is getting very powerful here, let us go into the shade."

There was a wall built on the brow of the hill, which enclosed the property of Florentius; the young girls went to sit close to it, and were thus sheltered from the noon-day heat; they grouped themselves round Flora, and looked down upon Rome. The Palatine, the Janiculum, the Esquiline were in sight, and the city of the seven hills lay proudly enthroned among them, little dreaming that to that group of fair young girls she would one day owe her glory.

\* \* \* \* \* \* \*

A few days passed, and a dense population crowded round the foot of the Latial Mount. Morning and evening, priests toiled up the steep ascent, carrying offerings to the temple at the summit. Tripods were placed along the road; from these the smoke of incense rose unceasingly; each grateful adorer dropped a few grains on the fire as he passed. In the wood where the pine trees, consecrated to the mother of the gods, diffused a delightful fragrance, temporary altars had been erected. The very road, trodden by the votaries, bore the divine initials, which two thousand years have not effaced from the lasting stone; the Via Numinalis showed then, as now, the letters V. N. engraved on its huge blocks of pavement. Then, as now, the whole of the Latian Campagna extended on one side of the hill, the Roman on the other, forming to those who stand on the summit a panorama of fields, forest, and plains; where the two lakes of Albano and Nemi, although far asunder in reality, seem, when viewed in perspective, to lie side by side, as is ever the case with memory, which softens the asperities of life, and makes its bright parts shine on the surface like mirrors. Then, as now, there glittered at the horizon the gold-reflecting waves of the far-off sea, its murmurs hushed in the distance, and its beauty alone visible. Over the whole there seemed to be diffused a bright luminous atmosphere, half of earth, half of heaven, where the perfume of the flowers seemed to blend with ethereal sweetness, and the tree tops, touched with brightness, emitted an odour like unto nature's incense. Such was the invigorating, joyous feeling which penetrated the votaries of that mount, which seemed like an open temple, where a universal homage was offered up—a faint reminiscence of the One God, who even when falsified and misunderstood, holds His sway, nevertheless, as Sovereign of Nature in the heart of man. Half way up the Latial Mount, there is a surface of table-land which has preserved the name of Hannibal's camp, where, it is said, the warrior was stationed, when, receiving the order to leave Rome and succour his native country, which Scipio had attacked, he was obliged to return. How great must have been the anguish of that brave heart, which had to prefer duty to glory! Hannibal looked down on the plain of Rome, so near at hand, so easy a prey, could he have seized it; yet he gave orders to fold the tents and depart. We might almost imagine that the famous "Delenda est Carthago" had been flung back by the patriot general on his enemy's country, and that, before leaving this encampment, he had vowed the soil to destruction, for not a blade of grass will grow on that uneven, parched earth, and the peasants say that a huge charnel-house lies hid under the surface; for all their efforts towards cultivation only succeed in digging up dead men's bones. Are these the remains of many a bloody fight? Who can tell?

On this very spot, the people now thronged in all the joyousness of a festival day; food was prepared for them at rural tables, as in the days of Homer; trees had been cut down from the forest, and wild boars were being cooked before the huge blazing logs.

The old people sat down to partake of the good cheer, beginning the repast by a libation to Latial Jove. The minstrel, so loved by the ancients, was not wanting at the banquet, the bard who fired his hearers by the recital of their ancestors' glorious deeds. On this occasion, however, no praises were sung but those of Jove. Under the trees, youths and maidens joined in the choral dance, and performed plays in the style of Greece: all wore crowns in honour of the gods. Now and then a peal of merry laughter resounded in the ranks of the spectators as they listened to the satirical allusions of some favourite comic actor; but the sport which attracted the greater number, and which was indeed the prominent feature of the day, was that of the swings fastened between the trees, where the young people balanced each other in graceful, unaffected attitudes.

"Florentius, I salute you," cried Adrias, recognising his friend among a group of spectators, and coming to join him; "I thought you were too much of a philosopher to condescend to take part in this feast."

"I have come out of respect to our Sovereign Lord, the Emperor. I have seen him and spoken to him; he is so good that he well merits the title of divine."

"So you do not despise court favour although a philosopher?"

"Gordian has been nobly munificent to me and mine though I have never been at court."

"Yes! I heard of his visiting Aricia and granting the pardon of those two poor young people at Flora's request. It was nobly done of your little maiden to plead for them. Where is she? Is she here to-day?"

"Yes! there she is in that group of maidens with lilies on their heads."

"Strange flower to wear in honour of Latial Jove; it is not consecrated to him."

"Little do I care! My daughter is a flower in herself, at least in my eyes—the flower of all maidens here present."

"Well, I must own you are right for once! How kind and gentle she is to poor Lucilla! I see she has her by her even now."

"But where are your children, Adrias, and your wife? Take me to salute Paulina."

Florentius was endeavouring to divert his friend's attention from his daughter and her Christian companions, whose secret being entrusted to him he felt bound to watch over. He drew away Adrias towards a meadow, where youths were exercising themselves in the foot race, and arrived just in time to see his own adopted son, Laurentius, bound on before him, his feet hardly touching the ground, overstep his companions by far, reach the goal, and, with a small pointed lance in his hand, bear off an egg which was fixed on a pole as a symbol of victory; he was proclaimed to have won the crown of green leaves, which he received amid the loud acclamations of the judges. His eye ran round the crowd, where he recognised his father, and running up to him at once, he affectionately laid the prize at his feet.

"Well done, my boy," cried Florentius, "I had hardly expected this of you; I thought you were not sufficiently strong to try the race."

"I do not like it particularly, father, but I hoped to afford you pleasure by trying my skill in manly exercises."

"You have succeeded beyond my hopes; and I am the more proud of your success, that some of my friends have been expressing their fear to me, lest the training you have received were calculated to render you effeminate."

"But you do not think so, father, and therefore please disregard them. I am justly proud of having been brought up at home under your care and that of my adopted mother. The most illustrious of our Roman heroes were formed by early tuition at their mother's knee. Oh, if ever I become a poet, I shall take for my favourite theme the exalting of woman's character, which has been too often lowered by ignoble praise and silly verse."

"Rightly spoken!" cried a merry juvenile voice behind him. "Were it not for that wise speech and that you are my friend, I could not forgive you for winning the prize of the race-course from me. Why, I am twice as strong as you; and, besides, you are entirely clothed when running, unlike us. You are very hot."

"You require refreshment, my dear boy," interposed his father. "Go and take some with your good friend, Hippolytus, who is so generous a rival. I must go to present my respects to the Emperor. I am surprised we have not met him; perhaps he may be at the summit of the hill preparing to offer sacrifice."

Florentius directed his steps up the Via Numinalis; but, before leaving Hannibal's camp, he turned aside a little to speak to his wife and daughter. The Christian ladies had gathered together, forming a pleasant group, and sought recreation in innocent pastimes apart from the idolatrous crowd. The blind girl was indeed the only pagan amongst them, but she clung to Flora with a tenacity of affection which would not allow of any separation; and the exertions made by the latter to save her sister increased her gratitude tenfold. She was an object of compassion to all that young circle, who at first had been kind to her out of regard to Flora; by degrees they learned to love Lucilla for her own sake when they saw the good they could develop in that young nature, which had been concentrated in itself and rendered fierce by sorrow; and the daily contact with those Christian girls worked visibly on Lucilla. In her absorbing love for Flora, she would listen to anything from her, even bearing patiently with a gentle chiding; for her sake she learned to repress the outbursts of an impetuous nature. They got to be so accustomed to her presence that they often forgot she was a pagan, and words would fall from their lips which they had learned at the highest and purest sources of Christianity. They spoke together of the happiness of suffering, of the joys of penance, the strength that grows from humiliation. Lucilla listened in silent wonder at first, but with that intuitive perception which is the gift of those that live alone; those lessons fell on her untutored mind as a ray of light which, penetrating a closed cave, discloses the hidden gems that cast a prismatic reflection upwards; thus did the first ray of faith dawn on the young pagan's mind.

Flora was the first to see her father drawing near to them, and she immediately left her companions to go and meet him. The glow of health was on her cheek, and her simple white stole became her so well that her father looked at her with pardonable pride: "I have been watching you from a distance," said he, "and rejoiced to see you take so active a part in the day's amusement. I see that no one has molested or even noticed your party; in this crowd you can pass unperceived."

"Dear father, we have followed your prudent suggestions to the letter. We took care to arrive after the hour fixed for the sacrifice so as not to participate in it."

"Then you are not aware that it has not taken place at all. The Emperor, who ought to perform it, has not appeared, and the cause of his absence is not known."

"Long life to Gordianus! Long life to the good Emperor, the second Trajan, the protector of innocence, the forgiver of injuries! May the thread of his life be spun of gold!"

Thus sang a chorus of manly voices, juvenile yet deep-toned, louder and louder rang the notes as they ascended the hill and drew near; there was one voice that led the song, varying the Emperor's praises at every verse, then all joined in the burthen, *Vivet in æternum!* They passed out of a thicket which had somewhat sheltered them from view, and came up the steep road in order. He who was at their head wore white garments, a crown of lilies on his head, a palm branch in his hand; his demeanour was grave and modest; while his companions sang with the exuberance of joy. His bearing was that of a deep, well regulated feeling; indeed, so subdued was his manner that he did not raise his eyes on the festive scene, but went on his way steadily, and would have passed by the place where Florentius was standing had not the latter greeted him, calling out: "All hail, Icilius, thou here! why, the gods be praised!"

The young man turned round at once on hearing his name called upon, and looked much agitated; some memory seemed to be evoked within him connected with the mental derangement from which he had suffered so much, but Flora was by her father's side, and the sight of her calmed him at once. He asked his companions to go on without him, and, standing alone, with his arms folded on his breast: "Florentius," he said, "allow me to thank your daughter, or rather, help me yourself to fulfil my debt of gratitude. Noble maiden, you have been doubly my benefactress. May the remembrance of what you have done for me be your reward until your dying day, while I promise to pass my life in the manner which, I know, will please you best. May it be often given you to perform deeds worthy of yourself."

"I accept the promise, Icilius," she said, "and am indeed so happy that I need no further reward. I did not know what had become of you since" . . . she hesitated, then asked, "Have you seen Hippolytus?"

"Yes!" he said with a bright smile, and a look of unutterable thankfulness.

She understood he had received baptism, which she had requested Hippolytus to undertake to prepare him for. She glanced at his white spotless toga, and said: "Oh, I am so thankful you have seen Hippolytus".

"Who is calling me?" cried a merry voice, and the youth we have seen following Laurentius from the race-course, came up, still with his friend, and finding himself suddenly in the midst of acquaintances he had not expected to meet, looked a little bashful.

"Why, here you come again with the speed of an arrow," said Florentius, laughing. "I left you both running off to the games; have you wings to your feet?"

Both were so struck with the sight of Icilius that they could not hear any one else: "I rejoice with you from my heart, Icilius," was the pleased salutation of Laurentius. One look from his sister showed him there was more subject of joy there even than the recovery of health and reason.

Wishing to place them all at ease, she said: "Forgive me, Icilius, if I recall to you a painful remembrance, but there is one stands before you to whom you owe much. Hippolytus is the son of the centurion who had the command over the Mamertine prison; he did a great deal towards consoling you during your captivity, and I feel sure no one rejoices in your liberation more than he does."

Icilius, with the humility he derived from his new faith, bowed to the young soldier without any token of familiarity, not knowing how far Hippolytus would like the acquaintance of one who had been so lately his prisoner: "I feel deeply the weight of the obligation I have incurred towards you, Hippolytus," he said. "Kindness in affliction is a boon beyond thanks. May the happiness most desired at your age be yours; may every success attend you in the career you have chosen."

The young soldier was touched; almost without perceiving it he gave his hand to Icilius, and in so doing his eyes were raised to Flora, though only for an instant. That look did not escape Icilius; he guessed at once what was the secret spring of Hippolytus' actions, so prone are we all to fathom the hearts of others by our own.

"And where are you going?" resumed Florentius. "You were at the head of a joyful band just now, singing a fine ode, as I thought."

"Yes; the first act of my liberty has been to assemble such of my friends as could the best sympathise with my feelings, and go to meet Gordianus with the song of gratitude on our lips, and an undying love in our hearts. Much as I shall suffer in beholding him I have injured, yet I do wish to show him how deeply I regret an act which I can hardly call my own, but that of a madman."

"That is a right distinction and a difficult one to define, my young friend; nevertheless, you have hit it off well. Two natures in one person; an act performed without the concurrence of the understanding can hardly be said to be complete, if not complete it is not performed at all. Let me see!" Here the philosophical Florentius fell into one of his musing fits, which might have lasted indefinitely had not Laurentius diverted his attention by adroitly interposing with the remark—

"Icilius has undertaken a solemn duty in going to meet the Emperor, perhaps it would be better not to delay him."

"True, but where can the Emperor be? My son, come with me, and let us enquire."

They went out towards a tent covered with purple and snowy white draperies; servants were stationed round, as if guarding the sacred person of the Emperor, but the tent was empty; the menials awaited the arrival of their master. Meanwhile the voice of prayer resounded on the Via Numinalis, as also that of song and joy.

The feast of Latial Jove was to last three days, but

those who had ordered the pastime took no share in it. Misitheus had been seized with a sudden and violent fever; Gordianus, with the kind-hearted thoughtfulness we have seen him show to his old minister, had forgotten every other concern to watch by the bed-side of him who was about to close his long and useful career. Thanks to him, the reign of the young Emperor had been one of the most peaceful and virtuous that ever graced the throne. Even at this hour, when the old man felt, in the rapid decay of his faculties, the symptoms of an approaching dissolution, he entertained his royal pupil with great and noble plans: "Beware," he said, "to whom you give your confidence in future, you will find many to flatter you, few that will love you for yourself, as I have done. Beware, Gordianus, for you are easily influenced."

"Oh, but you will recover, Misitheus. You must live! You have not accomplished yet all your heart desired."

"The fates are inexorable, Cæsar, the thread of my life is spun. I feel quite struck down. Remember how often we have thought and worked together for the welfare of Rome; you must now execute what we together conceived. Your expedition to the East! . . . do not put that off. Yet I regret your leaving Rome, for you have no one to take your place during your absence; this fickle people forget their Sovereign when he is not in sight; if even there were an Augusta to represent you! . . . I wish you were married, Gordianus."

"That was the subject of our last conversation

together; the very motive of our assembling the people at this feast in honour of Latial Jove."

"Is it so? I had forgotten. My memory fails me. All within me dies first . . . the body will follow. Why are you here, Cæsar? Go, show yourself to the people."

"Not while you, my best friend, require my company and my help."

"You can do nothing more for me."

"What? can I not comfort you by my presence? You are, in truth, a poor flatterer, Misitheus."

A faint smile played on the sick man's lips: "I would," he said, "that my couch were drawn near to the window, that I might look again on the plains of my dear country. Nay, Cæsar, I did not mean you to do it, my dear Sovereign; call a slave." He tried to put away Gordian's hands, but the latter only pressed his affectionately, saying, with a melancholy smile: "Even as you tended my youth, so would I have watched over your old age . . . if" . . . He moved with great ease the light iron bedstead of Etruscan workmanship, on which the minister, a foe to luxury, reclined; he opened the casement with his own hand, and a flood of rich, mellowed, softened light poured into the room, and played round the head of the dying man: "Is it too much for you?" he asked anxiously.

"No, no, only shade my eyes, for I am very weak. Yes, I see it all. Latium . . . and, in the distance . . . far away, lies Rome, I know; but I cannot see her as I used. . . . Had I thought to die, I should have preferred not being removed here, Gordianus; I would fain have expired within her walls . . . even as a son returns home to die on his mother's breast!"

He fell back, weary and exhausted, gently murmuring: "The first and the last love!"

A long silence ensued, interrupted only by the short breathing of the elder man, and the suppressed sobs of the younger, who struggled to conceal his grief. Suddenly the former raised his head, and said with a strong effort: "Commit no injustice, Gordianus!"

"We have not wronged anyone, I think."

"I hope not, but" . . .

Another pause, the fever was at its height, Misitheus began to speak wildly: "Where am I going?" he asked.

"To Elysium, where you will meet the shades of the heroes, where you will join those who have done much good in their lives."

"Who has told you so?"

"Who? I do not know . . . the oracles, the poets."

"What are they that we should believe in them? . . . It is not sleep I am going to . . . Why should I sink into dark, perpetual night? when there is a feeling within me which revolts against destruction and craves to live? . . . Prince, we have studied many questions together, . . . why have we left this, the last of all, unfathomed?"

The young Emperor was at a loss; he thought the mind of his friend wandered, and endeavoured to calm him by making use of an argument which was his favourite theme: "We have laboured for the happiness of Rome," he said.

"Rome!" repeated the other bitterly, "and what has been my reward? What will fame avail to my dust? Rome! can she give me one hour of life? . . . Alas! alas! I have heard of children dying triumphantly, saying they were going to claim an eternal reward, what could that be?"

The Emperor was silent. He called for assistance, alarmed at the rapid change which was coming over the dying man. His utterance grew choked, nor could Gordianus, lovingly bent over him, distinguish any meaning in those imperfect sounds, indistinct like the wailings of childhood; for there is a strange similarity in our entrance to, and our exit from, life. The light grew fainter; golden rays no longer poured in, but deep-coloured violet and crimson hues shed a mysterious tint of warning. Gordianus feared lest the last moment should pass unperceived, for the blood of life had retired to its last stronghold and total exhaustion had succeeded to the ravings of fever. Some time yet elapsed, . . . . the Emperor felt the once strong frame of his beloved friend quiver in his embrace, while words escaped him uttered in that slow, uncertain manner with which dreamers speak in their sleep. Misitheus was indeed sinking into his last rest as he said: "Seek, Gordianus, seek . . . . that immortal reward those children spoke of!"

The pagan had expired. A little light flickered yet in the west; another light, dim, yet prophetic, had dawned, but too late, upon his soul.

# SELECTION

FROM

# BURNS AND OATES' CATALOGUE OF PUBLICATIONS.

---

**ALLIES, T. W.**
See of St. Peter . . . . . . . . £0 4 6
Formation of Christendom. Vols. I., II., III. . each 0 12 0
Church and State as seen in the Formation of Christendom, 8vo, pp. 472, cloth . . . . . . 0 14 0

"It would be quite superfluous at this hour of day to recommend Mr. Allies' writings to English Catholics. Those of our readers who remember the article on his writings in the *Katholik*, know that he is esteemed in Germany as one of our foremost writers."—*Dublin Review.*

**ALLNATT, C. F. B.**
Cathedra Petri; or, The Titles and Prerogatives of St. Peter, and of his See and Successors, as described by the Early Fathers, Ecclesiastical Writers, and Councils of the Church, with an Appendix, containing Notes on the History and Acts of the first four General Councils, and the Council of Sardica, in their relation to the Papal Supremacy. Compiled by C. F. B. Allnatt. Third and Enlarged Edition.
Cloth . . . . . . . . 0 6 0
Paper . . . . . . . . 0 5 0

"Invaluable to the controversialist and the theologian, and most useful for educated men inquiring after truth, or anxious to know the positive testimony of Christian antiquity in favour of Papal claims."—*Month.*

Which is the True Church? New Edition . . 0 1 4

## ALZOG.

History of the Church. A Manual of Universal Church History, by the Rev. John Alzog, D.D., Professor of Theology at the University of Freiburg. Translated, with additions, from the ninth and last German edition by the Rev. F. J. Parbisch and the Rev. Thomas S. Byrne. With Chronological Tables and Ecclesiastico-Geographical Maps. 4 vols., demy 8vo £1 10 0

## ANNUS SANCTUS:

Hymns of the Church for the Ecclesiastical Year. Translated from the Sacred Offices by various Authors, with Modern, Original, and other Hymns, and an Appendix of Earlier Versions. Selected and Arranged by ORBY SHIPLEY, M.A. In stiff boards . 0 3 6
Also, a limited Edition in cloth, printed on large-sized, toned, and ribbed paper . . . . 0 10 6

## B. N.

The Jesuits: their Foundation and History. 2 vols. crown 8vo, cloth, red edges . . . . 0 15 0

"The book is just what it professes to be—*a popular history*, drawn from well-known sources," &c.—*Month*, July 1879.

## BORROMEO, LIFE OF ST. CHARLES.

From the Italian of Peter Guissano. 2 vols. . . 0 15 0

## BOTTALLA, FATHER (S.J.)

Papacy and Schism . . . . . . . 0 2 6
Reply to Renouf on Pope Honorius . . . . 0 3 6

## BRIDGETT, REV. T. E. (C.SS.R.)

Discipline of Drink . . . . . . . 0 3 6

"The historical information with which the book abounds gives evidence of deep research and patient study, and imparts a permanent interest to the volume, which will elevate it to a position of authority and importance enjoyed by few of its compeers."—*The Arrow*.

Our Lady's Dowry; how England Won and Lost that Title. Second edition . . . . . . 0 9 0

"This book is the ablest vindication of Catholic devotion to Our Lady, drawn from tradition, that we know of in the English language."—*Tablet*.

Defender of the Faith: the Royal Title, its history and value . . . . . . . . . 0 1 0

## BRIDGETT, REV. T. E. (C.SS.R.), Edited by.

Suppliant of the Holy Ghost: a Paraphrase of the 'Veni Sancte Spiritus.' Now first printed from a MS. of the seventeenth century composed by Rev. R. Johnson, with other unpublished treatises by the same author. Second edition. Cloth . . . 0 1 6

## CASWALL, FATHER.

Catholic Latin Instructor in the Principal Church Offices and Devotions, for the Use of Choirs, Convents, and Mission Schools, and for Self-Teaching. 1 vol., complete . . . . . . . £0 3 6
Or Part I., containing Benediction, Mass, Serving at do., various Latin Prayers in ordinary use . . 0 1 6
(A Poem) May Pageant: A Tale of Tintern. Second edition . . . . . . . . . 0 2 0
Words of Jesus (Verba Verbi). Cloth . . . 0 2 0
Poems . . . . . . . . . . 0 5 0
Lyra Catholica, containing all the Breviary and Missal Hymns, with others from various sources. 32mo, cloth, red edges . . . . . . . 0 2 6

## CISNEROS (GARCIAS).

Book of Spiritual Exercises and Directory for Canonical Hours . . . . . . . . . 0 5 0

## COLERIDGE, REV. H. J. (S.J.)

Life and Letters of St. Francis Xavier. (Quarterly Series.) 2 vols. Fourth edition . . . 0 15 0
Life of our Life: the Harmony of the Gospels. Arranged with Introductory and Explanatory Chapters, Notes, and Indices. (Quarterly Series.) 2 vols. 0 15 0
Public Life of Our Lord Jesus Christ. (Quarterly Series.) 8 vols. already published . . each 0 6 6
Vol. 1. The Ministry of St. John Baptist.
Vol. 2. The Preaching of the Beatitudes.
Vol. 3. The Sermon on the Mount (*to the end of the Lord's Prayer*).
Vol. 4. The Sermon on the Mount (*concluded*).
Vol. 5. The Training of the Apostles (Part I.)
Vol. 6. The Training of the Apostles (Part II.)
Vol. 7. The Training of the Apostles (Part III.)
Vol. 8. The Training of the Apostles (Part IV.)
*⁎* Other Volumes in Preparation.

"It is needless to praise the matter of such a work, and the manner of its performance is admirable."—*Cork Examiner.*
"No Catholic can peruse the book without feeling how large is the measure of gratitude due to the richly-endowed intellect which has given a contribution so noble to our standard Catholic literature."—*Freeman.*

The Sermon on the Mount. Three vols. (the second, third, and fourth vols. of the above bound up separately, for convenience of purchasers. (Quarterly Series) 0 15 0

## COLERIDGE, REV. H. J. (S.J.)—*continued.*

| | |
|---|---|
| Life and Letters of St. Teresa. Vol. I. (Quarterly Series) | £0 7 0 |

"Father Coleridge states that he is anxious to enlarge the knowledge of St. Teresa among English readers, as well on other grounds, as because a large number of English Catholic ladies in the days of persecution found a home in the communities of her Order abroad, established by their own countrywomen. He has made much use of the labours of Mr. David Lewis, whose translation of the Life of St. Teresa of Jesu, written by herself, was published eleven years ago."—*Tablet.*

| | |
|---|---|
| Prisoners of the King, a Book of Thoughts on the Doctrine of Purgatory. New edition | 0 5 0 |
| The Return of the King, Discourses on the Latter Days. (Quarterly Series) | 0 7 6 |
| The Mother of the King. (Quarterly Series) | 0 7 6 |
| The Works and Words of our Saviour, gathered from the Four Gospels. Cloth | 0 7 6 |

"No English work that we know of is better calculated to beget in the mind a love of the Gospels, and a relish for further and deeper study of their beauties."—*Dublin Review.*

| | |
|---|---|
| The Chronicle of St. Anthony of Padua, the "Eldest Son of St. Francis" | 0 3 6 |
| Dialogues of St. Gregory the Great. An old English Version | 0 6 0 |
| History of the Sacred Passion. By Palma. Third edition. Cloth | 0 5 0 |
| The Life of Mary Ward. By Mary Catherine Elizabeth Chambers, of the Institute of the Blessed Virgin. (Quarterly Series.) 2 vols., each | 0 7 6 |
| The Baptism of the King. Considerations on the Sacred Passion. (Quarterly Series) | 0 7 6 |
| Holy Infancy Series :— | |
| Vol. I. Preparation of the Incarnation | 0 7 6 |
| Vol. II. The Nine Months. The Life of our Lord in the Womb | 0 7 6 |
| Vol. III. The Thirty Years. Our Lord's Infancy and Hidden Life | 0 7 6 |

## COMPARISON BETWEEN THE HISTORY OF

| | |
|---|---|
| the Church and the Prophecies of the Apocalypse | 0 2 0 |

## DARRAS.
History of the Church. From the French. A General History of the Catholic Church from the commencement of the Christian Era until the Present Time. By M. l'Abbé J. E. Darras. With an Introduction and Notes by the Most Rev. M. J. Spalding, D.D., Archbishop of Baltimore. 4 vols. 4to . . . £2 8 0

## DEHARBE (S.J.)
A History of Religion, or the Evidences for the Divinity of the Christian Religion, as furnished by its History from the Creation of the World to our own Times. Designed as a Help to Catechetical Instruction in Schools and Churches. Pp. 628 . . . . . . reduced to net 0 8 6

## DUPONT, THE LIFE OF LÉON PAPIN, THE
Holy Man of Tours ; being Vol. VIII. of the "Library of Religious Biography," edited by Edward Healy Thompson, M.A. This work is not a Translation, but has been composed, after a careful study of the Abbé Jauvier's full and complete Life of the Holy Man, and that of M. Léon Aubineau. Cloth . . . . . . . . . 0 6 0

"It is an original compilation, written in that well-known style of devout suggestiveness and literary excellence which characterise the writer's former volumes of religious biography."—*Dublin Review.*

## FABER, VERY REV. FATHER.
All for Jesus . . . . . . . . 0 5 0
Bethlehem . . . . . . . . . 0 7 0
Blessed Sacrament . . . . . . . 0 7 6
Creator and Creature . . . . . . . 0 6 0
Ethel's Book of the Angels . . . . . . 0 2 6
Foot of the Cross . . . . . . . 0 6 0
Growth in Holiness . . . . . . . 0 6 0
Hymns . . . . . . . . . 0 6 0
Notes on Doctrinal and Spiritual Subjects, 2 vols. each 0 5 0
Poems . . . . . . . . . . 0 5 0
Precious Blood . . . . . . . . 0 5 0
Spiritual Conferences . . . . . . . 0 6 0
Life and Letters of Frederick William Faber, D.D., Priest of the Oratory of St. Philip Neri. By John Edward Bowden of the same Congregation . . 0 6 0

## FOLEY, HENRY (S.J.)

Records of the English Province of the Society of
Jesus. Vol. I., Series I. Demy 8vo, 720 pp. net £1 6 0
Vol. II., Series II., III., IV. Demy 8vo, 622 pp. net 1 6 0
Vol. III., Series V., VI., VII., VIII. Demy 8vo, over
850 pp. . . . . . . . net 1 10 0
Vol. IV., Series IX., X., XI. Demy 8vo, 750 pp. net 1 6 0
Vol. V., Series XII. Demy 8vo, nearly 1100 pp., with
nine Photographs of Martyrs . . . net 1 10 0
Vol. VI., Diary and Pilgrim-Book of the English College, Rome. The Diary from 1579 to 1773, with Biographical and Historical Notes. The Pilgrim-Book of the ancient English Hospice attached to the College from 1580 to 1656, with Historical Notes. Demy 8vo, pp. 796 . . . . . net 1 6 0
Vol. VII. Part the First: General Statistics of the Province; and Collectanea, giving Biographical Notices of its Members and of many Irish and Scotch Jesuits. With 20 Photographs . . . . . net 1 6 0
Vol. VII. Part the Second: Collectanea Completed; With Appendices. Catalogues of Assumed and Real Names; Annual Letters; Biographies and Miscellanea . . . . . . . net 1 6 0

"As a biographical dictionary of English Jesuits, it deserves a place in every well-selected library, and, as a collection of marvellous occurrences, persecutions, martyrdoms, and evidences of the results of faith, amongst the books of all who belong to the Catholic Church."—*Genealogist.*

## FRANCIS DE SALES, ST.: THE WORKS OF.

Translated into the English Language by the Rev. H. B. Mackey, O.S.B.

Vol. I. Letters to Persons in the World. Cloth . 0 6 0

"The letters must be read in order to comprehend the charm and sweetness of their style."—*Tablet.*

Vol. II. On the Love of God. Founded on the rare and practically unknown English Translation, of which the title-page is as follows: A Treatise of the Love of God, written in French by B. Francis de Sales, Bishop of Geneva, and translated into English by Miles Car, Priest of the English College of Doway. 1630 . . . . . . 0 9 0
Vol. III. The Catholic Controversy . . . . 0 6 0
Devout Life . . . . . . . 0 1 6

## FRANCIS DE SALES, ST.: Works of—continued.

| | | | |
|---|---|---|---|
| Manual of Practical Piety | £0 | 3 | 6 |
| Spiritual Combat. A new and careful Translation. 18mo, cloth | 0 | 3 | 0 |
| The same, pocket size, cloth | 0 | 1 | 0 |

## GALLWEY, REV. PETER (S.J.)

| | | | |
|---|---|---|---|
| Precious Pearl of Hope in the Mercy of God, The. Translated from the Italian. With Preface by the Rev. Father Gallwey. Cloth | 0 | 4 | 6 |
| Ritualism: Lecture I., Introductory | 0 | 0 | 4 |
| 2. Is the Blessing of Heaven on Ritualism? | 0 | 0 | 4 |
| 3. The Sanctity of the Ritualistic Clergy | 0 | 0 | 4 |
| 4. Are Ritualists Protestants or Catholics? (extra size) | 0 | 0 | 6 |
| 5. Ritualism and St. Peter's Mission as revealed in Holy Writ (double size) | 0 | 0 | 8 |
| 6. Do Ritualists owe Obedience to their Directors? Do the Anglican Clergy hold the Place of Christ? | 0 | 0 | 4 |
| 7. Ritualism and the Early Church. The Faith of St. Leo the Great | 0 | 0 | 6 |
| 8. The Faith of the English Church Union, A.D. 1878; of Clewer, A.D. 1878; of the Council of Ephesus, A.D. 431 | 0 | 0 | 6 |
| 9. Anglican Orders. Part I. | 0 | 0 | 4 |
| 10. Anglican Orders. Part II. | 0 | 1 | 0 |
| 11. Anglican Orders. Part III. | 0 | 0 | 8 |
| 12. Anglican Clergy in the Confessional | 0 | 0 | 6 |
| All the above Lectures bound in 2 vols. . . net | 0 | 8 | 0 |

## GIBSON, REV. H.

| | | | |
|---|---|---|---|
| Catechism Made Easy. Being an Explanation of the Christian Doctrine. 2 vols., cloth | 0 | 7 | 6 |

"This work must be of priceless worth to any who are engaged in any form of catechetical instruction. It is the best book of the kind that we have seen in English."—*Irish Monthly.*

## HERGENRÖTHER, DR.

| | | | |
|---|---|---|---|
| Catholic Church and Christian State. On the Relation of the Church to the Civil Power. From the German. 2 vols., paper | 1 | 1 | 0 |

## HUMPHREY, REV. F.

The Divine Teacher: A Letter to a Friend. With a Preface in Reply to No. 3 of the English Church Defence Tracts, entitled "Papal Infallibility."
Fifth edition. Cloth . . . . . . £0 2 6
   Sixth edition. Wrapper . . . . . 0 1 0
Mary Magnifying God. May Sermons. Fifth edition . 0 2 6
Other Gospels; or, Lectures on St. Paul's Epistle to the Galatians. Crown 8vo, cloth . . . 0 4 0
The Written Word; or, Considerations on the Sacred Scriptures . . . . . . . . 0 5 0
Mr. Fitzjames Stephen and Cardinal Bellarmine . . 0 1 0
Suarez on the Religious State: A Digest of the Doctrine contained in his Treatise, "De Statû Religionis." 3 vols., pp. 1200. Cloth, roy. 8vo . . . 1 10 0

## LIGUORI, ST. ALPHONSO.

New and Improved Translation of the Complete Works of St. Alphonso, edited by the late Bishop Coffin:—
Vol. I. The Christian Virtues, and the Means for Obtaining them. Cloth elegant . . . . 0 4 0
Or separately:—
  1. The Love of our Lord Jesus Christ . . . 0 1 4
  2. Treatise on Prayer. (*In the ordinary editions a great part of this work is omitted*) . . 0 1 4
  3. A Christian's Rule of Life . . . . 0 1 0
Vol. II. The Mysteries of the Faith—The Incarnation; containing Meditations and Devotions on the Birth and Infancy of Jesus Christ, &c., suited for Advent and Christmas . . . . . . . . 0 3 6
  Cheap edition . . . . . . . 0 2 0
Vol. III. The Mysteries of the Faith—The Blessed Sacrament . . . . . . . . 0 3 6
  Cheap edition . . . . . . . 0 2 0
Vol. IV. Eternal Truths—Preparation for Death . 0 3 6
  Cheap edition . . . . . . . 0 2 0
Vol. V. Treatises on the Passion, containing "Jesus hath loved us," &c. . . . . . . 0 3 0
  Cheap edition . . . . . . . 0 2 0
Vol. VI. Glories of Mary. New edition . . 0 3 6
With Frontispiece, cloth . . . . . 0 4 6
  Also in better bindings.

## MANNING, HIS EMINENCE CARDINAL.

Blessed Sacrament the Centre of Immutable Truth. A new and revised edition. Cloth . . . . 0 1 0
Confidence in God. Third edition . . . 0 1 0
England and Christendom . . . . . 0 10 6

## MANNING, HIS EMINENCE CARDINAL—continued.

| | | | |
|---|---:|---:|---:|
| Eternal Priesthood. Cloth. Popular edition | £0 | 2 | 6 |
| Four Great Evils of the Day. Fourth edition. Paper | 0 | 2 | 6 |
| Cloth | 0 | 3 | 6 |
| Fourfold Sovereignty of God. Second edition | 0 | 2 | 6 |
| Cloth | 0 | 3 | 6 |
| Glories of the Sacred Heart. Fourth edition | 0 | 6 | 0 |
| Grounds of Faith. Seventh edition. Cloth | 0 | 1 | 6 |
| Holy Gospel of our Lord Jesus Christ according to St. John. With a Preface by His Eminence | 0 | 1 | 0 |
| Independence of the Holy See | 0 | 5 | 0 |
| Internal Mission of the Holy Ghost. Fourth edition | 0 | 8 | 6 |
| Love of Jesus to Penitents. Seventh edition | 0 | 1 | 6 |
| Miscellanies. 2 vols. | 0 | 15 | 0 |
| Office of the Holy Ghost under the Gospel | 0 | 1 | 0 |
| Petri Privilegium | 0 | 10 | 6 |
| Praise, A Sermon on; with an Indulgenced Devotion | 0 | 1 | 0 |
| Sermons on Ecclesiastical Subjects. Vols. I., II., and III. . . . . . . . . . each | 0 | 6 | 0 |
| Sin and its Consequences. Sixth edition | 0 | 6 | 0 |
| Temporal Mission of the Holy Ghost. Third edition | 0 | 8 | 6 |
| Temporal Power of the Pope. New edition | 0 | 5 | 0 |
| The Office of the Holy Ghost under the Gospel | 0 | 1 | 0 |
| True Story of the Vatican Council | 0 | 5 | 0 |

## MANNING, HIS EMINENCE CARDINAL, Edited by.

| | | | |
|---|---:|---:|---:|
| Life of the Curé of Ars. New edition, enlarged | 0 | 4 | 0 |

## MIVART, PROF. ST. GEORGE (M.D., F.R.S.).

| | | | |
|---|---:|---:|---:|
| Nature and Thought. Second edition | 0 | 4 | 0 |

"The complete command of the subject, the wide grasp, the subtlety, the readiness of illustration, the grace of style, contrive to render this one of the most admirable books of its class."—*British Quarterly Review*.

| | | | |
|---|---:|---:|---:|
| A Philosophical Catechism. Fifth edition | 0 | 1 | 0 |

"It should become the *vade mecum* of Catholic students."—*Tablet*.

## MORRIS, REV. JOHN (S.J.)

| | | | |
|---|---:|---:|---:|
| Letter Books of Sir Amias Poulet, Keeper of Mary Queen of Scots. Demy 8vo | 0 | 10 | 6 |
| Troubles of our Catholic Forefathers, related by themselves. Second Series. 8vo, cloth | 0 | 14 | 0 |
| Third Series | 0 | 14 | 0 |
| The Life of Father John Gerard, S.J. Third edition, rewritten and enlarged | 0 | 14 | 0 |
| The Life and Martyrdom of St. Thomas Becket. Second and enlarged edition. In one volume, large post 8vo, cloth, pp. xxxvi., 632, price 12s. 6d.; or bound in two parts, cloth, price | 0 | 13 | 0 |

## MURPHY, J. N.

Chair of Peter. Popular edition. 720 pages. Crown 8vo . . . . . . . . . . £0 6 0

## NEWMAN, CARDINAL.

| | | | |
|---|---|---|---|
| Annotated Translation of Athanasius. 2 vols. each | 0 | 7 | 6 |
| Apologia pro Vitâ suâ . . . . . . . | 0 | 6 | 0 |
| Arians of the Fourth Century, The . . . | 0 | 6 | 0 |
| Callista: An Historical Tale. New edition . . | 0 | 5 | 6 |
| Difficulties of Anglicans. Two volumes— | | | |
| Vol. I. Twelve Lectures . . . . . . | 0 | 7 | 6 |
| Vol. II. Letters to Dr. Pusey and to the Duke of Norfolk . . . . . . . . | 0 | 5 | 6 |
| Discussions and Arguments. . . . . . | 0 | 6 | 0 |
| Doctrine of Justification . . . . . . | 0 | 5 | 0 |
| Dream of Gerontius. Twenty-second edition, wrapper | 0 | 0 | 6 |
| Cloth . . . . . . . . . . | 0 | 1 | 0 |
| Essay on Assent . . . . . . . . . | 0 | 7 | 6 |
| Essay on the Development of Christian Doctrine . | 0 | 6 | 0 |
| Essays Critical and Historical. Two volumes, with Notes . . . . . . . . . each | 0 | 6 | 0 |
| Essays on Miracles, Two. 1. Of Scripture. 2. Of Ecclesiastical History . . . . . . | 0 | 6 | 0 |
| Historical Sketches. Three volumes . . each | 0 | 6 | 0 |
| Idea of a University. Lectures and Essays . . | 0 | 7 | 0 |
| Loss and Gain. Ninth Edition . . . . . | 0 | 5 | 6 |
| Occasional Sermons . . . . . . . | 0 | 6 | 0 |
| Parochial and Plain Sermons. Eight volumes . each | 0 | 5 | 0 |
| Present Position of Catholics in England. New edition | 0 | 7 | 0 |
| Sermons on Subjects of the Day . . . . . | 0 | 5 | 0 |
| Sermons to Mixed Congregations . . . . | 0 | 6 | 0 |
| Theological Tracts . . . . . . . | 0 | 8 | 0 |
| University Sermons . . . . . . . | 0 | 5 | 0 |
| Verses on Various Occasions. New edition . . | 0 | 5 | 6 |
| Via Media. Two volumes, with Notes . each | 0 | 6 | 0 |
| Complete set of his Eminence's Works, half bound, in 36 vols. . . . . . . . . net | 14 | 0 | 0 |

## NORTHCOTE, VERY REV. J. S. (D.D.)

Roma Sotterranea; or, An Account of the Roman Catacombs. New edition. Re-written and greatly enlarged. This work is in three volumes, which may at present be had separately—

Vol. I. History . . . . . . . . 1 4 0

## NORTHCOTE, VERY REV. J. S. (D.D.)—*continued*.

| | | | |
|---|---|---|---|
| Vol. II. Christian Art | £1 | 4 | 0 |
| III. Epitaphs of the Catacombs | 0 | 10 | 0 |
| The Second and Third Volumes may also be had bound together in cloth | 1 | 12 | 0 |
| Visit to Louise Lateau. Written in conjunction with Dr. Lefebvre of Louvain | 0 | 3 | 6 |
| Visit to the Roman Catacombs: Being a popular abridgment of the larger work | 0 | 4 | 0 |

## POPE, REV. T. A.

| | | | |
|---|---|---|---|
| Life of St. Philip Neri, Apostle of Rome. From the Italian of Alfonso Capecelatro. 2 vols. | 0 | 15 | 0 |

## QUARTERLY SERIES (Edited by the Managers of the "Month").

N.B.—*Those printed in Italics are out of print, but may be reprinted.*

| | | | |
|---|---|---|---|
| Baptism of the King: Considerations on the Sacred Passion. By the Rev. H. J. Coleridge, S.J. | 0 | 7 | 6 |
| Christian Reformed in Mind and Manners, The. By Benedict Rogacci, of the Society of Jesus. The Translation edited by the Rev. H. J. Coleridge, S.J. | 0 | 7 | 6 |
| Chronicles of St. Antony of Padua, the "Eldest Son of St. Francis." Edited by the Rev. H. J. Coleridge, S.J. | 0 | 3 | 6 |
| Colombière, Life of the Ven. Claude de la | 0 | 5 | 0 |
| Dialogues of St. Gregory the Great: an Old English Version. Edited by the Rev. H. J. Coleridge, S.J. | 0 | 6 | 0 |
| English Carmelite, An. The Life of Catherine Burton, Mother Mary Xaveria of the Angels, of the English Teresian Convent at Antwerp. Collected from her own Writings, and other sources, by Father Thomas Hunter, S.J. | 0 | 6 | 6 |
| Gaston de Ségur. A Biography. Condensed from the French Memoir by the Marquis de Ségur, by F. J. M. A. Partridge | 0 | 3 | 6 |
| Gracious Life, A (1566–1618); being the Life of Madame Acarie (Blessed Mary of the Incarnation), of the Reformed Order of our Blessed Lady of Mount Carmel. By Emily Bowles | 0 | 6 | 0 |
| History of the Sacred Passion. By Father Luis de la Palma, of the Society of Jesus. Translated from the Spanish. With Preface by the Rev. H. J. Coleridge, S.J. Third edition | 0 | 5 | 0 |

**RAWES, THE LATE REV. Fr., Edited by**—*continued.*
*Little Books of the Holy Ghost:*—
 Book 2. Little Handbook of the Archconfraternity of the Holy Ghost. Fourth edition, 111 pp. . . £0 1 0
  Gilt . . . . . . . . . 0 1 2
 Book 3. St. Thomas Aquinas on the Lord's Prayer. 139 pp. . . . . . . . . . 0 1 0
  Cloth gilt . . . . . . . 0 1 3
 Book 4. The Holy Ghost the Sanctifier. By Cardinal Manning. 213 pp. . . . 1s. 6d. and 0 2 0

**RICHARDS, REV. WALTER J. B. (D.D.)**
 Manual of Scripture History. Being an Analysis of the Historical Books of the Old Testament. By the Rev W. J. B. Richards, D.D., Oblate of St. Charles; Inspector of Schools in the Diocese of Westminster.
  Part I., 2 maps. Second edition . . . . 0 1 0
  Part II., ,, . . . . . . 0 1 0
  Part III., ,, . . . . . . 0 1 0
  Part IV. . . . . . . . 0 1 0
   Or, the Four Parts bound together. Cloth . 0 4 0
 " Happy indeed will those children and young persons be who acquire in their early days the inestimably precious knowledge which these books impart."—*Tablet.*

**RYDER, REV. H. I. D.**
 Catholic Controversy: A Reply to Dr. Littledale's " Plain Reasons." Fifth edition . . . . 0 2 6
 " Father Ryder, of the Birmingham Oratory, has now furnished in a small volume a masterly reply to this assailant from without. The lighter charms of a brilliant and graceful style are added to the solid merits of this handbook of contemporary controversy."—*Irish Monthly.*

**SOULIER, REV. P.**
 Life of St. Philip Benizi, of the Order of the Servants of Mary. Crown 8vo . . . . . . 0 8 0

**ULLATHORNE, BISHOP.**
 Endowments of Man, &c. New and revised edition . 0 10 6
 Groundwork of the Christian Virtues: A Course of Lectures . . . . . . . . 0 10 6
 " A good and great book by a good and great man. This eloquent series of almost oracular utterances is a gift to men of all nations, all creeds, and all moral systems."—*The British Mail.*
    *Ready shortly.*
 Christian Patience, the Strength and Discipline of the Soul. Being the third and final volume of this series 0 10 6

www.ingramcontent.com/pod-product-compliance
Lightning Source LLC
Chambersburg PA
CBHW032044220426
43664CB00008B/850